Praise for Catherine Watson

"Catherine Watson is the consummate travel writer—both an assiduous, accomplished reporter and an eloquent, evocative storyteller. These tales bring the wide world home with an adventurous spirit, a discerning intelligence, a rich attention to detail and a soaring heart."

Don George, Global Travel Editor,
Lonely Planet Publications, and author, "Travel Writing"

"Catherine Watson leads us gently by the hand to unusual places—and to new understandings. That is what the best travel writing does. These evocative, sensitive and, above all, honest stories most assuredly fall into that category."

Catharine Hamm, travel editor,
The Los Angeles Times, Los Angeles, California

If you're the sort of traveler who believes that the treasures of travel can be found in the people, the details and the life-lessons learned, you're in for a treat. Watson's descriptions are almost poetic. She doesn't overdo it with flowery prose but always seems to find just enough choice words to paint the scene without detracting from the storyline. Historical lessons and her veteran commentary are added like spice. Each tale is satisfying, yet leaves you fiendishly peeling back the page to see what the next tale is about. You figure you'll just skim the first few sentences. Too late. You're hooked.

Doug Lansky, travel editor, lecturer,
author, *Rough Guides'* "First-Time Around the World"

Reviews of *Roads Less Traveled*

Booklist

Across 30 years and seven continents, Watson, the Minneapolis *Star Tribune*'s first travel editor and self-identified "tourist in life," takes the reader to the road with ease. Watson is a traveler who is meant for writing. Kick back and listen as she shares life stories, reflections and insights on cultures the world over. Stand in line for a witch doctor's cleansing in Mexico City's Sonora Market; have a closer look at polar bears in Churchill, Manitoba; participate in a community cleanup project in Winslow, Arizona; join hikers and see Machu Picchu, the lost city of the Andes. Here are romantic cities, great rivers, and trips on the wild side, Lebanon, Minnesota, and Nepal in one rich volume. The essays that make up this anthology fit every itinerary—perfectly! Travel readers in the know have probably already made Watson's acquaintance. For those who haven't, this is first-class travel reading at its best.

Minnesota Literature

Watson . . . writes with an unabashed zeal for places and people that comes through in her prodigious talent for more-than-photographic detail. Taste this, she seems to urge, feel this. She is also refreshingly down to earth. . . . Always ready to be surprised, she reminds us that what is exotic to us is only home to the people who live there. As she reluctantly leaves the mysterious . . . city of Petra, Dean Burgen's "rose-red city, half as old as time" and the site of the Grail temple in Indiana Jones and the Last Crusade, she is joined by a Jordanian man who rhapsodizes about his visits to Kansas. "'You know why I love Kansas?' he said, his eyes growing a little dreamy. 'Kansas is flat like here—only GREEN!' So much for rose-red cities."

Roads Less Traveled

Dispatches from the Ends of the Earth

Catherine Watson

To Mary — may all your rambles bring you joy — Catherine Watson

SYREN BOOK COMPANY

Minneapolis

Published by
Syren Book Company
5120 Cedar Lake Road
Minneapolis, Minnesota 55416

Printed in the United States of America on acid-free paper

ISBN-13: 978-0-929636-45-0
ISBN-10: 0-929636-45-7

LCCN 2005927225

Cover photo, Taj Mahal, by Catherine Watson
Back cover photo by *Star Tribune*
Cover design by Kyle G. Hunter
Book design by Wendy Holdman

To order additional copies of this book, see the form
at the back of this book or go to www.itascabooks.com

For Al and Lucky and Galena

Contents

Author's Note

———

WHEN YOU GROW UP at the end of a runway, jet engines always sound like home. Their throaty rumble soaks into your soul, until leaving seems as natural as staying put. When your neighborhood also includes the Mississippi and Minnesota Rivers and the mile-long Mendota Bridge, becoming a traveler is just about inevitable.

By high school, I thought of myself as a "tourist in life," someone whose actual earthly purpose was going away. Only later, when I'd become a journalist, did I comprehend the rest of the assignment: coming back and telling about it. That's what I tried to do in more than 30 years of travel writing for the *Star Tribune*; the essays in this book are drawn from its pages.

Because travel was the theme of my life, there are a lot of people to thank, starting with my parents, Richard and LaVonne Watson. They believed in travel. She was born in Canada and went to college in California; he was from Montana and spent World War II in Europe. Because of their stories, we kids knew about Ontario and Berkeley and England and France long before we understood that the earth was round.

Our happiest family times were long driving trips—several thousand miles each summer, towing a shiny aluminum trailer behind the station wagon. Our own personal Starship Enterprise.

Thanks also to the other passengers—my beloved siblings, Steven, Elizabeth, John and Jane. And to Al Sicherman, my life partner, steadfast support and keenest editor. My traveling companions, Mary Ann Ringwelski and James Warner Bjorkman. Old friends Karen Anderson, Trudi Hahn, Kirsten Ingerson, Patricia and Jack Doyle in Galena, Illinois, and Rosario and Antonio Lobo and their family in Costa Rica.

I owe a great debt to Fort Snelling, my strange, historic, ephemeral hometown; to American Field Service, for sending me to school in Germany, and to the Minnesota SPAN Program, for the dig in Lebanon that showed me I was meant for writing, not archaeology.

To Stuart Telecky, my high-school German teacher, whose challenging standards remain an inspiration. Tom Walz, the college professor who introduced me to Third World travel and first suggested writing about "the family of man." Wallace Allen, the managing editor of the *Minneapolis Tribune*, who entrusted me with the best job in the world. And my colleagues at the *Star Tribune*, especially the travel section team, Sharon Emery, Chris Welsch and Nancy Entwistle.

The people I can't thank here, or perhaps anywhere, number in the thousands and are scattered across the globe, from Honduras to Helsinki, Nome to New Zealand. They shared their life stories, their cultures and their insights with me, so I could share them with others. Thank you all, always.

Catherine Watson
Spring 2005

Roads Less Traveled

Dispatches from the Ends of the Earth

Eyes of the Forest

1992

———

W E T R O L L E D S L O W L Y, the tok-tok throb of the two-cycle motor echoing off the jungle walls, up a river the color of strong coffee, along a corridor of chartreuse leaves.

Trees like skyscrapers towered overhead, the sentinels of Borneo's coastal rain forest. Startled by our boat, monkeys shrieked and crashed into the foliage as we passed—mostly macaques but sometimes their rarer cousins, proboscis monkeys, looking like miniature Jimmy Durantes with fur.

It was hot, strange, exotic—exactly what my companions and I had hoped for. We had come to the third-largest island in the world, one of the last outposts of true wilderness, to study its most famous residents: wild orangutans. We did not yet understand that they would be studying us.

Four hours upriver from the coast, after the dark river had shrunk to the width of a creek, we pulled up to a weathered wooden platform and began to unload our gear—tropical hiking boots, rain ponchos, gallons of mosquito repellent.

We were prepared for just about anything. But we weren't prepared for Pola, under the big dock, soaping up. Pola was an adult male orangutan, a creature strong enough to pick you up and throw you against a tree trunk if he wanted.

What he wanted right then was a few slurps of soapsuds, something as tasty to Camp Leakey's orangutans as boiled rice and green tea to the other resident primates.

Pola glanced up at us, small eyes gleaming in a face like a black leather platter, decided we weren't interesting and serenely returned to his task—working a pilfered bar of soap over his hairy red forearms until they were white with foam, then bending his huge head and schlukking off the suds.

Whatever expectations we had about orang behavior, Pola had just schlukked them to smithereens. He was giving us a classic example of imitation—a new behavior learned by observation. Learned, in this case, by watching humans take baths in the river.

Pola was a camp regular, accustomed to people. He looked so cute covered with soap suds that I didn't take him seriously. I don't think any of us did. Instead, we were focused on wild orangutans—the original wild men of Borneo, the old men of the forest, and their old ladies, their babies, their aunts, uncles, cousins and just plain hangers-on.

Our group included a veterinarian, a retired doctor, a computer consultant, a restaurant owner, two lawyers, two teachers, a psychiatrist, a real-estate agent, a journalist and a designer of automobile interiors. We had come to Borneo from the United States, England and Australia with Earthwatch, a Massachusetts-based clearinghouse that connects lay volunteers with academic researchers around the world.

The camp's staff led us from the dock to "the team house," one of a cluster of white frame cottages in a clearing. We unrolled our sleeping bags on its attic floor, laid out flashlights and toiletries, arranged our shrouds of mosquito netting and eventually bedded down.

Next morning, and every morning for our two weeks at Camp Leakey, this is what we woke to: Clammy air. Dull light. And noise. Ear-splitting noise.

The poker-faced orangutans were silent in the morning, but everything else screamed its head off the moment the moon faded. The macaques sounded like madmen, sending out cascades of shrieks, hollers, burbles and whoops. What the macaques started, the cicadas finished, searing the air like insect chainsaws.

And then we'd hear something fainter, a dry scuttling, just under the eaves, and slowly a long red hand would come into focus against the chicken-wire window. Like nearly everything in this jungle, it was nothing fearsome, just Davida, a young female orangutan, hanging around, wondering if anything interesting was going on. Besides herself, that is.

So I'd struggle out from under my mosquito net, pull on a semi-dry T-shirt and yesterday's jungle-grubby trousers, lumber down the team house ladder, ladle river water into a basin for face-washing and watch Davida watching me.

She watched closely. Some mornings, she copied us washing our hair or brushing our teeth. Once I awoke to human laughter and a sound that was even stranger: Davida was gargling.

Named for the renowned primatologist Louis Leakey, the camp is directed by the youngest of his three female protégées and the only one still doing active field work.

Unless you are a primate groupie, you're not likely to have heard of Birute Galdikas, but you'll probably recognize the other two women in the triad of researchers nicknamed Leakey's Angels: Jane Goodall, who studied chimpanzees in

Tanzania, and Dian Fossey, who studied mountain gorillas in Rwanda (and was murdered in the effort—the movie "Gorillas in the Mist" was based on Fossey's life).

Galdikas is known as "the Professor" to every English speaker at Camp Leakey, but she is "Ibu," an honorific meaning "respected mother," to her adoring Indonesian staff. By any name, though, she wasn't there. She was in Jakarta, fighting to free ten captive juvenile orangs from a tangle of red tape so they could be released into the wild again.

To the ritualized routine of the camp, the Professor's absence made little difference. We followed an unvarying schedule, with its own, never-challenged jargon:

Volunteers who were going "to search"—look for orangutans—got to sleep until the morning noise started and then waited for the 9 a.m. breakfast gong and a meal of rice and tea.

If you were going "to follow"—continue tracking a wild orangutan spotted the day before—you rose before dawn, dressed in silence and trudged down barely visible paths and into a nightmare landscape of dry swamps, tripping over roots and stumbling into curtains of vines, hoping to reach the orangutan's nest before the occupant woke up.

It would have been worse if the seasonal rains hadn't been late. Then we'd have had to contend—as Galdikas had done for years—with blood-sucking leeches and swarms of malarial mosquitoes.

Orangutans spend nearly all their time in the treetops. So "followers" spent theirs looking up into the treetops and writing down whatever the orangutan did, in minute-by-minute life-bites for two hours at a stretch. We moved when the orangutan moved. We stopped when the orangutan stopped. If it stopped long enough, we got to sling a hammock around a couple of trees and try to get the kinks out of our necks.

We searched and followed in pairs, each pair accompanied by an Indonesian assistant, nearly all of them Dayaks, members of a once-fierce local tribe. The assistants took the best notes, never got lost and never seemed to sweat.

We sweated as if we'd invented it. The temperatures were 90-plus, and the humidity matched. Each morning I stocked my backpack with three quarts of boiled river water, all I had bottles for, laced it liberally with powdered Gatorade and still had to ration it to make it last the day.

All day, no matter where I turned, the dry jungle was the same—a dusty greenish-gray screen of trees that looked thin but managed to swallow up my companions whenever we were more than a dozen steps apart.

The place felt infinite, a forest universe, and I could not conceive of trees going on and on without end. They were ending, of course, all over Borneo, and they continue to. Even in the protected wilderness around Camp Leakey, we caught the smell of smoke from distant forest fires, set by farmers desperate to clear land, and we all knew that what wasn't threatened by burning was falling to the chain saws of loggers. We knew that the forest and the orangutans who depend on it were running out of time.

Even so, I kept peering into the leafy blankness, expecting it to give way, Hansel-and-Gretel-like, and reveal something familiar, something normal—a restaurant in the center of the jungle, perhaps, with a thatched roof and barstools and cold lemonade.

By late afternoon, my scientific curiosity ebbing with my supply of drinking water, all I wanted was to go back and take a cooling bath in the river. We all did. But the Professor's rules decreed that our days ended, not when the sun set, but when our orangutan decided to make a nest for the night. Snap, crackle, smash—a few bent branches was all it took, and our subject was safely snuggled down. Then we could mark the site and tip-toe home. In the darkness, I noted more than once, the jungle vines looked just like pythons, looping across my path. I was always too tired to be afraid.

What made it all worthwhile were rare moments of discovery. Like the night we heard the "long calls"—the strange booming sounds that adult male orangutans make to signal their presence to others. Deep and low, the calls rumbled through the quiet forest; it was like listening to the echo of an earthquake, more felt than heard.

Another time, a teammate and I observed a wild male orangutan using a twig to scrape something off a branch and put it in his mouth. "Ants," our Indonesian assistant murmured, as if he'd seen it many times. "Eating ants."

We were electrified. We were watching tool use—the very observation that propelled Jane Goodall into the primatological spotlight. It proved that other species also use tools, which shattered a basic definition of being human. For continued thrills like that, I too might have been willing to spend my life wading swamps.

Orangutans are constant eaters—think of human teenagers—so they have to move a lot, looking for food. When they find it, they stay for a while, munching flowers, crunching seeds, prying open green fruit and generally making a steady mess, until the next treetop beckons.

Usually they forage alone, but that doesn't mean they're antisocial. They get along pretty well when they're pulled into groups by a common interest, such as food. But they're not like chimpanzees, who live in close-knit bands and will attack and kill outsiders. We humans seem to be more closely related to the killers: About 99.5 percent of our genetic material matches that of chimps, while only 98.5 percent matches that of orangutans.

The shrinking forest and the need for food made Camp Leakey a transition zone, a place where two worlds meet: the world of the wild orangutans and the world of humans. Nearly 40 "ex-captives"—orangutans released from zoos or reprieved from the illegal pet trade—were living in its vicinity. Some had returned completely to the forest, but many of them, like Pola, had chosen to linger between the worlds.

Until I got there, I'd expected the ex-captives to be rather like pets. I pictured bonding with them, the way I would with a responsive dog. Wrong. Face to face, they were rascally opportunists, curious, smart and only as domesticated as they wanted to be.

They were also brazen. Princess, a senior female, broke into the team house while we were away, ransacked our supplies—she ate all the chocolate and grabbed the soap—and met us at our own front door when we returned. She sauntered out with real nonchalance, as if nothing had happened. A guilty dog would have been cowering under the couch.

There's not enough natural food in the surrounding forest to support all the ex-captives, so every afternoon about 4:30, the camp cooks boiled up a vat of rice and milk and trundled it down to a feeding platform beside the dock. The ex-captives—mostly females, some with toddlers or infants in arms—were already waiting. So were 20 or 30 macaques, scampering like rats along the dock, watching for a chance to filch a few bites. Sometimes there was a wild boar the size of a Volkswagen, rummaging under the platform for leftovers.

And usually there were a couple of what we called "the big

guys"—fully wild adult males, drawn to the feeding platform by the semi-tame females the way certain other male primates are drawn to singles bars. The big guys liked to show off for the ladies—shaking branches, roaring, acting macho. It helped account for all the new babies.

Except at feeding time, it wasn't easy for us to spot a 200-pound guy with bright red fur in a big green tree. Seen against bright sky, orangutans are just fuzzy black shadows. "You look for things that don't match," one of the staff advised.

Like what? Like a hand. Like a shadow with eyes.

It is the eyes that have stayed with me. Every time one of our Indonesian assistants would spot an orangutan, we'd train our field glasses into the forest canopy and have this kind of conversation:

"Where?"

"There."

"Where?"

"There!"

"No, really, where?"

"You don't see? There!"

When the blur finally coalesced into an orangutan, the animal was always—always—staring straight back. I never got used to that. Never got used to those bright eyes looking into my own, across the gulf of a couple of million years of evolution.

No, there's more. What I never got used to was the expression in those eyes. The orangutan always gazed back as a human might, with puzzlement, concern and confidence. It gazed back as an equal.

Just how equal was a lesson I learned from the ex-captives. Very near the end of our stay, a Canadian researcher arrived, and what she said showed me I'd underestimated them. They weren't just funny, they were remarkable, said Anne Russon, a research psychologist from Toronto. They were constantly observing us and mimicking what they saw. "It's like the orangutans are bicultural," Russon explained. "They can use the forest if they feel like it or interact with humans, but it's voluntary—it's not forced."

Earlier researchers had capitalized on this by trying to teach sign-language to some of the ex-captives. Princess, for example, still practiced a little of what she'd learned. "Food," she would sign, and charmed volunteers would instantly offer her raisins and cashews. Princess hadn't found the sign for "tuning fork" nearly as useful.

More interesting were the human behaviors that the apes had chosen to copy on their own. Soapsuds, for example. Camp Leakey's orangutans had observed a regular parade of human beings like us, going down to the river each afternoon to rub soap all over their puny, hairless bodies. The orangs decided to investigate. A couple of them swiped a bar of soap, and the rest is ex-captive history. Now they even teach soapsuds-slurping to their babies.

Russon had documented about 350 human behaviors that the orangutans at Camp Leakey chose to copy. At least 50 were unexpectedly complicated, going well beyond soapsuds. Just how complicated were they?

"Well," Russon said proudly, "one of them knows how to start a fire."

And what would have happened to the world, I wondered, if these peaceable creatures had figured that one out before we did?

On the Road to Santiago

1998

——

THE TOWN WITH the fortress church was named Portomarin, which sounded vaguely like "portal," but it didn't
have to be a gateway to please me; I arrived content. I had come
to it the day before, late in the afternoon, walking down a very
long hill through gold and green countryside.

My hiking companions went on, but I stopped just where
the hillside started down and sat for a while on a lichen-painted
wall of gray stone—not so much because I was footsore, but
because I felt good and happy, and I wanted to sit in the Spanish sun and prolong that feeling. It was one of the best moments of the trip.

I remember that a couple of hotshot Italian bikers zipped
past me while I sat on the wall, their gears set for maximum
speed as they began the downward run. It was a perfect hill for
bikers as well as walkers, but nothing in northern Spain—or
maybe anywhere else—can really be counted on, especially if
you're going too fast. I encountered them again at the bottom
of the hill, one helping the other with a newly ruptured tire.
He'd hit a rock, where the road swerved suddenly for the new
bridge.

In another place, on another journey, I might have thought smugly that they got what they deserved: The Camino de Santiago is a sacred way, even if it does make for good biking, and they certainly weren't going at it reverently or humbly.

But I was trying to, and some of the lessons of that ancient pilgrim path were sinking in. I felt sorry for the time the two bikers were going to have to lose—prying the tire off, gluing on a patch, reassembling the thing, pumping air back in and hoping the patch would hold. It was better to be on foot, I thought, as I swung across the bridge and up the bank beyond, where the red-roofed houses clustered.

That night, I stayed with my friends in a modern white *posada,* one of Spain's famous inns, sleeping soundly in clean sheets. We were on our way to the great shrine of St. James in the city of Santiago de Compostela, which made all of us pilgrims of some sort. But we weren't religious ones; blisters and stiff muscles aside, we saw no merit in suffering.

Portomarin stands near the end of the Camino. It's a moved town, a reconstruction: A ruined medieval bridge and the skeleton of the original village lie beneath—just beneath—the waters of a dammed-up river. It was mid-September, and the water was low; stubs of abutments and the outlines of walls broke the surface. If we hadn't known, the flooded buildings would have made us wonder what had happened there.

Before the dam was finished and the village drowned, the government managed to move—stone by historic stone—a small but high-walled chapel, boxy-looking and all but windowless because in the Middle Ages it had doubled as a fortress, protecting pilgrims. It now stood in the central plaza of the new village, lending authenticity.

In the morning, while my comrades downed bread and

milky Nescafé in a tiny restaurant under the arcade of the plaza, I headed for the shiny green doors of the church.

I wanted the place to myself—and would have had it, the hour was so early. But a boy in a red windbreaker came in when I did. I passed him on the steps, just as he dismounted and leaned his bike against the church wall. The bike had saddle-bags, which meant he was another long-distance traveler, another pilgrim. But he wasn't with the Italians; the boy was riding alone.

What struck me was his youth, but I couldn't be sure how young. He might have been 22, though I'd just as readily have believed 31 or 17. He had a plain, pleasant face, slightly freckled, with a wide mouth and sandy hair.

His presence in the church made me feel a little self-conscious. He must have felt the same way: As if by agreement, we walked in opposite directions, or as opposite as you can get in a place the size of a living room.

The chapel's high walls were plastered smooth and white, and the scarcity of windows was just as odd inside as it was out. The few it had were small and high up, so marauders couldn't get in. The windows were too high to shoot arrows out of, but there is a profoundly spiritual difference between defense and protection, between a fort and a refuge. You could feel it there.

The light I remember came from a single round window high above the altar—morning light, warm and lemony. It flooded the place, so even the shadows were soft and pale.

After a few minutes, I sat down near the front and closed my eyes and prayed. While I'm not devout, I am drawn to spiritual places, so sitting in foreign churches was not new. But I was doing it more often than usual on this trip. It seemed to be part of the path.

"Behave as if," a psychologist once advised me, in a context I no longer recall, but the thought has stayed with me and evolved into this: Behave as if you mean it, because sometimes doing that will help you mean it. On the Camino, "behaving as if" means prayer, simply because so many others have done so before you—millions, most likely, over nearly a thousand years.

I wasn't praying for anything. Requests didn't feel right on this trip, and besides, my habitual cravings had evaporated. I was just saying thanks—for the good afternoon the day before, for the repose of the current moment, for the rhythm of the days: the alternation of rest and walking, of food and hunger, of solitude and conversation.

Then I sat still. There was peace in that place, and I let it seep into me, basking in it a little, storing it up. I felt my heart relax. I hadn't, till then, known that it still needed to.

When I stood to leave, I saw that the boy in the red jacket was also sitting down, farther to the front on his side of the aisle. He didn't see me rise or notice that I paused to watch him. He was staring upward at the window above the altar, as if the answer to life lay in it. Maybe for him, it did.

The light seemed liquid, like a purifying bath, a mikvah for the soul. It was transforming him, and maybe me, as well. I felt a rush of inexplicable tenderness for the boy—the man, the child, all the ages he had been and would be. It was as if I'd known him all his life, as if I'd been his mother, sister, lover, friend, and they were all the same.

I stood there frozen by the thought, cradling him in my mind, sharing a lifetime with him in that moment. And then, like a bubble, the moment broke. The holy light was still streaming in, the clean space still felt pure, but time had snapped back to normal.

The boy stood up then, his body moving into the aisle before he pulled his gaze away from the high window. As he turned, his eyes met mine, and his face broke into a smile—a wonderful, open, whole-hearted smile, as pure as the light itself.

He had been lonely, I saw, and now he wasn't anymore. Now he would be all right, I thought. He'd gotten what he needed in that chapel. In different ways, we both had.

I watched him walk back along the aisle and out the door, both loving him and letting him go. When I walked out, he was already gone, his red jacket disappearing on the far side of the cobblestones. I never saw him again. And never needed to.

My friends were still drinking coffee when I found them. I ordered a cup too, dropped three small white bricks of sugar into it and stirred to cool it down. How was the church, they wanted to know. It was nice, I said, telling the truth. It was very nice.

The Taj Mahal

1974

—— · ——

To get from New Delhi to the Taj Mahal, a friend and I hired an antique limo, the Indian version of a 1940s Packard, complete with an inattentive driver who wanted to watch us instead of the road.

I remember the drive to Agra as a blur of open windows, dust coming in, blinding sun overhead, and one clear image embedded in the driver's unending chatter: a snake charmer, teasing a tired cobra out of a basket at one of the rest stops. We stopped to watch for a while. I felt sorry for the cobra.

Then journey's end, a dismally modern motel with no hint of Agra's fabled luxury. Its plain beds wore incongruous red plaid blankets, but then, it was January—winter in India too, even if it felt like summer.

Agra itself seemed a dingy town, though we didn't give it much of a chance. We went straight to the Taj and hung around it for the rest of our stay, like summer insects around an exceptionally appealing porch light, leaving it only briefly for food and sleep.

The trip came to sum up India for me—a blend of ugliness and breathtaking beauty, of death and joy, that I have encountered nowhere else and have never understood. Out of the grime of Agra emerged this white fantasy, cool and lovely as an ice palace—pure, serene, untouched, a kind of miracle.

That is fitting. The Taj Mahal is a monument to love, built three centuries ago by one of India's great Mogul rulers, Shah Jahan. It is the tomb of his favorite wife, Mumtaz Mahal, who died in 1631, after the birth of her 14th child. ("Fourteen!" I overheard a middle-aged American woman gasp, reading a sign by the main gate. "She *deserved* the Taj Mahal!")

Every cliché about its beauty is true. It really does shimmer by moonlight. It really does seem to float in early morning mists. And it really is the most beautiful building in the world. It was intended to be. From her deathbed, the woman known as "the crown of the palace" had asked her husband for just such a memorial.

The Shah mourned her deeply and built her mausoleum across a bend in the Jumna River from his palace. He is said to have contemplated the Taj—and his lost wife—every morning and every evening. Did he imagine, I wondered, that it would last like this, seducing its viewers, transcending differences of culture and religion, for centuries to come? He must have. Surely it seduced him. Perhaps it seduced him too much.

There is a legend, repeated in Agra like a current rumor, that the Shah had planned a matching tomb in black marble for himself; it is said you can still see the foundations. But Jahan fell into disfavor and was overthrown by his son, who imprisoned him in the palace, though he was still allowed his view of the Taj. When the old shah died, the son decided the Taj was good enough for two and crowded his father's sarcophagus in beside Mumtaz Mahal's, skewing the elegant symmetry of the innermost chamber.

The Taj Mahal came under official protection during the British Raj, and the Indian government still takes good care of it, forbidding the wearing of shoes on the marble floors; fretting about occasional cracks (the best place to build a Taj is not a soft river bank); covering the precious dome during times of war and threatening harsh treatment for carving names in the monument.

That last, like many rules in India, doesn't prevent people from trying. What keeps the Taj Mahal from looking like a latrine wall is the hardness of the marble itself. You can see faint scratches where people have attempted to cut their names but failed.

From a distance—and certainly from the windows of the shah's palace apartments—the Taj looks like a snowy dove resting on the riverbank. Up close, the white walls wear a tracery of color: green malachite, the red-orange of carnelian, golden agate and the intense cobalt blue of lapis lazuli.

Such inlay work is still done in Agra. Any taxi driver will show you the workshops of real, live, direct descendants of the Taj builders (not impossible, since about 20,000 laborers worked on the building for 22 years). They are still at it, cutting colored stones into tiny pieces and embedding them in white marble souvenirs—tabletops, plates, little boxes. It is difficult work and often beautiful. Even the best, though, is shamed by the real thing.

The Taj changes color, just as it is supposed to, with the hours of the day—fragile blue fading into pearl as the river mists lift; so blazing white at mid-day that it is hard to look at and harder to photograph; faintly gold and sunny pink in late afternoon. But the best time of all is night, especially the night of a full moon.

Then the place seems haunted. More than that—it seems alive. Warmed through the day by the Indian sun, the marble holds the heat for hours. Even at midnight, it is as warm as living flesh. When I touched it then, I half expected to hear the building breathe.

I found a dark niche in the main chamber, where I could look through the lace of a marble screen and see out across the quiet gardens. I leaned against the warm wall—the stone felt almost soft—and stayed there, alone, for a long time.

Eventually two old men, guards in tattered uniforms and head cloths, discovered me. They had been shuffling around the tomb, picking up rupees left by tourists, minding the candles burning on the marble coffins, mumbling to themselves. Now they had someone else to talk to.

Clearly, they had never gotten over the miracle of the Taj. They were personally proud of it. "Look," one said, holding a flashlight against the surface, "the light in the stone!" The marble glowed as if incandescent.

But what I never got over—maybe what nobody gets over—wasn't the visual beauty of the Taj that night. It was the *sound* of the Taj. The dome has an echo. One of the stooped old men awakened it. He leaned back and began, in a deep, rich voice, to sing the Muslim call to prayer.

As he sang, the dome picked up the sound and stretched it out, higher and softer, until the stone seemed to be humming, until the marble rang like bell metal, until the prayer evaporated like a sigh.

Taking the Cure

1995

——

IT WAS 10 O'CLOCK at night, and around us, the shopkeepers were snapping off their lights, stall by stall, until the whole market was dark, except for the stall where we stood. Light from bare bulbs fell on shelves crowded with bright-colored boxes and bottles, making us feel as if we were standing at a glowing hearth. At the counter, a man was carefully sifting glitter onto fat cylindrical candles.

My friend Mary Ann and I were in the depths of Mexico City's Sonora Market, waiting for that man. We had been waiting for nearly an hour, feeling conspicuous and uneasy, and we were prepared to wait much longer. We knew him only as "Don Hector." He was a witchdoctor, and we were waiting to become his patients.

Mexico makes fine distinctions among the practitioners of Don Hector's craft. Technically, he and his wife were *curanderos*—healers—people who cure in many ways. They can issue good-luck charms, remove curses, treat illnesses and forestall others, nurse the soul with blessings and ritual.

We were in line for one of their specialties—*una limpieza*—a cleansing—recommended by a Mexican friend we'd met that afternoon while watching Mayan dancers in the Zócalo. Drawn by throbbing drums that echoed for blocks around Mexico City's vast central plaza, we marveled at the dancers' faces and costumes. Their profiles, their ornaments, their long feathered headdresses could have come straight off a carved stone monument or a temple painting in the Yucatan. It was like watching archaeology come to life.

"Are those original dances?" we asked an onlooker. No, the man replied, sounding wistful, most of Mexico's dances were lost in the Spanish Conquest, so these were modern recreations. But other folk customs had survived, he said. The incense the dancers were burning, for example, was *copal*—the same stuff that the ancient Maya used in their ceremonies 1,300 years ago.

That gave me goosebumps, as the idea of survival always does—survival of belief, of custom, of human threads that can be traced back and farther back, back beyond history.

I'd thought Mexico's original religions had been completely eclipsed, either blended with Spanish Catholicism or reduced—as in our country, as in Europe—to scraps of superstition. Our new friend shook his head and smiled. No, he said, the old ways are alive in Mexico. Call it folk medicine, call it witchcraft, but it was still there, and a lot of people believed in it, himself included.

That surprised me. The man was about 30, well-dressed, with an educated accent—not someone I'd expect would believe in much of anything. It surprised him too, he admitted. But he'd had a lot of trouble with migraine headaches, and modern doctors hadn't been able to cure them. He got desperate enough to try a witchdoctor—and the headaches stopped.

"Now I *believe*," he said. His wonder-worker was Don

Hector. ("Don" and the female "Doña" are affectionate hon-
orifics in Spanish, used with first names only. English has no
real equivalents.)

Don Hector was authentic—someone Mexican people
depended on, not someone who put on displays for tourists
or, for that matter, got involved with tourists at all. "Why not
find out for yourselves? He has a stall in the Sonora Market.
Ask for *una limpieza*."

The Sonora was a long one-story stucco building on Fray
Servando. Most of it was like any other Mexican market—
aisles of fruits and vegetables, ranging from the familiar to the
absolutely unidentifiable; aisles of cut flowers, cool with scent;
aisles that stank of cloudy-eyed fish and blood-clotted meats,
and strange aisles of dried herbs and spices, in bags and bins
and piles.

In every market, a few of the spice stalls sell more than
spices: peculiar stalks, dried leaves, rattlesnake rattles, animal
pelts, bird claws and feathers—things used in cures or curses.
What made the Sonora different was that it devoted a whole
department to these things: the Herbolaria, a sort of herbalists' warehouse.

It was dark when we got there; the whole place looked
closed, and we almost turned back. Its wide parking lot was
empty, except for a litter of corn husks and lettuce leaves and
flimsy plastic produce bags that drifted across the asphalt like
small ghosts.

But the herbalists' entrance was still open. We asked for
Don Hector at the first booth we came to—a tourist's mistake. Never heard of him, snapped the shopkeeper, a young
guy in a baseball cap and undershirt, with gold front teeth that
gleamed under the naked light bulbs.

"He's a *curandero*," Mary Ann explained in Spanish.

The young man gave us a sharp look. "There are no curanderos here," he growled. Never mind that his own stall was crammed with bundles of herbs, plastic skulls, demon masks and bottles of scented oil.

We should have waited to ask until we were farther inside, where tourists were less likely to venture. So we moved down the aisle, asking every few stalls for Don Hector and getting only head shakes and silence. Eventually, we must have walked past suspicion. When we said his name again, a woman sweeping her stall smiled and pointed to the last one in the row.

I expected Don Hector to be a wrinkled gnome, draped with charms and chanting curses over a fire. But the man we found looked like a successful California lawyer or maybe a TV chef.

He was about 45, tan and fit as a tennis player, with a neatly trimmed ring of salt-and-pepper hair around the back of his balding head, and a warmly confident smile. He wore a denim shirt with the sleeves rolled up and a trendy denim apron. No mystery here, no magic, though he did glow a little: He'd gotten tiny flakes of candle glitter on his face, the way a busy cook gets smudged with flour.

We told him we had come for a cleansing. "My wife does that," Don Hector said kindly and left off gilding candles long enough to go find her. It took a while. Yes, she would do it, she said, but there were at least five people ahead of us, and we'd have to wait our turn.

The Spanish verb *"esperar"* means "to wait" as well as "to hope." A fellow traveler in Latin America once told me that you couldn't really understand the verb until you'd waited for something so long that you gave up hope. That night, we came close to understanding the verb.

The wait, we decided, must have been a kind of test: Only the sincere would keep on standing there, in the darkened market, while Don Hector blessed candles and chatted with clients. Customer after customer stepped up to place orders: candles for a wedding; a blessing candle for a child; a pair of frog charms, one red, one green, for a young couple. Don Hector advised them to keep the frogs in their pockets or purse at all times.

While he worked, his wife—a handsome, dark-haired, 40-ish woman in slim blue jeans—took other customers into a room at the back of the stall for consultations. Finally Don Hector's wife sent her last customer on his way and smiled at us. Our turn. "You go first," Mary Ann said, and I stepped past the counter into the space behind—a tiny cubicle, its walls lined, floor to ceiling, with candles and rainbow-colored bottles.

Doña Hector stepped in beside me. The floor space was no bigger than the top of a desk. This close to another person, you either need strong defenses or complete trust. It had to be trust.

She asked me gently, in Spanish, what was wrong. She was completely serious, and suddenly so was I. I poured out every complaint I could think of, from my own migraines to frequent stiff necks and a pinched nerve that made my right hand clumsy.

She listened intently, sometimes asking a question, sometimes gently touching me—my lower back, my shoulders and the knuckles of my hand—to find out, as a physician would, whether this place or that place hurt.

Then she called Don Hector in, and they discussed my medical problems. They concluded that I needed a special *teita*—a little tea. She listed off the herbs she wanted, and he went out to the counter to mix them.

"Now," she said, "you want to have a *limpieza?*" Yes.

She called out front for a special bouquet and the egg of a black chicken. A young girl assistant, whom I hadn't noticed before, quickly handed them in: a raw egg with a brown shell and a nosegay of fresh-smelling green leaves bunched around a single white daisy and a red carnation. It looked like something a winter bride might carry.

La Doña took a bottle of pink liquid from a shelf, poured some into my hands and told me to rub it over my face and hair. It reminded me of glycerine and rosewater.

Then she picked up the bouquet as if it were a whiskbroom and began to sweep me, stroking my body with the flowers as if she were dusting off a precious relic—first one side, then the other: head, neck, throat, breasts, both arms, both legs, even the soles of my feet.

While she swept, she murmured. I expected an incantation, but this was a prayer—a long whispered speech that my curandera spun around me like a thick web. Over and over, she asked the Virgin Mary, Jesus and all the saints to help and protect me.

She swept and murmured for a long time, and I closed my eyes and relaxed under the soft strokes of the bouquet. The process was somewhere between massage and caress, and it was startlingly sweet, with a few surprises.

When I was deeply lulled by the sweeping, la Doña suddenly pressed the bouquet hard against my eyes, and I jumped. "That you may not see evil," she said. Then she put her hands over my ears: "That you may not hear evil." Then she held the bouquet firmly against my lips. The leaves felt cool, and I could smell the sharp fragrance of the flowers: "That no calumny come from your mouth."

When she had swept me spiritually clean, she laid the bouquet on the floor and had me trample it, crushing the flowers and scattering the leaves.

Next she picked up the egg and, still praying, passed it over me, working from head to toe, making little crosses with it on my forehead and above each breast. I understood that whatever evils remained in me were now going into the egg. The idea pleased me. All of this did.

Finally she gave my arms a little squeeze. "Good," she said, the way a mother might after combing a daughter's hair, and I knew we were done.

I had just been given half an hour of intense, concentrated, professional attention aimed at healing both body and spirit. I felt refreshed, at ease and cared for, as if I'd visited a doctor, a pharmacist, a shrink and a priest, all at once—as, in fact, I had. No wonder the old ways had survived, I thought; they made you feel better.

"How was it?" Mary Ann asked as we traded places. "Great," I said, and meant it.

Out front, Don Hector presented me with a big yellow plastic bag full of what looked like salad—different shades of chopped green leaves, segments of horsetail rushes, clumps of corn silk. My prescription. I was to let it dry—only in the shade—then take a handful of it, add it to boiling water and drink the resulting tea in place of water, every day for a month.

The price of the whole experience—cleansing, *teita* and all that time—was $6. At home, it would have required visits to at least four separate professionals and cost as much as my round-trip airfare.

We left the Sonora Market feeling unexpectedly calm and good. "Cleansed" was an accurate word for it. The glow lasted for several days, but the herbs lasted longer. Too long, as it turned out.

I lugged the yellow plastic bag of damp vegetation across Mexico for the next week and a half, opening it each night at my hotel and fluffing up the contents, hoping it would dry better. The salad changed colors, but it didn't dry. I did get one pot of tea out of it; it tasted like a cross between licorice and mint. Then I accidentally left the bag on a sunny windowsill for an afternoon, and it began to rot.

I'd briefly considered trying to take it home, although a U.S. customs agent wasn't likely to believe that my bag of mysterious leaves was really homeopathic medicine. Now that it was turning into compost, I abandoned the idea. But I couldn't just toss it into a wastebasket; that seemed somehow sacrilegious.

There was a fireplace in my hotel room, and the night before I headed home, I pulled handfuls of the fermented leaves out of the bag, threw them into the flames and watched the perfumed smoke drift up the chimney. It reminded me of the incense in the Zócalo, and like the *limpieza* itself, it made me feel peaceful. I think Don Hector and his wife would have approved.

Polar Bear Country

1993

———

THE SURF WAS BREAKING on the beach behind the hospital, each wave tossing more chunks of ice onto the whitening shore. Hudson Bay was starting to freeze, and I wanted a closer look.

In Churchill, Manitoba, in late fall, that isn't a good idea. Polar bears might be there—hungry bears, ambling along the tide line or sleeping among the boulders, waiting for freeze-up so they can go out on the bay ice and spend the winter hunting seals.

From a distance the bears look like cuddly toys—big creamy white creatures that belong under an oversized Christmas tree. Even up close, viewed from one of the ponderous sightseeing vehicles called Tundra Buggies, the bears still look cute, with their roly-poly bodies, their black button eyes, their black noses wrinkling as they try to figure out who (or what) you are.

It was hard to remember, looking at them, that these appealing animals are the world's largest land carnivores. Yes, grizzly bears are about the same size, and polar bears are thought to have evolved from them. But grizzlies eat berries and a lot of other stuff that isn't meat, making them omnivores. That leaves polar bears in the carnivore lead—kind of like Tyrannosaurus Rex with fur.

Polar bears are not really dangerous, people up here will tell you—as long as you don't run into one. Which is sort of like saying race-car driving is perfectly safe, as long as you don't start the engine.

Local people do take the bears seriously, but they also take them in stride, staying away from the rocky beaches and sticking to well-lighted streets at night. Caution is something Churchill children are taught as soon as they are old enough to go outside. "It wasn't 'don't talk to strangers' or 'watch out for cars' when we were growing up," one woman told me. "It was 'watch out for bears.'"

But I saw no animals on the beach that morning, not even dogs, so I broke the Polar Bear Alert rules and edged closer to the breaking waves and the white-frosted shore. And closer. And closer.

Then I heard a deep rumbling on the sand behind me and swung around. No bear—just a big van with two uniformed members of the bear patrol ready to deliver a safety lecture. "It's for your own good," one of the officers explained, shooing me away. That's pretty much the same strategy they use on bears. At least I didn't get sent to the Polar Bear Jail. It already had 17 inmates.

If little Churchill were anywhere else, you wouldn't give it a glance. But the town is half-way up the west side of Hudson Bay, beyond the tree line, and that makes this cold, bare, wind-worried hamlet one of the most exotic places in the world.

"The accessible Arctic," it's called. And it does get tourists, drawn by migrating beluga whales in summer, the polar bears in fall and a year-round sense of remoteness.

The town grew out of an 18th-century Hudson Bay Co. fur-trading post, and the Bay maintained a presence here for the next 270 years. Today it's like TV's "Northern Exposure," only without the mountains, the trees and the architecture. What's left is a village of blandly modern buildings, perched on permafrost and home to about 1,000 people. More or less: Some folks say 900, some say 1,200. "It depends on people's feelings," one resident said. "People who feel more depressed will quote you a lower number."

Either way, it's a very small town—the kind of place where townsfolk make bets on when the ice is going to break up. Where "down south" means Winnipeg, not Dixie. Where insurance companies sell policies against polar-bear damage. Where the hospital puts up signs in Inuit. And where local attitudes toward cold weather can make even a Minnesotan feel like a wimp.

The problem isn't so much the winter temperatures, people say, it's the wind—so fierce that it can harden snow like cement. I was dumbfounded when someone mentioned a windchill of 2800, then realized it wasn't calculated in degrees. It's in watts lost per square meter—the more, the worse—a more accurate measure than the one Americans are used to, a staffer at Churchill's government weather office explained. Windchills of 2800 to 3200 are the "dangerous" range, capable of freezing exposed skin in less than a minute. Churchill's school and government complex close then, and people are supposed to stay indoors.

Which leads to the question that shivering visitors, including me, invariably ask: "What do you do here in the wintertime?"

The answer, from just about everybody, is "lots"—everything from curling competitions to city council meetings, to say nothing of bingo, hockey, Christmas parties, snowmobiling, dog sledding, volunteer work, children's plays and dances most Saturday nights. "To live here, you have to like winter," said Lorraine Brandson, curator of Churchill's Eskimo Museum. "The real sense of the north is winter."

About half the community is Canadian Indian—predominantly Cree, but also Metis, who are of mixed white and Indian descent, plus some Dene—an Athabaskan group distantly related to the Navajo—and a few Inuit who come from villages farther north and west. "Churchill is considered to be fairly unique in Manitoba because there are a lot less racial tensions," Brandson said. The main reasons: "They all went to school together—no segregation—and they go hunting together."

The community divides along other lines, however, depending on a person's commitment to the place. Churchill includes people who were born and raised here, both Indian and white; transients, including the doctors and nurses at the health center, who come from other parts of Canada to work on long-term contracts; seasonal workers, some of whom come back year after year to work at the port, and permanent transplants—those who were only going to stay a short time but changed their minds.

That last group is particularly loyal. "I like it here," said Vera Gould, a Toronto native who came up with her late husband and stayed on to run the town's first bed-and-breakfast. "You're safe, you know. Everybody knows you. If you're in trouble, I don't think there's anybody wouldn't give you a hand."

Even in peak bear season—late October and early November—Churchill is hardly overrun with the animals. But bears often stray into town then, and the Department of Natural Resources puts on extra staff and opens a special hot line for townspeople to phone when they spot one.

All this fuss isn't the bears' fault. "Somebody built a town in the wrong place," said Laurent Brouze, chief of the local Polar Bear Alert program. The bears bump into Churchill on their annual migrations to and from winter hunting grounds on the frozen bay.

Fall is the worst time because the bears haven't eaten all summer. "They're hungry," Brouze said, "and they get into all sorts of trouble" while they wait for the ice to freeze. The bears take off as soon as it can hold their weight—typically 400 to 1,000 pounds, though the largest bear recorded at Churchill was 2,200 pounds.

"Hunting" is too active a verb for how they spend the winter. The bears locate breathing holes that seals keep open in the ice, then lie in wait for a seal to come up for air. When one does, they give its head a mighty clout with a big, black-padded paw, drag it out of its hole and feast.

When hunting goes well, the bears can double their weight over the winter. They need to. Come summer, Churchill's bears go into a peculiar phase of life called "walking hibernation." They don't dig dens and sleep. They just linger near where they came ashore when the ice thawed, lazing around like bored children out of school, snoozing a lot and conserving body fat. (It's different for polar bears in the high Arctic, where the sea ice is permanent. When ice stays all year, bears can hunt all year.)

When the polar bears begin collecting on Cape Churchill in late fall, so do tourists, by the thousands. If they don't fly in, they come by train, as I had. The journey from Winnipeg takes two nights and a day, one way, through a landscape that looks like an endless Christmas tree farm. Nobody arrives by car, because the roads don't come this far north.

Tourists usually stay a couple of nights in a Churchill motel and spend their days bear-watching along the coastline east of town. But they're not allowed to set foot out there. They go in organized groups in Tundra Buggies—the locally built off-road vehicles that resemble ungainly school buses with six-foot tractor tires. Designed to handle rutted, partly frozen ground, they make slow, lurching, noisy progress. The ride I was on nearly made me seasick: The last three miles of the 20-mile trip took an hour and a half.

Given how big the region is and how relatively few bears there are—the polar-bear population of the entire western side of Hudson Bay is estimated at under 3,000—it does not take a tourist long to wonder why the Tundra Buggy drivers always know exactly where to find some.

First, bears tend to collect on Cape Churchill, because it juts into the bay and the ice freezes there first. Second . . . well, there are ways, and there are ways.

Feeding bears is against the law and violates the prime directive of the Polar Bear Alert program—to prevent bears from associating people with food. But tempting bears is another matter. Bears gather, for instance, around an unusual hotel called the Tundra Buggy Lodge—five of the long, balloon-tired vehicles linked together like train cars and parked on barren land near the coast during bear season.

What draws the bears are its kitchen smells—food being cooked for guests, of course, but also an occasional open can of sardines or a hot panful of bacon that just happens to be set outside on a viewing platform, where the bears can smell it but not reach it. Polar bears within sniffing distance zero in on the lodge. So do the mobile Tundra Buggies, if they haven't run onto a bear of their own somewhere else.

Arriving by buggy at the lodge one morning, my group found a lone white bear facing four other tundra vehicles, their windows bristling with tourists and telephoto lenses. The bear was unfazed.

An overnight stay at the Tundra Buggy Lodge is a rare experience—and a cold one if the heater in the bunkhouse goes out, as it did one night while I was there. Even so, it was magic. In the distance, the lights of Churchill's grain elevators glittered on the horizon like pink stars. Overhead, the witchery of the aurora borealis danced and shimmered—the real lights of the north—while a wind like all the banshees in the world howled and chafed at the corners of the rig, strong enough sometimes to rock the cars.

It was exciting to know that all around us in the darkness, polar bears were waiting. Arctic foxes were waiting too. Dainty as butterflies, white as snow, the foxes are the bears' pale shadows, darting almost under their paws if there's a promise of a meal. When they rest, the foxes curl up so tightly that they look like white fur hats dotting the gravel.

There were four bears near the lodge when I was there, each a study in furry patience, all hanging around the dining car, all looking forlorn. From time to time, a bear would lick hopefully at the frozen runoff from the kitchen drain. Another picked up a rock in his mouth and gazed up at me, as pathetic as a dog with an empty dish. A third, young and thin, pressed his front paws together as he lay down near the dining car; he looked as if he were praying for food.

Once a plastic ice-cube tray blew off a viewing platform— no need for indoor freezers here—and a bear trundled up to paw it. It was something new, at least, if not something edible. Then a plastic bag wafted past, caught by the wind, and another bear ran after it, looking like a fat, pigeon-toed puppy.

And once, to get a picture, someone threw a piece of potato off a platform. Two bears converged on the illegal morsel, but the nearest one inadvertently sat on it, so they tussled briefly, growling, over food that neither could find. When they gave up, the waiting arctic foxes dashed in to clean up.

For me, the best moment came one twilight, when I was alone on a viewing platform, gazing straight down on a polar bear. It looked up and noticed me and then rose fast and smoothly to its feet and stood, one paw braced on the nearest tire, broad white face staring into mine.

I knew it couldn't reach me, but my heart jumped anyway. The great animal was almost within touching distance. We stayed that way for a few miraculous moments, until another lodge guest interrupted our communion. "How'd you like to get mauled by that?" he said. "Frankly," I said, "I'd consider it an honor." Then the bear gave a snort and went back to its own world, and I went indoors to mine.

Eatin' On a Corner

2002

———

W E W E R E G O I N G to Winslow, Arizona, to get groceries: Veronica, from New York City, who had the grocery list; Linda, from Los Angeles, who was trying to remember the rest of "Standin' on a Corner in Winslow, Arizona," and me, the driver, with what the other two thought was that cute accent like in the movie "Fargo."

We were volunteers, part of a community cleanup project on an Indian reservation in the northern part of the state. Our group needed supplies and more food, and Winslow was the nearest place with a big store.

It was an hour-and-a-half drive through the kind of country that always lifts my heart—a vast pale-blue dome of Western sky, sweeping desert and an array of buttes and mesas that looked like purple paper cutouts on the horizon. The road ran arrow-straight as far as I could see, and there was nobody on it but us. It was safe to drive fast, and I did. We cruised into Winslow in record time.

Winslow, population 9,520, is a classic Western town whose best years were in the heyday of old Route 66, the historic highway that was once its main street. Except for "Get your kicks on Roo-oot 66," we didn't know the words to that song, either.

Because I'm from the heartland, albeit the part with water, I felt obliged to interpret this bit of inland Americana to my coast-bred companions. Neither had been in the middle before.

So I did what my father used to call "casing the town"—criss-crossing its web of streets, north to south, east to west, back and forth the way people used to darn socks. This works great in bigger towns like, well, Fargo.

But in Winslow, where railroading is still a mainstay, it got us tangled in a stretch of tracks so wide I couldn't find a way through. Eventually we got into a neighborhood of 1920s cottages, concrete-block ramblers and sunburnt lawns, and finally we got back to downtown, only a couple of blocks big.

This process provoked some East Coast-West Coast muttering about what kind of people made their homes in Winslow. Or, as West Coast put it, "Who would *live* here?"

I said it was just like any small farm town, only drier. They didn't buy that. I said it looked pretty good for a Western town. No dice. I said people who lived in small towns usually loved them. Silence.

On one of my criss-crosses—you can't make many before you run out of Winslow—we passed the Santa Fe Whistle-stop Diner on 3rd Street.

"We should have lunch there," I said.

The Whistlestop was as classic as the town, a nicely preserved Depression-era diner with a dozen red vinyl stools, nearly all occupied, and a menu containing nothing but hamburgers, shakes, sodas and fries. It looked like the kind of place that would still toast the buns on the griddle. The motto on the menu read "burgers that stop trains."

"I'd like a salad," East Coast said. Heads, some of them wearing cowboy hats, turned.

"I'd like one, too," said West Coast. "I don't eat meat."

You don't hear sentences like that in Winslow every day. But the sweet-faced high-school girl behind the counter took this calmly.

"We don't have salads," she said.

"Well, where could we get a salad?"

She said she didn't know.

Now the patrons of the Whistlestop Diner got involved and started kicking this question around. They came up empty. Nobody knew of any place in town that served a salad.

"We saw a restaurant called Sue's," East Coast said. "Would that have a salad?"

A woman customer nodded. "If any place has a salad, it'll be Sue's."

So I said "Sorry" to the waitress, and we walked out.

We found Sue's, which did indeed have a salad on the menu. Just one. "What kind?" East Coast asked. "Iceberg lettuce," the waitress said. Both Coasts had been hoping for romaine and arugula.

So I said "Sorry" to the waitress, and we walked out. Again.

"It's OK," West Coast said. "We can go back to the place you wanted. I'm not that hungry."

East Coast said she wasn't that hungry, either, so they'd just watch me eat.

Back at the Whistlestop, we slid onto a trio of stools at the counter. This time the manager came over.

"We're back," I said, feeling stupid. "Can you tell we're tourists?"

"Oh, yeah," she said.

But she'd have known it even if we hadn't opened our mouths because, she said, she knew everybody in town. She was a third-generation native whose grandmother settled in Winslow in 1909.

"What's Winslow like?" I asked.

A great town, the manager said, a place where people can count on each other: "Wouldn't live anyplace else." See? I wanted to say to the others, but they were busy with their menus.

I ordered a hamburger with grilled onions. The bun came toasted.

West Coast, who doesn't eat meat, ordered a burger with everything.

East Coast, the salad lover, announced to the entire diner that she had PMS and therefore had to have a chocolate malt.

The manager and I shared a glance. "Make that a double," I said. And then everybody smiled. Just not for the same reasons.

———

(By the way, the famous corner in Winslow is at 2nd and Kinsley Sts. The title of the famous song is "Take It Easy," written by Jackson Browne and Glenn Frey and recorded by the Eagles in 1973. The famous verse goes, "Well, I'm a standin' on a corner in Winslow, Arizona/ and such a fine sight to see:/ it's a girl, my Lord, in a flatbed Ford/ slowin' down to take a look at me.")

On the Isles of Aran

1999

———

O NE MOMENT the tiny plane was surrounded by clouds, the next I caught a glimpse through the pilot's windshield of a gray shape on silver water, and then our wheels were reaching down for bumpy land.

We clambered out onto the grassy field that serves as an airstrip on Inishmaan, the middle island, and came face to face with Aran reality: rock and sky and sea. Mostly rock.

There are more stones than earth here, never-ending stones, and island farmers have always had to struggle with them. So they made fences—miles and miles of gray stone fences. The fences are the trademark of the Aran Isles.

Everywhere I looked, they stood—stone walls as high as my chest, as high as my head. Stone walls along every road and village lane. Stone walls that turned the landscape into puzzles, the pastures into fortifications. Safe within them: white cottages thatched with grass; sheep grazing on tiny emerald fields; children.

There are dry-stone walls all over Ireland, but Aran's made me uneasy. It took a museum diagram to explain why, and then it was obvious: Except near people's houses, there aren't any gates. Instead, there are "Aran gaps"—places where the stones are stacked at a different angle, like a weaving flaw in a length of rough gray cloth. If you want to drive your sheep or cattle through, you pull down the stones of the gap, then build them up again behind the herd.

Wherever I went on Aran, I could not shake the sense that I was constantly peeking over something. Even when there weren't any fences, I had peeked over so many already that I felt as if I were invading privacy with every glance, as if I were seeing secrets everywhere I turned my eyes. Only once did anything on Aran peek back; it was a donkey, and I took its picture as if it were a rock star.

Though it's usually spoken of in singular, there are really three parts to Aran: Inisheer, the smallest island; Inishmaan, the middle-sized one, and Inishmore, the biggest, with cliffs on the west side and a gentle slope to the sea on the east, where Kilronan, the biggest village, stands.

If the stone fences are the most impressive feature on this trio of islets, the next most striking thing is sky—the cease-lessly changeable sky, which tosses up weather in fits of mist and rainbows.

The main island, Inishmore, is only nine miles by three, but the weather can be wildly different in different places: sun, cloud, rain, cold, warmth, drizzle, sun again—and always wind. The mini-climates make each day feel like many days. For all its wildness, islanders say the weather on Aran is better than on the mainland. "It never gets hot," one resident said, "and we have no frost."

After the sky of Aran, there is the quiet. Aran as a whole gets 2,000 to 3,000 visitors on summer weekends, but the quiet survives. And the rest of the year, when tourism drops off, the islands revert to their own pace.

It was so quiet one October afternoon that, sitting on a park bench in the center of the largest town, I could hear small separate sounds—sea birds crying, the mild rush of low surf on the beach, a car motor, a dog's bark in the distance, the crackle of a potato-chip bag being passed around by young tourists on the next bench, the hooves of a horse pulling an old-fashioned jaunting cart down the street.

Beyond the walls and the weather and the welcome quiet, there is Aran's history and prehistory and, if there is such a thing as pre-prehistory, I am sure Aran has that, too. It rightly claims to have more ancient sites and religious ruins than any other place its size in Ireland.

Among its treasures are seven massive stone forts, all about 2,000 years old; four are on the main island alone. On my first night there, I walked up to one, following a muddy trail behind my bed-and-breakfast—between green fields, between gray walls—until I came to the cliffs. The ruined fort of Dun Aonghasa glowered there, on the edge of a 300-foot drop. A fierce wind whipped my hair and coat and made going closer a terrifying idea.

That wind had distance in it. "There'd be no other land out there, to America," a tour guide explained next morning. The guide's name was Jerry Flaherty—the surname shared by most of the people I met, none of them close relatives.

"I think Flahertys have been here since forever," one of the women told me. "I was a Flaherty before I was married, and I married an O'Flaherty." Such tight connections made for coincidences. So did the tiny population. There are only 900 people on Inishmore, far fewer on the two smaller isles.

One night, I went to a pub to hear Irish music; the next day I mentioned it to a woman staffing the local museum. Did I remember the flute player, she wondered. Yes, I said, he was good.

She beamed. He was also her husband. Spend a week on Aran, I concluded, and you'd end up knowing half the population.

Aran's mix of quaint and quiet has long appealed to outsiders, including writers. The best-known in the 20th century was Leon Uris, who stayed at my B-and-B while working on a book called "This Terrible Beauty." But he was only one of many celebrities, the mistress of Kilmurvey House told me with pride. "All the Kennedys stayed here," Brigid Hernon said. "All the Shrivers."

Sturdy, white-haired and bright-cheeked, Hernon first came to Aran to study Gaelic; she married an islander and in 1947 began taking in guests, making hers one of the first families to rely on tourism.

I asked her who the people were in the oldest of the old pictures on her parlor walls—a man in a red coat and white wig, a woman in an 18th-century dress. Ancestors of her late husband, she said: They established his branch of the family on Aran. "They were a wild tribe. They were known as the Furious O'Flahertys." Of course.

It was another O'Flaherty who explained the sweaters to me. The sweaters are Aran's best-known ambassadors. You'll certainly have seen them: thick wool, solid colors, complicated patterns. They came to world attention through a 1956 article in Vogue magazine, and they've been popular ever since. Anybody can knit one now, anywhere, and many do, from Minneapolis to Taiwan. But the result is still called an Aran sweater.

The names of the traditional stitches write their own poem: blackberry, diamond, honeycomb, moss, lobster claw, ladder, plait, bobble, link, basketweave, tree of life. . . . There are almost two dozen, and the combinations are infinite.

The sweater legend I'd heard was that Aran women knitted them for their fishermen-husbands, each using her own particular design, so that if a boat capsized, the drowned men could be identified by the patterns on their backs.

But Aran's modern knitters scoffed at that. Yes, they said, the thick sweaters were worn by fishermen—still are—but that was because they're warm and rugged, not because they held some dismal code.

As in lots of distant, northern places, sweaters were just an inevitable part of life: You had sheep, you had wool, you had time, and you had need. "Knitting was something you had to do," said Mary O'Flaherty, who sells her sweaters from her white-walled cottage on Inishmore.

Now middle-aged, O'Flaherty learned to knit from her mother and grandmother when she was tiny. "I knit continuously," she said. "On a wet day in winter, except for getting our meals, I'd be knitting until 11 or 12 at night, depending on what's on TV." An elaborate adult-sized Aran sweater takes her just four days.

Sweaters are one of Aran's newer traditions, introduced only a few centuries ago. Other traditions are much older, preserved as if in amber by the islands' isolation. Gaelic is the best example. Ireland's ancient language not only survives here, it's the language of instruction in the islands' schools.

Old customs survive as well. During my visit in October, for example, residents were gearing up for one of the oldest traditions in Europe: Pucai—pronounced "poochee"—the Aran version of Halloween. "It's more serious here" than on the mainland, said Rachael Conneely, a young woman who came to the islands with her family on vacations and eventually married a local.

"Every adult dresses up," she said, "not so much a costume

as a disguise. You disguise everything, even your hands, and nobody talks. You go into a pub, and nobody talks to you. They don't even order their usual drink. A man who drinks Guinness'll be drinking a martini. A man that doesn't smoke will be smoking. You don't know who anybody is. Oh, you can bother anybody. Adults could go into the neighbor's house. It's actually scary. Even when you dress up, you're scared. It's a nervous time."

But when I was there, Pucai was half a month away, and Aran felt utterly safe, even on the lonely lanes, even after dark. I chalked that up to all the walls, but it may simply have been all those close family ties in a tiny population.

This has unpredictable results. One recent immigrant, a mainland girl who moved to Aran to write poetry, complained that the local writers' group won't give good criticism. It isn't that they're too harsh, she said. They're too kind. They have to be, one of the group finally explained to her: Aran's a small place, and hurts would last a long time.

Including Kilronan, which looks like a proper town, there are 14 villages on the big island, most of which don't look like towns. They're just loose groups of perhaps 20 houses apiece, set at the intersection of paths and small roads through stony pastures.

Farms are small, 20 to 40 acres, and a single "farm" may consist of several separate plots in different places. That way, Jerry Flaherty said, "nobody has all the bad land, nobody has all the good land. They'd be scattered around that village, like." And well-fenced, of course. "They say there are 7,000 mile o' stone walls on the island," he said. "Nobody's counted 'em."

Actually, the local museum has. The total for the tiny inhabited islands is still more than 700 miles. No wonder I kept feeling like a peeping Tom.

It isn't just the stone walls that make Aran feel so private. It's a matter of simple geography. The islands lie on the edge of Europe, six miles west of the Irish shore as the gulls fly but 12 by boat, because of tricky currents.

In the old days, such distance made this place a kind of limestone life raft, an isolated backwater whose people lived starkly self-sufficient lives. The local museum sums up the old life in two terse lists:

This is what the islands imported a century ago: Cattle and horses. Long grass for thatched roofs. Peat for fuel. And "poitin"—what we'd call moonshine.

This is what Aran exported: Seaweed for making iodine and fertilizer. Salted fish. Potatoes. Cattle and horses. Stone for making lime. Slabs for gravestones.

Life was marginal at best, and by the end of the 19th century, the little farms and the old ways of fishing—done from small boats or the tops of the cliffs—couldn't support the islands' rising population. In 1886, the parish priest sent a desparate message to the outside: "Send us boats or send us coffins." The boats came, and many islanders left.

The descendants of those who stayed are less self-sufficient now but a lot more comfortable and far more connected to the outside world. Running water arrived in the 1960s, telephones and electricity in the 1970s. Now a supply boat makes daily runs from Galway in summer, three times a week in winter. Mail comes in daily by plane. There are three primary schools and a technical school. All three islands have their own nurse, and there's a doctor on Inishmore. A covered lifeboat, designed to stay afloat in any sea, is kept at Kilronan to transport emergency cases to the mainland when the weather's too bad for flights.

How do islanders make a living now, I asked. "I would say fishing and the tourists, like," my guide said. Many families do both. Rachel Conneely was a good example: She worked for Aer Arann, the islands' mini-airline, a job sustained by tourism, and her husband is a fisherman. Life has changed on Aran in the past few decades, as it has everywhere in the world, she said, but "you don't hear people complaining that it was better before."

But islanders are human too, which means there's always room for grousing. I asked an old man, shuffling slowly up the road to a pub with an incongruous name—The American Bar—how the island had changed since his youth. "Motor-cars!" he growled. "The island is completely spoilt by the tour buses!"

Well, progress always has a price. I paid a little of it myself on the final night at my B-and-B. The evening was cold and rainy, and the wind was snarling around the corners of the square stone house. I settled down to savor it in the toasty front parlor—a classic tableau of an earlier Ireland: A turf fire smoldered fragrantly in the grate; a pair of plush sofas flanked the hearth; crowded bookcases stood in the corners; bric-a-brac and lace doilies dotted every surface.

I curled up on one of the sofas, at peace with pen and journal—until a resident youngster bounced in, commandeered the TV set and turned it up till the sound drowned out the wind. Suddenly Aran felt just like home. Just like anywhere.

COSTA RICA

A Journey with Mamá

2001

M AMÁ MET ME at the airport with *besos* and *abrazos*—
kisses and hugs—just as she always does. Usually, my
sister Jane is along to help absorb this shower of affection, but
Jane had visited in April and a return in December was too
soon, so this time I had come to Costa Rica alone.

The excuse for my trip was a wedding: The first of Mamá's
eight grandchildren was getting married. But it turned out
that Mamá and I each had hidden agendas. She revealed hers
right away: "You have come to be spoiled by Mamá!" she said,
patting my arm as we rode to her home.

She's not my real mother—she isn't old enough—but I've
been calling her Mamá and she has been mothering me, long
distance, for more than 25 years.

For that, I thank a twist of fate and a high-school exchange
program. Mamá and her late husband were my sister's host
parents when she was an American Field Service student in
Costa Rica in 1973. When Jane went back for a college project
a few years later, I went along to spend a couple of months
studying Spanish and living with her adopted Mamá and Papá.
Ever after, their family has included me, too.

Over the years, Jane and I have gone back several times, and Mamá, Papá, four of their five grown children and several of the grandchildren have visited us in Minnesota. The time between visits has averaged out to several years, but we've stayed close enough for both sides to feel that they have an extra family—a family in reserve, even in hard times.

After Papá died a few years ago, for example, Jane invited Mamá to spend Christmas up north with us. (She had always said she wanted to see snow.) Her children lovingly supported her choice.

On this visit, if Mamá's hidden agenda was to spoil me, mine was to travel. I wanted to see the country.

It was about time, I thought. Costa Rica is only one-quarter the size of Minnesota, but in all these years—except for family jaunts to a couple of Pacific beaches and three attempts to see the crater of Poás Volcano, invariably obscured by fog—I'd never been beyond the central valley, around San José, the capital. I'd never seen any of Costa Rica's famous rain forests, let alone gotten to Limón on the Caribbean side of the central mountains, and I'd developed a real craving to see Limón.

The reason I'd never explored the country on my own is that our adopted family is so close-knit. Most of Mamá's children and their families live within a few blocks of one another, and everybody is in virtually continuous contact with everybody else.

When the grandchildren were younger, they gathered at Mamá's house every day on their way home from school. At least half a dozen relatives routinely dropped by for afternoon coffee several times a week. Mamá regularly served lunches and suppers to eight or ten people, when she had planned for three or four, without batting an eye or running out of food.

Once we went on a spontaneous picnic that ended up including 18 people.

What always amazed me was the way everybody got along—blood kin and in-laws alike. I've never heard anyone argue, except over politics—Costa Ricans love arguing over politics—or utter a harsh word or scold a child. Some of this is cultural. More of it is Mamá.

Because all events, all trips, all touring always involved so many people, we seldom went very far. But this time, I promised myself, I'd make a real effort to get out on my own. After the wedding, I intended to rent a car and really *see* Costa Rica.

What I didn't see was that I was overlooking a rare gift. It took a trip and a small adventure to remind me how lucky I was to know this family and especially to know Mamá.

Her name is Rosario Lobo. She is a small, dark-haired woman with a kind smile, a talent for hard work, lots of common sense and boundless patience. She is also a survivor. She surmounted a childhood that could have left her bitter: the loss of her mother when she was ten, a stepmother who rejected her, a variety of temporary homes after that.

"I didn't resent it," she told me during this visit. "That was just how life was. I had to accept it and go forward . . . and I always knew there were people who loved me."

Accept, go forward, love: That became her philosophy. She teaches it daily. In the three years since I'd seen her, I had lost sight of that, so she taught it to me all over again. First she spoiled me. Then she guided me.

She spoiled me the way only mothers can—the way I'd not been spoiled since my own mother died, the way I didn't think I'd ever be spoiled again. She made my favorite breakfast every morning (*gallo pinto*—black beans and rice). She insisted

I put on a sweater when the evenings got chilly (down to, oh, 65 degrees). She made me take naps when I looked tired.

But most of all, she talked—about people, about kindness, about going ahead no matter what curve life throws you. She talked, in short, like a mom.

We were all older, but otherwise the tight-knit family was exactly as I remembered: lots of people, lots of kissing each other hello and goodbye, lots of good-natured talking—all at once, in a blur of fast Spanish that I still miss most of. The wedding, which drew in other granddaughters' boyfriends and the groom's former roommates, simply intensified the closeness.

The same night I flew in, Mamá and I went over to the house of her daughter Sandra, the mother of the bride, to see the latest wedding gifts. The next day we went over to Sandra's three more times to see more wedding gifts, each time kissing different combinations of family members.

The wedding itself was lovely—the young bride was radiant, the groom adoring, the church beautiful, the reception elegant. There was so much food and so much dancing that we didn't get home till 2:30 in the morning.

The day afterward, almost everybody went back over to Sandra's, to snack on leftover wedding cake and talk about the great event some more. And I asked Mamá if she'd like to come with me to the Caribbean side of the country.

I knew she'd say yes. I also knew she'd be a great guide and a good companion. At 74, she is an indefatigable traveler, curious about the world and unafraid of it. She has confidently traveled alone around the United States by Greyhound bus, sometimes on ten-hour stretches, even though she speaks no English.

But because she's 74, her children have become protective—too protective for her taste. Limón made the family nervous—

it's a banana-shipping port with a rough reputation—but Mamá sold them on our trip by saying that she had to go along to protect me.

To protect both of us, I shifted our target to a place 30 miles south, Cahuita, a tiny beachfront community tucked into the palm trees on the edge of a national park. My guidebook said it was far more pleasant than Limón.

The family wasn't happy about that, either, which puzzled me, until I called my sister to update her on the wedding and the trip. "We're going to Cahuita," I said.

"But that's where those murders were!" Jane said, genuine horror in her voice.

Mamá explained matter-of-factly: The previous spring, two American college girls had been murdered near Cahuita. The tragedy appalled Costa Ricans. Their country is widely considered the safest place in Central America, where things like this aren't supposed to happen. Two perpetrators were quickly arrested and police patrols stepped up in the area, but Cahuita's reputation was destroyed.

This made me falter. What real business did I have, dragging somebody else's mother into potential danger? But Mamá just said it would be fine. And that was how the whole trip went: me getting anxious, Mamá leading me forward and making me feel safe.

I rented a car, and we set out over the Cordillera Central, the mountain spine that runs down the center of the country. The mountains aren't high, but they're covered in rain forest; the highway is twisty and frequently wet, and Costa Rican drivers are known for attempting the impossible—passing on uphill outside turns, or passing you while you're passing someone else, usually at high speed.

I promised the family that I'd drive only by day, but even

then, I white-knuckled my way across the Cordillera. Mamá, who doesn't drive herself, wasn't nervous at all.

Beyond the mountains, the land dropped swiftly to the tropical flats—hot, humid banana-growing country. Mamá knew the region; Papá had worked on the plantations there when they were first married.

It was late afternoon when we rolled into Cahuita—a straggly collection of one-story wooden houses along a couple of gravel streets. We chose a small inn at the far end of town, just across a tiny footbridge from the 15 kilometers of palm-fringed white beach that make up Cahuita National Park.

Our room was big and plain and spotless, with dark wood walls and new mosquito nets over the beds. The proprietor was a genial, gray-bearded Spaniard who spent his free time sitting outside, flanked by two dogs and a pet parrot, drinking beer, chain smoking and painting wonderful portraits of local kids.

The sun sets about 5:30 in Costa Rica in the winter, and there's almost no twilight, so it was dark by the time we'd unloaded the car. Cahuita isn't big on street lights. We strolled a block or two up the dimly lit main street until I got uneasy, then looked for a place to eat.

A long-haired local guy recommended a funky restaurant tucked off among some trees. It might have been cute in the daytime, but the darkness made its lane look sinister. Mamá told me not to worry. Right as usual: The staff was friendly, and the fresh, sweet shrimp were delicious.

We turned in early. In the middle of the night, an unearthly noise woke me—a booming, throaty roar, like a cross between thunder and the screams of a giant pig being slaughtered outside my window. The eerie sound came again and again, in waves, nearer, then farther, then nearer again.

I lay there frozen, silent and wide-eyed under my mosquito

net, struggling to figure it out. From the other bed, I heard two soothing words: "It's monkeys." Mamá had guessed I'd need assurance. Of course it was monkeys. What else could it have been? I went back to sleep.

The next day, we went up to Limón—it was indeed a rough-looking seaport—and from there took an all-day boat tour through jungle-flanked canals to Tortuguero National Park, a gem that is inaccessible by road. We saw alligator-like caimans, striped and spotted lizards, spider monkeys, black howler monkeys—the kind I'd heard roaring—and enough tropical birds for a National Geographic special.

We spent another night in Cahuita, this time without monkeys, and the next morning we walked barefoot a couple of kilometers down the exquisite, empty beach. Then we packed for home.

Everything had been fine, just perfect, in fact, just as Mamá had foretold—until about noon, when I turned the ignition key.

Silence.

I hadn't left the lights or anything else on, but the battery was dead. I asked our Spanish hotel keeper about a garage. There wasn't one in Cahuita—the village is too small—but he knew a guy "who knows something about cars." Nobody could find the guy.

I called the car rental company, which offered to send a replacement from San José, but it wouldn't get to us until nearly dark. If I'd been traveling alone, I wouldn't have worried, but—cross the mountains at night with Mamá in my care?

She sat me down in the hotel garden, told me I was getting unnecessarily *tensa* and presented a solution: We should forget the car, she advised. Just leave it behind. Drop the keys with the Spaniard and tell the car company we were taking the bus home. Relieved, I called the rental company back, and the car rep said, "That makes sense." Mamá already knew that.

Costa Rica has a good network of buses, and they're cheap. The 4:30 p.m. express to San José left Cahuita's main street in a cloud of dust at precisely 4:30, and it cost us less than $6 apiece. When we hit fog in the mountains that evening, it was a relief not to be at the wheel.

All afternoon, starting before we left Cahuita and continuing at every rest stop the bus made, I kept urging Mamá to call home and let the family know the car had broken down and we'd be late. She refused. If she did that, she insisted, everybody would just phone everybody else, and the result would be the family equivalent of calling out the National Guard.

So she didn't tell anyone until we got to the bus depot in San José and had to call Sandra and ask her to pick us up. Mamá's phone call was a masterpiece of motherly management:

"We had a wonderful trip!" she gushed. Everything was just wonderful, everything! The lovely, empty beach! The Spaniard who ran the inn! His paintings! Our room! The food! Not one single problem! Oh, well, there was this tiny thing with the car. . . .

Judging by the shocked reactions, if we had called home to report our car trouble, the family's worry would have melted the national phone lines. The smile Mamá gave me was as good as a wink.

So we'd had our trip together, we'd shared an adventure and a gentle conspiracy, and we'd come home safe. And thanks to Mamá, I can now say I've seen a lot of Costa Rica. But also thanks to Mamá, I know that I'd been seeing the real Costa Rica all along, through all those years—every time I looked into her face.

The American War

1996

———

I WAS STANDING in front of the old U.S. embassy in Saigon and looking up, through the over-arching branches of the shade trees, at the staircase on the roof.

Clearer than the building in front of me, I was seeing the televised images of a helicopter plucking desperate people from the top of that staircase on April 30, 1975, the day Saigon fell to the North Vietnamese.

Just then an elderly woman came up and stood directly in front of me. She was tiny—I could still see the embassy staircase over her head—and she looked like a wartime stereotype:

She wore a conical straw hat, with her gray hair pulled back in a bun, and she had on the dark trousers and long-sleeved blouse that the American press always described as "pajamas," but which were really standard Vietnamese peasant clothing.

"Where are you from?" she asked softly in French. The old people often speak French to foreigners; they got their schooling before 1954, when Vietnam was still a French colony.

"America," I answered. "*Amerique.*"

She smiled broadly, took both my hands in hers and

bowed over them. *Bienvenue à Vietnam,* she said. "Welcome to Vietnam."

This kind of thing had happened often in the day and a half I'd been in the city. I was touched by it—and mystified.

Yes, this was the South, and America's government had sided with South Vietnam's, so maybe I was more welcome here than in Hanoi. But maybe not: Before the war was over, we'd abandoned the southern cause, and thousands of people in the South had suffered.

"My country had a bad war with your country," I said to the old woman. "But everywhere I go, people are nice to me. Why?"

She smiled again and said, very simply and quietly, "The war has been over for 20 years."

Just not for us, I thought. Just not for us.

The Vietnam War is now as distant in time as World War II was in 1965—about the time we were getting in over our heads in Southeast Asia.

But in different ways, and for different reasons, Americans still are dealing with the Vietnam War, still reacting to it, still reacting to others' reactions to it.

The Vietnamese seem to have moved on—emotionally, politically, economically. They had another long bloody war in Cambodia after our war ended. And they'd had many other wars before we showed up.

"The history of Vietnam," a Vietnamese tourism entrepreneur told me, "is the history of war."

Everybody I met—whether from North or South, resident or refugee, tourist or returned vet—had a war story to tell, and everybody seemed to have had a different war.

I began to think in plurals: so many wars, so many Vietnams.

Here's one of them, from a cyclo driver who stopped to talk to me in a Mekong Delta town. In a soft voice and good English, he recited the names of all the U.S. officers he'd worked for at MACV (Military Assistance Command Vietnam) in Saigon.

"I remember," he said, speaking their names in whispers so nobody else could hear. The man had lost his future when the North won, went through postwar "reeducation" and then was assigned—apparently forever—to pedaling one of the ubiquitous pedicabs.

But he had come to terms with what happened, and he sounded as if he meant it. "This is my life now," he said gently and smiled. "I am very happy. Very happy."

Being in Saigon brought my own memories flooding back—memories of a place I'd never been. And had never wanted to go. They were memories in black and white, drawn from the black-and-white photographs that streamed into newspaper offices every day during the war. I'd pictured the country in black and white ever since.

Irrationally, that was what I expected to see when my plane sank down through the cloud cover on its way into Saigon's Tan Son Nhut airport. While my mind wrestled with the shock of that familiar name, my eyes registered a flat land, green as springtime, lush with rice paddies and trees, and spangled with snaky bits of water that glinted as the aircraft tilted. I felt an unexpected relief. Of course, it wasn't a black-and-white country—any more than it had been a black-and-white war.

Most of the Americans I met in Vietnam said they preferred Hanoi. But I liked Saigon best—perhaps because I saw it first, more likely because I'd heard so much about it.

Officially, it is District One of Ho Chi Minh City: HCMC is how it appears on government documents and airline tickets, and it's the name you use when you're in the more conservative North.

But like many American tourists, I kept calling it Saigon. "Sorry," I said, "it's habit." Don't worry, locals said, we call it that too.

I asked an American war veteran if the city had changed much since he was here in 1968. He said no, it had looked pretty much like this, but it had more bars then "and maybe it was a little cleaner."

Indeed, Saigon did look like its pictures: Those conical hats, the graceful tunic dresses called *ao dais*, everybody on motor bikes (with sun-conscious women in face masks and long evening gloves), terrifying traffic, teeming public markets and people everywhere—people spilling out onto the sidewalks, conducting business, eating lunch, tending babies, even sleeping.

It wasn't good press, but the war did give Vietnam big-time brand recognition among Americans—the kind other developing Asian countries covet, and it is one of Vietnam's major assets in the worldwide competition for tourist dollars.

Name the place, and most Americans over age 40 have heard of it: Not just Saigon, but Da Nang, Nha Trang, Cam Ranh Bay, Hanoi, Haiphong, the old imperial city of Hue.

Those Vietnamese places have been on our mental maps for 30 years, far more familiar than Chiang Mai or Phuket, the big tourist destinations in nearby Thailand.

Now Vietnam needs to replace the images that went with the names. Happily for the Vietnamese, that shouldn't be hard, given their startling friendliness and their country's astonishing beauty.

Friends who served in Vietnam had mentioned that at the

time. ("When the war's over, go to Da Nang!" one said, almost as soon as he got home.) But in the late 1960s and early '70s, beauty didn't seem very relevant.

Our grasp of Vietnam's geography probably takes a little rewriting, too. Every map shows a long, thin country—but how long is a surprise. It's nearly 1,000 miles from end to end, putting Hanoi and Saigon about as far apart as Minneapolis and New Orleans.

Even the climates are different: A normal fall day in Hanoi felt like mild June in Minneapolis, but every day in Saigon was like sweaty summer in Louisiana.

The cities were bubbling, and so were the people, but I kept tripping over reminders of our former presence. For starters, there were rows of old airplane hangars flanking the runway at Tan Son Nhut like big concrete Quonset huts. And there were the trucks.

One evening, in less than an hour, on the road from the Mekong Delta to Saigon, my taxi was passed by nearly 150 old U.S. Army trucks, still painted army green. At first I thought it was a military convoy, the kind you sometimes get stuck behind on the way to Camp Ripley in northern Minnesota. Not so. The U.S. military had left the trucks behind, and they had become the backbone of the Vietnamese transport industry.

(We left a lot more than that behind: The strangest fact I heard on the trip was that Vietnam still is one of the largest exporters of scrap metal in the world.)

The most painful monument to our countries' shared past was the War Crimes Museum—housed in the former U.S. Information Service complex, in case you need more irony. I went there on my first afternoon in Saigon because I wanted to get it over with early. It was awful.

Like war museums all around the world, it was full of atrocity pictures and grisly mementos, all shocking. What was worse, for me, was that, in this museum if not the whole country, the bad guys were us.

The bad guys also were people I knew and cared about. People I still know and care about. People who were good guys. An American vet who saw it when I did said simply, "The victors get to write the history books." And arrange the museums.

The Vietnamese don't call it the Vietnam War, by the way. They call it, logically, "the American War." So if you're a tourist from the States, it doesn't matter what your political views were at the time: The term "American War" takes in all of us, because it was our country that waged it.

I grew up with that war, graduated into the world with that war, and like most of my generation and our elders, regardless of our reasons, I wanted that war over.

When it finally ended, I wanted never to think about Vietnam again. Now I was in the middle of it, checking out—who could have foreseen this?—one of the world's most promising new travel destinations.

The souvenir shop at the War Crimes Museum—yes, there is one, the Vietnamese being astute business people—sells American-made bits of history:

Olive-drab cans of Desenex foot powder at $3 apiece.

U.S. Navy compasses for $50.

And Zippo lighters—lots of Zippo lighters. A whole shelf full, $15 each, no bargaining.

Graceful girls in blue and yellow *ao dais* were bending over the display cases, looking like flowers amid the war materiel, and sweetly urging tourists, nearly all foreign men, to buy.

The lighters had been made in the States but engraved in Vietnam for sale to U.S. servicemen during the war. Each carried a map and a place name on one side—Pleiku, Quang Tri, Khe Sanh—and a motto on the other.

The mottos were mostly unprintable, the kind of slogans that young men find funny in desperate situations: The humor helps ease the terror.

I asked to look at some of the Zippos, and the girls put a couple onto the counter, then a handful, then a dozen. I turned the lighters over, one by one, like flashcards, and read the mottos on the back:

"Always ripped or always stoned, I made it a year, I'm going home."

"If you think sex is exciting, try incoming."

"Fighting for peace is like screwing for virginity."

And then I turned over a Zippo that quoted Shakespeare: *"The quality of mercy is not strained."*

It made me catch my breath and choke up again, and I have been pondering its message ever since. Was the owner being sarcastic or sincere? Mentally, I added the second line, *"it droppeth as the gentle rain from heaven, upon the place beneath,"* and wondered whether he was thinking of healing—or of napalm.

I was glad when closing time came. Walking out of the museum felt like coming through the clouds at Tan Son Nhut all over again—out of a freezer, into warmth; out of the black-and-white war, into living color.

Late sunlight cast feathery tree shadows on the chipped stucco buildings and worn pavement. People were heading home from work, and the river of traffic was thick. Scooter horns bleated, bicycle bells chimed, and the sidewalks looked like a block party—schoolgirls with backpacks, women cuddling babies, vendors selling odds and ends, grandmothers and grandfathers perched on stools, everybody chatting in the mild air.

In front of the museum gates, a bunch of laughing, yelling little boys in dark blue school uniforms were playing shuttlecock. The game is like hacky-sack and has been popular in Vietnam for centuries.

I accidentally stepped into the action and nearly collided with one boy, but he dodged, beaming up at me as he made a particularly skillful save.

These kids weren't born when the owners of the Zippo lighters were stationed here, but other kids were playing the game then, and others will play it far into the future. It made me think about the permanence of little things.

Wars get waged, people die and others come to take their places. Big things change and keep on changing. But the little things of the world survive somehow: a style of dress, a beloved food, a children's game. Life *is* the little things.

In the end, what I took away from the War Crimes Museum wasn't the X-ray showing shrapnel in a face, or the awful photos of burned bodies, or the rusted U.S. tank decaying in the courtyard outside.

It was just these children playing hacky-sack, their laughter as golden as the afternoon light. I could hear their young voices for a long time as I walked away. The game hadn't ended just because an American stumbled through.

Mapping a Family

2001

———

FOR A MONTH NOW, I've been driving around with the United States in my station wagon. I'd forgotten how big it is. It fills the whole interior from the back of the driver's seat to the tailgate—front to back, edge to edge. And every time I slide behind the wheel, it makes me smile.

It's what my family called the Trip Map, always in capital letters. The Trip Map resided at my brother John's house for a dozen years after our father died, but now John was moving and wanted to pass it on to me.

"Wow," I thought, "the Trip Map!" I should have thought, "uh-oh, the Trip Map." My brother kept this awkward souvenir in his garage, and I guess I will be keeping it in mine, for the same reason: It won't fit anywhere else.

My family never did anything by halves, so *of course* the Trip Map is three and a half feet by nearly five. And it's heavy: My father glued it to a sheet of plywood and bolted it—yes, with steel bolts—into a heavy, homemade frame.

Even if he hadn't, it would have lasted. None of us can bear to throw it away. The Trip Map is the record of a dozen summers of our family's long driving vacations around the country.

We started out tenting, moved on to a 30-foot silver trailer—dubbed Watsons' Folly by our neighbors—and ended with a chassis-mounted camper on a Ford truck. Those rigs took our gang all over North America, from the Arctic Circle to the Guatemalan border—to every state in the Union, every Canadian province and nearly all of Mexico.

And every year, when the trip was over, my father would get out the Trip Map and carefully draw in our exact route, until a dense spiderweb of black lines radiated out from the Twin Cities, across the pastel blocks of the surrounding states.

The Trip Map testifies to a fact of Midwestern life and my father's attempts to cope with it: He was trying to vary the first few days of our travels, which—as every Minnesotan knows—always have to be across flat land.

Dad drove every possible route: due west, slightly northwest, way north and then west, and so on around the compass. The only real variety came when we went east, because we quickly ran into the Great Lakes. But we still had to drop down into the pancake flats of Indiana to avoid them.

Strangely, those slow, hot days of crossing the prairies are as vivid as our destinations. Whether we were heading for Anchorage or Yucatan, the landscape that was once our inland sea was so much the same (I am trying not to say boring) that there seem to have been more of those days than ones spent seeing Old Faithful or the Pacific Ocean.

That's what the Trip Map makes me remember—the ordinary days, the non-events, the commonplace stuff that no one ever writes down:

How we always left home not quite ready and always late,

on the premise that delaying yet another night would spoil
the trip, to say nothing of embarrassing us in front of the skep-
tical neighbors yet again. We once pulled out of our driveway
so late that we got only as far as Jordan, Minnesota, that night,
but at least we were underway.

How we packed light—just enough silverware, just enough
pots and pans, just enough clothing. No: not enough clothes,
not enough silverware, not enough dishes. And the dishes themselves, especially the colored aluminum tumblers that clanged if
you dropped them in the sink but never broke. I hated them
so much that I now own two complete sets—evil gifts from
friends who think they're funny.

But most of all, how we sounded. I look at the Trip Map
blocking the back of my car, and I can hear our voices again.
They're the voices of every traveling family. You know them,
too—how they start out cheerfully enough, then escalate as
the dusty prairies roll on and on:

"Everybody ready? Everybody been to the bathroom?"

"No fair! You got the front seat last time!"

"Settle down back there!"

"He hit me!"

Until finally, inevitably, we'd hear this: "Keep that up, and
I'll turn this car around and go home!" My brother Steve says
Dad once really carried through on that. He drove silently
in the wrong direction for perhaps two hours before Stevie,
on watch in the navigator's seat, finally figured it out and objected. The rest of us hadn't noticed: Flat is flat.

All this is why the Trip Map makes me smile, even while
it's keeping me from loading groceries into my car. I like to
think that other trips like my family's will be taking place this
summer, in other families' lives—despite two-job households,

despite the complications of Little League and kids' soccer, despite the gas crunch.

And I like to think that this winter, there'll be other parents carefully drawing black lines on big maps, making sure the continent sticks in other kids' memories—even if, when they grow up, they have to keep the continent in the garage.

Hunting the Falcon

2000

———

FROM MY HOTEL-ROOM window in Valletta, the sweeping view over Grand Harbour—one of the finest harbors in Europe—made me feel as if I were flying. It also made me marvel.

Daybreak, high noon, sunset, moonlight: At any time of day, in any light, it was beautiful—an immense living mural of deep-blue water and cream-colored stone. If I'd seen nothing else on this tiny Mediterranean island, Grand Harbour alone would have been worth the trip.

A couple of mornings, awake at dawn, I gazed at the panorama of stout stone buildings across the water for nearly an hour, watching the light and shadows playing over it. The view was so compelling that it was hard to pull away, even to get dressed.

One morning I stepped out of the shower, and a giant, out-of-scale white cruise ship was moving by, dwarfing even the tall, fortified cliffs that form the harbor walls. I reached for my camera while I was still dripping wet.

Another day, the ship moving past was a red-hulled freighter, coming home. The name on its bow read "Maltese Falcon."

That was the first such falcon I'd encountered in several days on Malta, and I was beginning to think it was as close as I'd get to the icon made famous in the 1941 Humphrey Bogart movie.

A black falcon statuette would be a natural souvenir for Malta, I thought, but apparently the Maltese didn't agree. I hadn't seen any in Valletta's shop windows, or for that matter, in any town. Maybe they had too much other history to think about.

Tiny Malta's national saga spans an immense amount of time—6,000 years—from Neolithic temples through World War II bastions and on up to the high-rise Hilton that overlooks the plush tourist neighborhoods north of Valletta. But no matter where you start, talk inevitably comes around to the island's greatest shaping force: the religious order known as the Knights of Malta.

The knights' history sounds like fiction—too over-the-top even for Hollywood. And that's before you get to the falcon. This is the nutshell version; Malta won't make sense without it:

The order was founded about 900 years ago, during the Crusades, as the Knights of St. John of Jerusalem, where it was headquartered. Its members were European noblemen who pledged to take care of Christians on pilgrimages to the Holy Land. But the region was in Muslim hands, held by Arabs and later Turks. The order soon militarized, becoming warriors for Christ as well as nurses for the needy.

Over time, the order grew wealthy and powerful, but Islam prevailed. The knights were forced out of one headquarters after another: out of Jerusalem in 1187; out of the Holy Land in 1291; out of Cyprus in 1310; out of Rhodes in 1522.

Finally, in 1530, the king of Spain gave them Malta. The

rent, it is said, was low but legendary: Every year, the knights would send the king a living falcon, to be used for hunting. Mystery writer Dashiell Hammett twisted the legend for "The Maltese Falcon," making one of the rent payments a golden statuette, later disguised by a coat of black paint.

Between battles (the worst was in 1565, when the Turks besieged Malta for four months), the knights spent their money and energy and power on buildings. All over Malta. For the next 268 years.

They built the towering battlements around Grand Harbour, the fortresses dotting the coasts, the church domes that dominate all horizons and the imposing Renaissance city of Valletta, their new capital. But they were needed less and less.

The French, under Napoleon, ousted the knights from Malta in 1798, only to be forced out themselves by the British a couple of years later. The Brits stayed for 170 years, fortifying the island until it resembled a baby Gibraltar. (By World War II, in fact, Malta was so strategic that the Germans bombed it harder than they bombed the East End of London.)

What is strangest about the saga of the knights, I think, is that they still exist. They are still high-born Europeans; they still do good works around the world, and their code of honor is still symbolized by the eight points of the Maltese cross.

Malta owes its history, including the knights, to its geography: In addition to having splendid harbors, it is a Mediterranean crossroads, located a little south of Sicily, halfway between mainland Italy and North Africa. It's always been a way station, whether for human voyagers or for the thousands upon thousands of birds that migrate across the Mediterranean every year.

On the plane from Rome, I had seen all of the miniature country, virtually all at once. Malta spread out like a three-island diorama on water so intensely blue that it looked solid: first, the island of Gozo, then Comino, then the main island, also called Malta.

Nearly all the national population of 360,000 is packed into the main island's northeastern half, so tightly that towns and villages run together, and only a Maltese can tell where one stops and another begins. There's still a little open land in the middle of the main island and along its southern coast, but the farm fields—rock-fenced like a sun-bleached version of Ireland—are not much larger than suburban American lawns.

I found it easier not to think of Malta as an island, but rather as a city completely encrusting a lump of limestone 17 miles long and nine miles wide. Even so, the place was overwhelming. The dense settlement, the complex history and the confetti of guttural place names on my map all combined to make Malta seem dauntingly big. Two things helped.

On my second night, still getting used to the distance distortion, I set out to walk around Valletta. I mean that literally: I walked around the entire city, on streets just inside the mighty ramparts. It took a mere 45 minutes.

After that, distances collapsed, and Malta shrank into something I could get my arms around. The nation of Malta, in fact, turned out to be the only place I've ever been where, if I asked somebody how far it was to X or Y or Z, and he said "five minutes," he was telling the truth.

The other key to Malta was a conversation with a tall, gray-haired former executive, Maurice de Giorgio, who directs the Foundation of Maltese Patrimony. Dedicated to preserving Malta's heritage, it arranges world-class exhibits of costumes, armor, silver, clocks, prehistoric art, even sedan chairs—treasures still in private hands.

"The best thing that happened to us was that the Knights of Malta got chucked out of Rhodes and came here," de Giorgio told me in elegant English, Malta's second language. Without the knights, he said, "we'd have been just another fishing island" instead of a rich repository of history, art and architecture.

The foundation's offices on Old Theatre Street were a perfect example of the knights' legacy. They're in the Manoel Theatre, an 18th-century jewel box that still holds performances. (Benjamin Britten's opera, "The Turn of the Screw," was playing during my stay.)

"We have an extremely varied culture," De Giorgio said. "So many nationalities have called in. We've had so many influences, and we've learned something from every one." Malta's callers included the Greeks, Phoenicians, Carthaginians, Romans, Arabs, Normans, the French, the British and now hordes of international tourists.

That's in addition to the knights, who were diverse in themselves. They belonged to eight major linguistic groups, called *langues* or tongues, and they may have provided Malta more than linguistic flavor. Although they had taken vows of poverty, chastity and obedience, just like nuns or priests, the knights grew rich and powerful and sometimes—well, less than celibate.

Every time I set foot outside my hotel, I saw clues to the cultural and historical mix that De Giorgio had talked about. Sleek modern yachts jostled for harbor space with old-fashioned wooden fishing boats, eyes painted on their bows for good luck. I bought toothpaste at a "chemist's"—Britain's term for drugstore. Menus read as if they'd been written by the European Union.

But the most disconcerting cultural combo hit me in church. Malta's shops and businesses close tight from Saturday afternoon to Monday morning, so there isn't much else to do on a sunny Sunday. I chose the 400-year-old Cathedral of St. John, a short stroll from where I was staying in Valletta.

It was built by the knights—of course—and they stinted on nothing. Frescoes adorned the ceilings; the dark walls were crowded with precious paintings and sculpture, and the floor was paved with tombstones—though that's too ordinary a word. They were memorial pictures made of inlaid marble— red, yellow, gray, black, white, green—depicting skeletons, armor, helmets, spears and battle flags; their inscriptions honor the men buried beneath them.

At the far end of the church, in a blaze of candles and gold, a priest was saying mass in Malti, the islands' distinctive language, virtually unintelligible to a foreigner. But there was one word I recognized, and it startled me. Though Malti is written in Latin letters, it's roughly 70 percent Arabic. So I sat in that 400-year-old Christian cathedral and listened to European Catholics praying to Allah.

Compact though Malta is, you still need wheels. I hired a taxi and traveled in loops around the main island—from the southern cliffs that look toward Africa, to the north coast, where St. Paul was shipwrecked in 60 A.D. I saw a lot, but I never saw a Maltese falcon, whether statuette or living bird.

At dusk on my last day on Malta, when it was dark enough to drive with headlights on but still light enough to see the forest of church domes against the sky, I was riding back to Valletta, lamenting the lack of falcons.

Then I noticed a small ad among many around the edge of my map. It was for a store called "The Maltese Falcon" in

Mdina, one of Malta's most picturesque places. An exquisitely preserved city inside a star-shaped, knight-built fortress, Mdina (pronounced Em-dina) is so small that it could snuggle inside Southdale, stone battlements included.

I'd already been there, and I hadn't noticed that store. But some of the streets had been closed off while a film crew shot scenes for "The Count of Monte Cristo." Maybe it was on one of those streets. . . .

"How far are we from Mdina?" I asked the taxi driver.

"About three miles. It's there," he said, pointing to church domes off to the south. I doubted we had time to get there before the stores closed, but I wanted to try. "Let's go," I said, and we left the rush-hour traffic converging on Valletta and raced across the island.

Cars can't drive into Mdina, so I dashed across the bridge over its moat on foot, through the magnificently carved main gate, past the baroque cathedral and up long, narrow Villegaignon Street.

Shops were closed or closing, but ahead was a solitary lighted doorway—and it was the right one. Inside, a whole shelf of black, brooding, hook-beaked ceramic statuettes glared down at me. They looked just like the one in the movie.

"These are the only Maltese falcons I've seen on the whole island," I told the young proprietor, as I set a big one and two small ones (Maltese sparrows?) on the counter.

That's because his family's store has a lock on the name, Paul Degiorgio (no relation to the foundation director) said with pride.

For a long time, he explained, the government would not allow any business to use the words "The Maltese" in its title. But his father had lived for a while in Canada and knew that the falcon was "very famous with the Americans, because of the movie."

The father pushed the issue when he moved back to Malta, and when the Maltese government finally eased its objections about 15 years ago, "he got it first," the son said. The figurine is modeled after the movie's, made in a Maltese crafts workshop nearby and sold nowhere else in the country.

"The Maltese falcon is very important," Degiorgio said. "We study it in school."

The movie? I was incredulous.

No, he said patiently, school children study the real Maltese falcon: "It's part of our history."

Unfortunately, there aren't any living ones left on Malta. "It used to be a perfect place—one of the best places for falcons in Europe. That's why there was the request from the king of Spain. The peregrine falcon is the best hunting bird, even nowadays." Then came World War II. "After the destruction here, they disappeared," and now the island has been so heavily built up that there is no place for them.

As I started to leave, Degiorgio offered me a sheet of information about the real falcon. It included something I hadn't known, and I got a shiver of serendipity: The falcon was to be paid to the king every year on November 1.

"That's today!" I said. It seemed like destiny. Degiorgio just smiled, and I stepped out into Mdina's darkened streets, my long-sought Maltese falcons firmly in hand.

Reunion in the Andes

2002

M Y NEPHEW JAMES spent his birthday at Machu Pic-chu. Not bad for any age, but he was turning 20, and there is no more magical place to launch an adult life. I felt honored to be with him there, along with his younger brother, Charlie, and their father, who is my younger brother, John.

For John and me, this trip was a travelers' reunion. We had seen South America's most famous ruins together when John was not much older than his sons.

Now, after 26 years, we'd come back to the Lost City of the Incas, and we were seeing it through many eyes: our own middle-aged ones, of course; James's and Charlie's young ones, and the eyes of memory—the eyes of our own younger selves.

In 1976, I had taken a leave of absence from my newspaper to spend a year exploring South America. My brother and a high-school friend, Mike Zika, both recently out of the Army, invited themselves along. "You speak Spanish," John explained, "and we figured you wouldn't mind two men as protection." They figured right.

We spent three months bumming around the Andes to-gether, riding rickety buses and staying in 50-cent-a-night hotels, most of them named the Bolívar. But it was worth it. Of many highlights, the absolute best was Machu Picchu, the mountain stronghold of the Inca Empire.

John and I started talking about going back to South America almost as soon as that trip was over. The idea got sidelined when careers and marriage and kids came along.

But when John's son James was about 4, the little boy became enchanted with his father's photos of Machu Picchu. "Dad," he'd asked, "someday will you take me to the mountain?"

John said yes. I said yes, too, even though I hadn't been invited: "If you ever do that," I told my brother, "I'm going along."

In March 2002, when James was a sophomore in college and Charlie a high-school junior, John decided it was now or never. I rendezvoused with them in Cuzco, the former capital of the Incas, high in the Peruvian Andes.

It was a trip land-mined with deja-vu. By the end of the first day in Cuzco, I'd written "when we were here before" so many times in my journal that I shortened it to WWWHB.

The boys, predictably, did not share our interest in seeing the very places where John and I had sight-seen, eaten dinner and slept WWWHB. But we couldn't help it. We made comparisons everywhere.

Much had changed. Cuzco was huge now, and it was crowded with tourists of all nationalities, even in the wake of Sept. 11. (Or possibly because of Sept. 11: Many international travelers—including me—thought South America would be a safer destination than the United States or the Mediterranean.)

But the bones of Cuzco were intact: its beautiful historic core, where ornate Spanish churches and white-washed palaces have stood for centuries atop powerful Inca foundations. Some of Cuzco's sights—the Koricancha, for instance, the

Incas' Temple of the Sun—were actually better because recent archaeology had revealed more of them.

And the roads were paved. WWWHB, when we wanted to go from Cuzco to the market town of Pisac, we'd caught a predawn ride in the open back of a pickup truck, and the trip took more than two hours over rutted dirt roads. Now, Pisac was barely half an hour from Cuzco by taxi.

Geography shrank as this new "now" collided with my treasured sense of distant "then." What hadn't changed was how places felt—and how we felt in them.

"It's like I never left," John said, sounding a touch dazed, as we worked our way through central Pisac, past market stalls where women in flounced skirts and fedora hats sold ears of corn and homemade freeze-dried potatoes—just like last time.

"Me, too," I said. I was having trouble keeping time straight, as if the two trips had tangled and the intervening 26 years had vanished.

Sometimes I even caught myself thinking the way I had back then, about what I'd do with my life when I got home. Maybe try grad school, or find a job that would let me travel. . . .

This time warp explained something John had said WWWHB. We were somewhere in Peru or Ecuador when he suggested we go to China. "Why not?" he had said. "It's just the world." And we were out in it, with no responsibilities, feeling as if we could go on forever. Everywhere was close, because everything was possible.

The morning of James's birthday, we took the early-morning train from Cuzco to Aguas Calientes, the village at the foot of the mountain that cradles Machu Picchu. Unless you're hiking the Inca Trail, a four-day trek, this town is the jumping-off place for the ancient city.

Aguas Calientes—"hot waters"—is named for an Inca bathing place, now the town's swimming hole. I remembered it as a tiny and somnolent village. But it, too, had morphed dramatically into a busy town of shops, restaurants, small hotels and smaller houses, crowded into a tight network of narrow gulleys.

Stalls full of T-shirts, llama figurines, flutes and wall hangings lined the path from the station. That was predictable. Tourism, after all, is the biggest industry in the world, and it shows everywhere. There are more human beings on the planet, and more travelers, and therefore more businesses to serve them.

But it made me worry about the changes I'd read about at Machu Picchu itself: a huge hotel, masses of exhaust-belching tourist buses, a proposed aerial tramway from valley to mountaintop. How much of this had happened?

We headed for a budget hostel—Gringo Bill's—which I'd found online and chosen because I thought the name was funny. We dropped our gear, got some food at an outdoor cafe and bored Charlie and James by talking about how different everything looked from WWWHB. Then we caught a bus uphill.

The changes at Machu Picchu weren't as bad as I'd feared. Tickets had gone up ($20 per person), but so had maintenance and security. The buses were bigger than before, but there were never more than a couple up there at a time. The hotel outside the gate was small and rather tasteful, and you could not see it from within the ruins.

Machu Picchu itself, impressive 26 years ago, now left me stunned and groping for adjectives: Gorgeous. Breathtaking. Mind-blowing. Incredible. All those are true, and so is a word that visitors, including archaeologists, have never been able to resist.

Face to face with this abandoned city in the clouds, the mind reaches instinctively for "mysterious." On every side, mountains fall away in green waves, and mists float up from the valleys, catching like scarves on the towering trees. The city's gray roof-less houses look more like cottages in an abandoned Scottish village than a last-stand fortress in the New World.

Local Indians, descendants of the ancient Incas, kept it se-cret for more than 400 years—until 1911, when they helped a Yale researcher "discover" it. It has been world-famous ever since. And rightly.

Machu Picchu means "old peak" in the local Indian tongue. In its best-known portraits, it lies across a saddle-like ridge with a green-clad mountain rising directly behind it. That is Huayna Picchu, or "young peak," whose picture had so en-chanted my nephew James when he was little.

The Incas had cut a path into the stone shoulder of Huayna Picchu, and it's still the only route to the top. It's so steep in places that now there are chains to help you pull yourself up. At the very peak, there's a small flat place carved into a boulder. It's called the Inca Throne, though it was more likely an altar.

My brother, our friend Mike and I had climbed this moun-tain twice in 1976, and I remembered the path up more clearly than anything else about Machu Picchu.

It hadn't changed: dark rocks slick with moisture, ferns and flowers growing from every crack, and narrow, breath-stealing steps that the Incas probably skipped up. At an alti-tude of roughly 8,000 feet, I didn't skip up them in 1976, and I didn't skip up them now. But James and Charlie did.

Just before the summit, you enter a tiny cave of fallen

boulders, pull yourself up and out and emerge on top of the world. Too many renowned sights turn out to be less than a traveler expects—Stonehenge, for example, is disappointingly small—but this view is far more than you expect or even deserve. Look down from the top of Huayna Picchu, and the whole ruined city spreads out at your feet, an archaeological miracle.

The Inca Throne was unchanged, and we took turns posing in it for pictures, the way John and Mike and I had when we were here before. But unlike last time, we didn't have the mountain to ourselves. Americans, Japanese, Brits and Australians streamed up with us, making it busy at the top. Most of the other tourists arrived, looked at the view and started down, paying no attention to the Inca Throne. That made us feel like old Machu Picchu hands—which, I guess, we were.

As the trip went on, we four fell into the same easy comradeship I remembered from the earlier trip. We stopped being adults and kids and became companions, our differences leveled by a shared adventure. It let me get to know my nephews and reconnect with my brother in a way that had not been possible in the intervening years, even though we live less than half an hour apart.

Hiking around the huge walls at Sacsayhuaman, an Inca site above Cuzco, for example, Charlie and I talked about his late cousin, my stepson Joe, who had been killed at age 18. Charlie was too young to remember the tragedy, and I was touched by his interest.

James and I spent the most time together. We were always getting separated from his brother and my brother, something we chalked up to personal travel styles. Charlie and John both traveled purposefully, while James and I . . . well, we didn't.

We were constantly distracted by details and assailed by

whims, stopping on impulse to make an important sketch or write a journal entry that couldn't wait or just sit down and talk.

The other-worldly silence of Machu Picchu invites introspection, and eventually we got around to talking about our lives and the quirks of our extended family.

I told him that I feel like my true self only on trips. At home, I always feel like an outsider, even within my family, though I'd never told them that.

James understood. He said he'd felt like that, too, growing up, but now, in college, he'd found out who he was and where he belonged, and he was truly, fully happy. It made me happy just to hear another Watson say that.

Our similarities got clearer as the trip went on. A day later, at Ollantaytambo, a different Inca ruin, James and I were doubling back to revisit a particularly interesting wall when we noticed Charlie and John heading for something new—far below us and in the opposite direction.

I felt torn. "I hate this—having to choose," I said. "I've always wished I could be in two places at the same time."

"Think how much that would suck," James said thoughtfully, "when you can't even be in one place at the same time."

Wow, I said, staring at him. Exactly!

Near the end of our last day at Machu Picchu, James and I rendezvoused—late, as usual—with my brother and Charlie at a place called the Gate of the Sun, where the Inca Trail enters the confines of the city. This is where hikers get their first view of the ruins. Seven came through the stone gateway while we were there, and each one stopped and gasped. It's almost as good as the view from the top of Huayna Picchu.

John and Charlie started back first, planning to walk all the way into Aguas Calientes on a shortcut trail that slices straight downhill through the switchbacks of the road.

James wanted to hike that trail, too, but not as much as he wanted to commune a while longer with the ancient city. We found a flat balcony of rock and sat down to watch tour groups emptying out of the ruins.

"I wonder if the city gets lonely for its lost people," I said, as the evening mists rose from the valleys and drifted toward us. Already, wisps of white had blotted out the peak of Huayna Picchu.

"Maybe they're coming back," James said. "Maybe the mists are Inca ghosts."

It was a nice thought to leave on. And we had to leave. It was getting dark, and the park gate would soon be locked.

We said goodbye to Huayna Picchu, goodbye to the stone houses, goodbye to the llamas grazing on the grassy plaza. We splashed cold water from an Inca pool on our faces one more time, in a final Inca baptism. And we took so many last looks on the way out that I felt compelled to mention Lot's wife. James asked what I meant.

"It's from the Bible," I said. "She looked back when she wasn't supposed to, and God turned her into a pillar of salt."

By now, I knew I could count on James for an offbeat response. "I'd have looked," he said.

And been turned into a pillar of salt? Yes, and it would have been worth it: "She was lucky," he said. "She got to stay."

Big Dry Train Ride

1986

SUDDENLY, THE MONOTONOUS landscape of sand and shrubbery realigned itself, and there they were, materializing from the flat beige background as if they'd been beamed from another world.

Kangaroos. Real ones. Just like the movies. They even hopped, all seven of them, fleeing the train. And I did what Americans do when seeing these beasts for the first time. I squealed, "Lookit! Lookit! Kangaroos!!!"

Australians find this sort of reaction amusing. They have had, after all, a couple of hundred years to get comfortable with the whole idea of giant hopping marsupials. Australians are just plain used to kangaroos, the way Minnesotans are to, oh, cows.

So my fellow train passengers took my outburst in stride. "What other Australian rubbish can we tell her?" one man remarked mildly to his friends, looking up from a round of Trivial Pursuit, Aussie style.

They had a bit of a think and decided to tell a Yankee joke—the one about the American tourist who tried chasing 'roos by truck and was impressed because "they're doing

40 miles an hour, and they haven't even put their front legs down yet!"

Kangaroos, which tend to cluster near garbage dumps like bears in American parks, were one of the highlights of crossing Australia by train. The train itself was the other.

Scenery, you'll notice, isn't on my highlight list. You don't take the train across Australia because of the scenery. You take the train across to say you've taken the train across. To learn something about the vastness of the island continent. To meet some of its people. And maybe to join them for a beer in one of the lounges or play a few rounds of their version of Trivial Pursuit when the scenery loses the last of its modest appeal.

I did both, and the game's questions opened new doors onto Australian life and history. Sometimes, though, I thought I was riding in a parallel universe.

———

"Where did Ned Kelly shoot three policemen in 1878?"
"Dunno."
"Stringybark Creek."

———

Scenery may not be the right word for what was outside the windows. Flat isn't the right word, either. It's beyond flat. On the Nullarbor Plain—the name means "no trees," and it's accurate—the limestone plateau is so level that the railroad track over it is called the Long Straight. It lasts nearly 300 miles— the longest stretch of straight track in the world.

I was traveling on the route of the Indian-Pacific, one of the world's great trains. Normally, it runs between Sydney, in New South Wales, and Perth, on Australia's West Coast, a distance of 2,460 miles, the rough equivalent of traveling from New York to Los Angeles. But a strike had disrupted the schedule, so I flew to Adelaide and caught the train there. Even so, the trip to Perth was 1,598 miles.

———

"What did the Australian government bury 20,000 of after over-catering for crowds at the opening of Parliament House in 1927?"
"Dunno."
"Meat pies."

———

We pulled out of Adelaide about noon, gliding for a while through wheat country. Like a lot of Australian geography, it looked familiar at first and then took an unexpected twist: long golden swells of land with green bits of trees in the creek bottoms—and then patches of what looked like snow.

The patches turned out to be dry salt lakes. "Do you have those where you come from?" asked one of my new Australian friends. Not in Minnesota, no.

We had to take to a siding whenever a freight—called a goods train Down Under—needed the single track. This put us into Port Pirie, a major railhead, nearly two hours late, and there were further delays as cars were added for the long hop westward.

When the train was finally made up, it consisted of the engines, four flatbeds of vehicles belonging to passengers bound for Perth, and 14 rail cars, including coaches, economy and first-class sleeping cars, a diner, a cafeteria/club car (for second-class passengers), a fairly plush lounge car (first-class passengers only) and a baggage car.

From Port Pirie, the train turned west and, after dark, shot arrow-straight for Perth and the Indian Ocean.

———

"What statue graces Five Mile Creek, near Gungadai, New South Wales?"
"Dunno."
"The Dog on the Tucker Box."

———

The dining car had served our evening tucker—Australian slang for food—during the Port Pirie stop. We rolled out of Port Pirie close to three hours late. Could we make up the time? Would it still be light the next afternoon, when we got into Kalgoorlie, the old gold-mining town where the train was supposed to stop long enough for sightseeing?

"Depends on if we hit any heat restrictions," the conductor intoned. Any what? "Heat buckles," he said. Those are places where Australia's fierce summer sun causes the track to expand and warp, and the train has to slow down so it won't fly off the rails. The maximum permitted speed is about 70 miles an hour, and the train averages just above 60. When the temperature is over 100 degrees, heat restrictions can limit the speed to about 45 mph. A hundred degrees is peanuts, by the way: "In the middle of the Nullarbor," the conductor said, "it can get up to 130, 140 degrees Fahrenheit."

———

"What was the first Australian state to introduce daylight saving?"
"I dunno."
"Tasmania."

———

Whether we hit heat buckles that night, I never knew. We did make several long stops on sidings, while goods trains rumbled past in the darkness, their headlights revealing a landscape of dust and what I would, in another hemisphere, have called sagebrush.

The day began with a chipper voice on the loud speaker: "Gud mornin', ladies and gentlemen, it is 20 to 7, train time. Passengers holdin' first seatin' cards, your breakfast will be served in the dinin' car at 7 a.m. train time. Repeat. . . ."

No one except the train crew paid much attention to train time. Perth residents, returning home, set their watches back to Perth time. I kept mine on Adelaide time. It didn't make much difference, as long as we got to the dining car in time to eat.

The scenery that morning was the Nullarbor Plain. It's pronounced "Nulluh-bore," which tells you something. "If I call this 'the middle of nowhere' in print," I thought during one of our unscheduled stops, "it would be true."

"What Australian aviator read his own obituaries when he finally reached England after a failed attempt to cross the Atlantic?"
"Dunno."
"Harry Hawker."

The highlight of that day happened soon after breakfast: An interlude at Cook, a railroad work camp where the trains stop to refuel. "Passengers will be allowed to detrain at Cook," the loudspeaker advised, "to stretch their legs while conductors water your cars."

Cook was a single wide street with about 30 houses along one side—frame boxes with deep verandas, galvanized metal roofs and a few bushes out front for shade. In the middle of town there was a dusty open space, like a plaza in a village in northern Mexico or desert Peru. In the middle of the plaza was a monument, a boulder with an aluminum plaque dedicated to the "Men of the Trees" who brought 600 trees to the town for its 60th birthday in 1982. Any resulting forest was invisible.

Near the plaza were the Cook School; the school playground; the Cook Community Complex; a post office housing a branch of the Commonwealth Savings Bank of Australia; the train depot; the telephone relay station and, nearest the tracks, a tiny trailer labeled "Cook Combined Charities." The trailer sold souvenirs: Cigarette lighters labeled "I Crossed the Nullarbor." T-shirts emblazoned "Trans-Australian" above a view of Cook. Collectors' teaspoons with a local wildflower painted on the handles; it was labeled "the Sturt desert pea."

At the far edge of town stood another building, a small hospital, one of the bases for central Australia's Flying Doctor service. In front of it, a roughly painted sign read, "If you're crook, come to Cook." I asked for a translation and found out that "crook" is Aussie slang for "sick." Not to be confused with "chook," as in "feeding the chooks," that is, chickens.

About 100 people lived in Cook. Nearly all were railroad employees and their families. "They're transients—don't stay long," one of them told me. "Guys like me, we only stay a fortnight. The ones with houses, a year. Some stay 15 years." Because they like the place? "No," he said, "because they've gone barmy."

"What ABC radio serial ran for almost 6,000 episodes?"
"Blue Hills."
(Ah! It's the Australian Broadcasting Company!)

The big event of the second night was Kalgoorlie, the town of 22,000 people that produces half of Australia's gold. The metal has been mined there since its discovery in 1893.

Although the train had made up a lot of time, we still arrived in Kalgoorlie after dark. No matter: A local tour company had sightseeing vans waiting anyway, and a dozen of us passengers hopped in.

Kalgoorlie lies in pure desert, getting only about nine inches of rain a year. It exists because of "the golden mile"—the richest mile of gold-bearing ore in the world. But it survives because of a pipeline that brings water from a supply nearly 350 miles away.

Even at night, you could see what the town had been. Its history showed in the extra-wide streets—made to give camel trains room to turn around—and in the Victorian brick storefronts, trimmed with white-painted cast iron and looking like frosted cakes in the lamplight.

You could also see what the town still is: A mining camp, a boom town, a place where paychecks are big and there isn't much to spend them on. "This is notorious Hay St.," the tour guide announced as we drove slowly past a row of doorways where women in scanty clothing stood bathed in purple, blue and magenta neon. "You're probably well aware of what we have here."

Prostitution wasn't legal, he said, but it was "tolerated" by local police: "When you go to a mining town that is mostly men, it's a well-known fact that this does keep the crime rate down."

———

"Who was the Sentimental Bloke's best mate?"'
"I dunno."
"Ginger Mick."

———

The next dawn brought different scenery—progressively greener and more populated as we approached the coast. There were hills now and vineyards and an occasional glimpse of the sea. Farmsteads appeared, then the farms shrank and gave way to suburban houses with green lawns and flower gardens and no dust on the leaves of the trees.

And then Perth station, and the hubbub of reclaiming luggage and saying goodbyes. In the first-class lounge car, one elderly passenger lingered at the electric organ, picking out the melody of "Now is the hour when we must say goodbye...."

One by one, my fellow Trivial Pursuit players missed the game-ending question. Too exotic, they complained. Finally it was my turn.

———

"What are the Twin Cities?"
"Minneapolis and St. Paul."
"Ooooh, no fair!"

———

The Rose-Red City

2000

———

IF THERE IS ONE PLACE on this planet that's guaranteed to make you feel like Indiana Jones, it's the *siq*—the knife-blade-narrow canyon that leads into the ruins of ancient Petra in the desert wilderness of southern Jordan.

The siq will also convince you that the Nabateans—the vanished people who were sovereign here 2,000 years ago—had Hollywood beat when it came to special effects.

The approach to the long-abandoned city of Petra starts in Wadi Musa, a modern town that could not exist without the ruins. Western tourists have been making their way here ever since Europe first heard about Petra in 1812—encouraged by an English poet who described it as "a rose-red city, half as old as time." Wadi Musa is where everybody stays.

The little town's blockish, desert-colored buildings cling to the sides of a steep valley. Near the bottom is the entrance to Petra National Park. The ancient city lies inside, but to get there, you have to walk through the siq.

This is the age-old entrance to Petra, a narrow slot canyon that twists like a roofless tunnel through nearly a mile of solid rock. You enter it through a cleft in a high, rough cliff, and instantly the world changes—from hot sunlight to cool shadow, from wide-open vistas to a narrow pale-pink path of sand, curving between towering sandstone walls up to two hundred feet high and sometimes as little as six feet apart.

It is like stepping into a cathedral: The siq simply *feels* silent. Light sifts from above like dust, and you want to lower your voice in respect, if not flat-out awe.

This helps explain a legend about it. It is said that, when Moses struck his staff on a rock and the Almighty sent forth water, the siq was gouged out by the miraculous runoff.

What's at the end of the siq is even more awesome. You are still in the dimness of the passage when you start to glimpse it—a slice of rosy light, sometimes revealed, sometimes hidden by the undulating walls. It looks like a pink ribbon, fluttering in an invisible wind.

Then suddenly the siq stops. There is no transition: You step from the dark defile into a bright box canyon, and there, glowing in the sun, stands the Treasury—a 130-foot-tall confection of columns, archways, doors, urns, statues and pediments, all carved out of warm pink sandstone.

It was designed to impress, built like the rest of Petra by the Nabateans. The Roman Empire assimilated their territory about 106 A.D.

The Treasury made me gasp, but it broke the heart of the college kid next to me.

At first, stopped in his tracks like everybody else emerging from the siq, he just beamed at it from under his slouch hat. Then he announced, to no one in particular, that he'd wanted to come here ever since he saw "Indiana Jones and the Last Crusade," and now he *was* here. "I gotta go see the inside," he said, starting forward.

"There's nothing to see in there," another tourist, a much

older man, said casually. True enough: The Treasury is no such thing, and any guidebook will tell you so. It's an empty tomb carved into a pink cliff, all facade and no depth.

Inside, there is only a shallow room with empty alcoves where the dead once lay. It is utterly unlike the movie's depiction: no secret cavern, no treacherous stepping stones, no whirling knives called the Breath of God—and certainly no 700-year-old crusader knight guarding the Holy Grail.

The kid in the Indiana Jones hat was stunned; it hadn't occurred to him that the interior he saw in the movie wasn't real. His naiveté touched the older man. "The interior was probably shot in some studio in California," the man said, soothingly. "I'm sorry."

"Rip-off!" the kid blurted out, disappointed and angry. "How could they do that?" Apparently, I thought, we need another sequel: "Indiana Jones and the Giant Reality Check." Or perhaps "Raiders of the Lost Childhood."

The more important omission in that Jones movie was the rest of the ancient city. From the canyon of the Treasury, the high walls of the siq fall back, and its sandy path turns into a thoroughfare flanked by tomb facades. Then you pass a huge amphitheater carved into the rock—it could seat 8,000—and the thoroughfare turns into a wide, shallow valley ringed with cliffs. Here the main part of Petra stood.

The valley floor is littered with partly excavated buildings, temples, Roman-style baths, even a stately street flanked by stone columns. This isn't as showy as that first glimpse from the end of the siq, but the valley and the surrounding heights are so rich in ruins that you could spend a week hiking Petra's trails, trying to comprehend it all. I spent two days rambling in its baking sunlight and wished for more time.

The valley forms a natural fortress in the heart of the great trade routes that connected India and China with the Middle East. No wonder the Nabateans grew rich. In their heyday, camel caravans came and went here, swaying their way through the siq, laden with silks and spices on their way from the Orient and with such local rarities as frankincense on the way back.

The siq had been nearly empty that first morning, when my guide and I walked in. Not so the rest of Petra. Large tour groups are timed to arrive extra-early so they can sightsee before the blast-furnace heat of midday.

So the key sights in the valley were swarming with tourists. That meant they were also swarming with local people trying to earn a living, usually by hawking rides on sturdy little burros or nasty-looking camels with tasseled blankets over their humps.

"You want donkey, lady?"

"Taxi to the top, madame?"

"Camel? Ten dollars . . ."

I shook my head and decided to hike the heights first and see the valley later, when I hoped it would be emptier.

Near a row of plain tomb facades, their tops carved in zigzags, my guide pointed to a narrow rock staircase rising straight into the cliffs. The rock was so colorful and the shadows so strong that I could barely make out the steps.

The steps twisted, changed to trails, changed back to steps, steadily lifting us up toward the Great Place of Sacrifice, a mountain whose top had been chopped off by the Nabateans to form a wide stone platform.

It boasted a staggering view—and a large French tour group. As we arrived, their leader suddenly sprawled out on the platform's low rock altar and pretended he was having his heart torn out, the way the Aztecs handled sacrificial victims in Mexico.

The French tourists laughed. My guide was disgusted. The offerings here would have been animals, he insisted, not people.

I was relieved to get back to the quiet of the trail. It wound past more tomb facades and many cisterns, basins for catching rainwater.

As many as 30,000 people had lived in Petra, my guide explained, and water was always a problem. That was why the Nabateans had carved so many cisterns and why the heights were laced with channels to lead water down into the city. They had even cut an irrigation trough into the sandstone walls of the siq.

At wide places in the trail, the modern world intruded again. Local tribeswomen in black clothes and dark scarves had often set up shop there, and they sprang at us, pleading with me to buy necklaces of agate and beads.

Once a trio of kids, riding bareback on donkeys, came clattering downhill, and we perched nervously on the outer edge of the trail to let them pass.

The rocks were mostly weathered to light brown, but where they'd been protected from rain and sun, the sandstone was tinted red, dark brown, coppery orange, pink.

Cats were prowling around up there—feral cats, my guide said, like house cats but wild—in almost as many colors as the rocks. They were the only wildlife I saw at Petra, except for one small lizard and a few birds wheeling in the hot, clear air.

Old stones get to look a lot alike, and I'd been ruin-chasing for almost a month before I got to Petra. I hadn't been expecting much. But once there, I couldn't bear to leave it.

I went back the second morning on my own, just to wander and absorb, but I had a deadline over my head. That night, I had to be in Amman, Jordan's capital, to catch a flight to Jerusalem; it meant leaving Petra in mid-afternoon.

The Treasury kept stopping me. I was besotted with it. I would start to leave, get into the siq, look at the Treasury over my shoulder, walk half-backward to stretch out the farewell. But the moment the stone walls blocked my view, I would rush back so I could see it again.

"Just one last look," I kept promising myself. "Just one more last look. . . ."

I played geological peek-a-boo with the Treasury half a dozen times and would have gone on longer, but a Jordanian man came up to me and started to chat. He was about 50, stocky and clean-shaven, in a snappy straw fedora, a white shirt and khakis. He spoke good but accented English: clearly a guide.

I told him I didn't want to hire another guide because I was leaving. "No guide," he said, "just friend."

He was walking out of Petra, too—and having much less trouble doing it than I was—so I took a *final* final look at the Treasury and joined him.

As we walked, he asked me if I knew what the sand could do. But what the sand had done was all around us: It had carved the siq. The most likely theory is that this skinny canyon had started as a crack along the fault line called the Great Rift, which runs through southern Jordan on its way down into East Africa. Then for eons, every cloudburst had churned sand into an abrasive slurry and driven it into the crack, scouring it out and smoothing its walls until they resembled sculpture. But that wasn't what the man meant. He meant the sand could work like dye.

Until a bypass was built, the siq used to have flash floods, often drowning whoever was in it, including more than 20 tourists in the 1960s. Even now, the siq's floor is wet where water seeps from the ancient irrigation trough, and there the sand is as red as old blood. My new friend reached down and grabbed a fistful.

"Give me your hand," he said. He rubbed the moist sand onto the back of my hand, and my skin turned the color of rust. "You can wash your hands—it will not come off," he said proudly. (He was right. There were still traces after my next shower.)

As we continued through the pinkish light of the siq, we established that I was an American, that I liked Jordan very much and that we both thought Petra was beautiful.

"But not like Kansas," he said. "I love Kansas!"

My mind stumbled. Of all the things I might have heard at Petra, that was the most unlikely.

"Kansas!" I yipped. "Why?"

He said he had guided a tourist from Kansas through Petra once, and they'd become friends. The tourist invited him to visit his farm near Abilene, and he went several times. He had even helped with the harvest.

"You know why I love Kansas?" he said, his eyes growing a little dreamy. "Kansas is flat—like here—only *green!*" So much for rose-red cities.

Villa Daze

1994

———

O<small>NE YEAR AT THE VILLA</small>, the most memorable event was watching a line of black ants transport slices of bright-green leaves and hot-pink bougainvillea petals past the swimming pool.

The ants were coming from somewhere near the mango tree and marching off toward the house, but we never found out exactly where they started or where they went. We could have checked, someone noted much later, but nobody thought of that.

We were in the pool at the time. The ants were trudging along the pool edge right past our noses, and we just hung there in the warm turquoise water and watched. It was like tuning in to the Discovery Channel without touching the remote.

And that, in a nutshell, is why I've spent 15 years of winter vacations renting the same house in Acapulco. Same house, same companions, same cook, same caretaker, same adventures.

Which is to say *no* adventures.

I go simply because it is beautiful, predictable, peaceful, *not home*, warm, sunny, beautiful, predictable. . . . We've done this trip so often, people complain when other people bring the same swimsuit two years in a row. Not enough variety.

We don't like variety in anything else, though. Every year is the same, and that's the great joy of this place: So far, at least, nothing that matters has changed.

Its not-so-great joy is the time-lapse effect of repeat visits: The lady who manages the house—and "lady" is the right word—ages gracefully from year to year, but ages all the same. Between visits, we age too.

And the visits connect like film clips, so we seem to age rapidly, as if God is flipping the corners on a stack of our snapshots. Waistlines thicken, wrinkles deepen, hairlines creep upward, jowls creep down. But it doesn't matter here. The villa's the same.

Going to the villa is like renting a summer cabin: You know somebody else owns it, and you pay to use it, but once you've paid, it's yours. And you can go as brain-dead as you like in the time you've bought. We go pretty brain-dead.

At the villa, painting your own toenails is an event. Painting somebody else's toenails takes planning. And wow! Somebody wants to have their hair highlighted? We'd better put that off till tomorrow, when we've got more energy.

Sometimes there are real events. One night we saw Queen Elizabeth's ship put out to sea and watched through binoculars until it became an uncertain smudge in the charcoal night.

On other occasions, we've seen whales—or rather the distant white plumes of their breath—and then gone nearly blind staring at the dazzling sea for the next hour, hoping to see them again. Once we saw a mother whale traveling steadily north, while her whale child—a black dot from our distance—frisked around and around her like a two-year-old in a toy store.

We frisk too. Being at a staffed villa is like being five years old. Only better. We have become friends with the people who take care of us each year. They set the schedule, we respond. This is all there is to do:

Get up in the morning, pull on your play clothes and show up for breakfast. Play by the pool or (if you feel that energetic) go to the beach till lunch time.

Eat lunch. Take an afternoon nap or (if you feel that energetic) write letters on the terrace.

When the sun is pounding full on the pool, go back for a long, lazy afternoon of reading (if you feel that energetic) or just lying in the water, with squadrons of frigate birds and vultures and pelicans drifting overhead against the blue, blue sky. It's not really true that the vultures come closer to check on us as the week wears on. We do move sometimes. Just not much.

And then comes sunset. It should be capitalized: SUN-SET. The biggest production of the day. While the cosmos is working on the clouds, the staff is working on margaritas, and we shower and dress for dinner to the sound of ice in the blender.

"Sunset alert," somebody announces, and we all turn to look. Are there enough clouds to make it gorgeous tonight? Does it rate a 10 this time or only the usual 9.6? Is it clear enough at the horizon to see the Green Flash?

Ah, the Green Flash.

The Flash is our Holy Grail. We have scanned the horizon for it for a decade and a half, and only a few of us claim to have seen it. The rest of us don't believe them. The flash is supposed to be caused by the last rays of sunlight shining through sea water as if through liquid emerald.

No, say skeptics, the Green Flash is in your head. Just a matter of nerve endings. When you've stared too long at the last tiny speck of sun, your eyes will see green when the red speck is gone.

The Green Flash argument is just one of our annual certainties. We know, for instance, that the suitcases of books we've packed won't be quite as appealing as the Agatha Christie or Vanity Fair somebody else brought. We know we'll end up trading novels and magazines, and we'll lament the trashy level to which our tastes have fallen.

(Once, before I knew better, I brought textbooks for a college course I was taking in anthropology. And spent the week studying yam consumption in Papua, New Guinea, while envying everybody else's New Yorkers.)

We know that one night per visit, our whole group will dress up and troop out to a nice restaurant. We know that halfway through the week, one or more of us will get a touch of *turista*, and we'll all discuss diarrhea at breakfast and blame it on the nice restaurant. And we know that we'll all take our nice pills and be fine again pretty soon.

We know that near the end of the week somebody will decide to go "into town," which means shopping for silver or ceramics at the downtown artisans' market, and that will touch off shopping frenzy in everybody else.

(One year the shoppers set up their own artisans' market in the hall outside our rooms. They spread all their treasures out on their beach towels, and the rest of the group got to shop without leaving the house. Our caretakers thought it was funny.)

We also know that we are not going to stay up till 3 to go disco dancing at Baby O's. That we will not watch the cliff divers jump off the rocks at La Quebrada. Or go to the bullfights. Or take the sightseeing cruise across the exquisite scallop of blue that is Acapulco harbor. Those worthy activities are for our occasional newcomers. We've already done them. Just don't ask us which year; the years sort of blur together.

This kind of vacation falls well below the tourism thresh-hold, and we know it. True, we had to get on a plane to get here, but it doesn't matter much where "here" is. Which is the point: When you take a villa vacation, you go somewhere to be—and to be taken care of.

It is an absolute break, and it could as easily be Hawaii or Key West or Phoenix or the Seychelles, for all we know. We didn't come to interact with the culture. (Although we do, in a way. The people who take care of "our" villa have put five kids through college on their share of the rent money, and that makes us feel as if we weren't complete parasites.)

One year I went into the villa the moment the taxi dropped us off at the gate and didn't leave the place for a moment, until the taxi came to take us back to the airport a week later for our charter flight home. When you have perfection, I figured, who needs to look any farther?

Another year, one of us forgot to leave his parka in Min-nesota, which means he had to carry it all the way to Mexico. He modeled the whole rig—gloves, scarf, hood—for the villa staff, so they'd understand what we were trying to get away from. Why live there then? they wondered.

That's the same question I ask myself in the middle of every winter—when my eyes get tired of gray and white and start longing for the Green Flash.

The World at Nineteen

1987

———

ABOUT TO FLY HOME from an assignment in Mexico, I had settled into a window seat and was running over the trip in my mind, considering which photographs would work best with which stories and generally feeling satisfied with the work I'd done.

"Excuse me," a young voice chirped, as its owner, a clean-cut college type, dropped into the seat beside me. He began to talk immediately, with so much urgency that he didn't notice takeoff.

He was from Canada, he said, Vancouver, actually; he was 19, and he was going around the world.

Not that he hadn't seen some of the world already, of course—his family had lived in England for a while, and they'd traveled together in Europe—but he'd never done any traveling completely on his own.

He was sure that it was good for him—letting him develop his inner resources, giving him a chance to find out what he could do without parental protection.

Besides, it was buying him time to think through what he wanted to do with his life: Should he go straight to medical school? Or take time off and work for a while? Or maybe switch career fields entirely?

Listening, I was impressed, not just with his optimism but with all his possibilities, all the roads he had to choose from. It made me a little nostalgic for age 19, when that had been true for me, too. I was beginning to wonder whether I'd pick the same path if I had to do it over.

Then he turned to his travels in Mexico. He'd loved the country and the people, especially the family he'd stayed with in Mexico City. They were so warm. And they'd had such good talks, covered so many subjects. He'd really felt a part of their lives.

"But it's still hard," he added sadly, "being away from your own family and friends for so long."

I nodded, recalling various homesick treks of my own, and asked how long he'd been on the road. Given how much he needed to talk, I figured several months.

"Three weeks," he said, and sighed, as if it had been a lifetime.

That, of course, was the other side of being 19: Life seemed to take so long then, and time was an endless ribbon that nothing could snip. I hid a smile and fought the temptation to give him a hug and say, "There, there."

The conversation made me remember another encounter between a 19-year-old beginner and a veteran traveler—only that time I was the 19-year-old.

It happened in Italy, in the middle of a hot, damp late-summer night, and my companion and I were tired. We had just finished a long ferry trip from Piraeus, the port of Athens, to Brindisi, on the Adriatic coast. We had taken deck passage because it was cheap, and the sea had been rough, so we hadn't slept.

Now we had boarded the night train from Brindisi to Rome—third class because it was cheap, so we wouldn't sleep there either—and we were stowing our humble gear in little racks over the wooden benches.

(Third-class benches have vanished from European trains, which is too bad. They belong in every traveler's past because, no matter what happens to you later, for the rest of your life you'll feel that you've come up in the world.)

Nearly all the passengers in our car were American students like my friend and me, homeward bound from a wandering summer in the Mediterranean, heading back to the States for school.

One wasn't. And she stood out.

She was about 55, thin, bright-eyed, very tan, in vigorous, handsome health—a woman of whom younger travelers thought, "She must have been beautiful once," while older travelers knew she still was.

Her clothes didn't suit her, though. She wore a simple wash-worn cotton dress, a head scarf, canvas slip-on shoes, no makeup, no jewelry. No pretensions of any kind, in fact, yet you'd never mistake her for a peasant.

She tossed a small duffel into the overhead rack, sat down opposite us and, in elegantly accented English, began to ask about our lives—not with the condescension older people sometimes use but with genuine interest: Where had we been? What had we been doing? What had we learned?

Nowhere near so much, we quickly realized, as she already knew.

When it was our turn to ask questions, we found out that she came from Argentina, that she was the wife of an American diplomat who had retired young from foreign service, and that they had loved so many places in the world that they didn't want to choose just one for a retirement home.

Instead of a house, they had bought a 40-foot sailing yacht, which they anchored in a different Mediterranean port for a year at a time. They used the boat as a base, traveling out from there to visit old friends and favorite cities.

They had just finished a year in Greece and were about to move to southern Italy. While her husband stayed behind with the sailboat, she was going to Rome to arrange the necessary immigration and docking papers.

We said something young and tongue-tied, like "Wow!" or "Neat!" or "Nice life!" Or maybe all three—I don't remember.

I do remember a rush of envy.

Because that woman was doing what all of us wanted to do and none of us could: wandering the globe, free as air, choosing exactly where to live and for how long.

We had youth, all right, but we also had very little money, degrees to finish, career choices to make and no guarantees that we would end up with that woman's rewards.

She must have sensed our thoughts. She added gently that there were drawbacks to her life.

"Look at my hands," she said, stretching them out, palms up, for us to examine. "They aren't pretty anymore. They're all muscles, from pulling on the lines."

That was true, but they looked strong, and we envied that, too.

We also had to remember, she cautioned, that a boat wasn't a house: You couldn't take very much with you.

"All we have room for are our sailing clothes"—she gestured with a hint of embarrassment at her dress and shoes—"and our evening wear."

Sequins and sailboats! We were awed. That image branded her on our memories forever.

It's been more than 20 years since that envious night on the Brindisi train, and my companion and I are well along the paths we chose for ourselves. They haven't led either of us—so far, anyway—to a yacht in the Mediterranean. But they have led to other experiences and other wisdoms, including one that our sailor-heroine personified:

Never underestimate the power of maturity.

Almost Shangri-La

2002

———

ATINY VOICE MURMURED something at my elbow. It sounded like "ohio-gozaimus." I looked down. A 4-year-old girl in a long brocade dress was smiling shyly up at me and leaning back against her father's skirts for confidence.

"No, not Japanese," her traditionally clad father said gently, "English! English!"

"Hello," she said, even more shyly.

"Hello," I said back.

She was learning, her father explained with pride, how to treat visitors to Bhutan. I'd been in Bhutan for a week by then, so I knew firsthand how the Bhutanese treat their annual handful of tourists. They treat them well. This little girl was just one more sweet example.

We met in the town of Paro, at the dance ground of the *dzong* that dominates the landscape—an ancient whitewashed building that is part Buddhist monastery, part fortress and part county courthouse, because in Bhutan, church isn't separate from state. Church *is* state.

It was the day after the full moon in April, and the great painting of Bhutan's patron saint had just been unrolled above

the dance ground for the first time in a year. The dancing had
been going on in its honor for four days.

Roughly 35 feet wide by 50 feet tall, the painting depicts
the holy man who, 1,200 years ago, brought Buddhism to this
small mountain-girded kingdom in the Himalayas. The Bhutanese believe he flew in on the back of a tiger.

The giant image, called a *thondrol*, had been let down like
an enormous window shade just before 4 a.m.—at the exact
moment when the full moon would shine directly on the por-
trait's face. Just seeing it is believed to take away your sins.

I was in the huge crowd at the *dzong* that night. I'd gotten
there with a few companions at 2:30 in the morning and then
had sat, chilled stiff, on cold stone steps amid the elaborately
dressed Bhutanese, waiting. I hoped their robes were warmer
than my jeans.

Then the moon rose, the monks untied the bindings, the
holy image unfurled, and the people sighed and flowed toward
it. I joined them, in a human stream so tightly packed that we
moved along in gusts, like leaves.

As they drew close, people handed gifts to monks holding baskets—money, rice, incense, packets of cookies—and
stretched out their hands to touch the painting's hem, to duck
under it, to pay homage at small shrines behind it, to let it trail
over their dark heads as they were swept past by the pressure
of others craving a turn.

The crowd grew through the morning, as more and more
Bhutanese poured in to see the revered image before it was
rolled up again and hidden away for another year.

They all wore traditional clothes, made of rich, handwoven fabrics in red, gold, blue, purple: the *kira*, a long wrap-
around skirt and short jacket for women and girls, and the *gho*,

a roomy kilt-length robe, tied at the waist and worn with knee socks and street shoes, for men and boys.

They were dressed normally. What they wear at home is up to them, but the Bhutanese always wear traditional dress to ceremonies, as well as to government offices and schools. It's not just picturesque, it's required, and that's one of the country's great charms for visitors.

The other, I realized that morning, is that in Bhutan, events like the dance festival still belong to the people. In Bhutan, by royal decree, tourists remain a tiny minority—truly invited guests, the way we should always be.

The only other place I'd seen anything so authentic was in Tibet, Bhutan's neighbor to the north, but there, you saw only what was left after the Chinese got through savaging its Buddhist shrines.

In Bhutan, you see the shrines, the monasteries, the maroon-robed monks and the people themselves—in all their living glory. And they smile. Just like my non-guidebook said they would.

Normally, I don't carry novels with me on trips; reality always turns out to be more satisfying than any fiction. But this time, on a whim, I'd packed a copy of "Lost Horizon," the 1933 classic that gave the world a new name for paradise: Shangri-La. In Bhutan, it proved as useful as a Fodor's.

Bhutan may not be Shangri-La—no human society could be—but it's certainly working on it. Tour promoters say it's like stepping back in time, but that's not true, either, because the old days weren't like this, anywhere. It was more like stepping onto the real-time version of Cloud Nine.

Bhutan is the last Buddhist kingdom in the Himalayas—a stronghold, in more ways than religion alone. Its great good fortune is a monarch who cares deeply about his people and has the authority to put policy where his heart is.

The king is a one-man amalgam of the progressive and the traditional: Jigme Singye Wangchuk was educated in England and has four wives. The four are sisters, and the national newspaper, the Kuensel, always refers to them as Their Majesties the Queens. It's a little disconcerting the first time you see it in print.

On the throne since he was 17, the king is known for living simply, for tooling around in a four-wheel-drive instead of a limo and for doing the right thing. Among his memorable pronouncements: "I care less about the gross national product and more about the gross national happiness."

In the early 1990s, worried that Bhutan would lose its culture the way other small countries have, the king issued a series of protective decrees. These are the reason that Bhutanese people still wear the *gho* and *kira* instead of blue jeans and polo shirts. Why students must be fluent in Dzongkha, Bhutan's official language, even though all other instruction is in English. And why new construction must be traditional-style and why existing concrete-walled factories are being Bhutan-ized with whitewash and ornate wooden eaves.

The decrees are also why Bhutan sets limits on tourism. "What we are looking at," a high-ranking tourism official explained, "is low volume, high yield—a certain class of tourist— minimizing the negative effect of tourism on our society, on our environment." It's the same upscale approach that worked for Bermuda.

Bhutan only opened to paying tourists in 1974, and growth has been deliberately slow. Fewer than 7,000 tourists came to Bhutan the year I was there, all traveling on government-approved guided tours that required each person to spend a minimum of $200 a day.

"Our king has a broad vision," another Bhutanese man told me. That was as evident as the national dress, and the more I heard about it, the more I liked it.

Environmental protection, for example, is taken so seriously that "all trees belong to the state, even the ones in your garden." New development is spread out across the country so rural people won't be so tempted to leave the land and migrate to the cities, the way peasants have done all over the developing world. Women have equal rights. Old people are admired. Schooling and health care are free. Family planning is a priority. That last item may be the most important on the list.

Bhutan is the size of Switzerland and has 750,000 people. Nearby Nepal is the size of two Switzerlands and has 23 million. You can see the difference from the air. The mountainsides of Bhutan are so thick with trees that they look black. But the hills of Nepal have been scalped for farm fields and terraces, and every rise of land except the snow peaks is topped by a house, or two, or three—the unmistakeable effect of runaway population growth.

I found the Shangri-La idea irresistible, right from the beginning. Coming north into Bhutan from the hot, crowded lowlands of India, the road rose through virgin forests where familiar-looking pines mingled with unknown hardwoods. The air cooled until it felt like spring at home.

Vistas opened at every switchback, a blend of Rocky Mountain National Park and the hazy beauty of the Great Smokies. Tiny white violets bloomed in the grass by the roadside, and rhododendrons as big as trees clung like pink clouds to the slopes. Sometimes what seemed to be flowers in the distance turned out to be fluttering prayer flags up close.

There were a few cattle in the pastures and once, near the road, a cluster of yaks—the shaggy, long-horned mountain work beasts usually associated with Tibet.

The few farmhouses looked like Swiss chalets, with thick white walls, slate or wooden roofs and stones weighing down the shingles. I half expected a Himalayan Heidi to come along. But the only people we saw were road crews from India—you could tell because they wore Western shirts and trousers.

I was traveling with a small group of North Americans and an official guide, required in Bhutan, even if you're a group of one. Our guide's name was Karma, the term for a Buddhist concept that Westerners often find hard to understand, let alone explain. Karma is a little like fate or predestiny, with the events of this life being direct outcomes of deeds in past lives.

We spent that night in Thimphu, said to be the only national capital in the world without a traffic signal. It had had one briefly, I'd read, but residents thought it was disruptive and ugly, so the government took it down.

Next morning, in the center of town, Karma showed us the signal's replacement—a uniformed policeman at a Bhutanese-style guardhouse, crisply directing main-street traffic, most of which was on foot.

A tour of any other capital would start at, say, the congress or the local equivalent of the Smithsonian. But religion is so important in Bhutan, so tightly entwined with daily life, that those things rank pretty low on the list of sights. Karma merely pointed out the parliament, in the same tone he used to point out the country's only golf course, while we drove to what really mattered: the first of many *dzongs*.

Old people, wearing winter jackets over their *kiras* and *ghos*, were worshiping there, fingering Buddhist rosaries, spinning prayer wheels, resting in the sun between slow circumnavigations of the shrines.

Their faces looked beautiful in the morning light, and I took out a camera, bracing myself for what I often get in other countries: resistance or a demand for tips. I was about to get another example of how different Bhutan is.

Before I could pantomime a request for permission, two of the old ladies volunteered. They gave their prayer wheels a whirl, grinned at me and posed. And every single person after that—everyone I wanted to photograph on the rest of the trip—did the same thing. No one ever said no. No one ever asked for a tip.

That had never happened to me before. Neither had this: I was standing beside a row of big prayer wheels when another elderly woman came slowly by, spinning them one by one and mumbling a prayer. With a jolt, I understood the words, and they gave me goosebumps: "*Om mani padme hum*," she was saying. "Oh, thou jewel in the heart of the lotus."

It is the great mantra of Buddhism. I had read it countless times but had never heard it said aloud by a true believer, let alone the way she was saying it, over and over, as if she were sighing. Shangri-La, indeed.

Bhutan's Buddhism is much different from the austere Zen variety. It's closer to the Tibetan version, full of incarnations and reincarnations, demons and protectors. Also like Tibet's, it includes elements of animism, the beliefs that preceded Buddhism. For example, Karma said, the national archery team—as important in Bhutan as the Super Bowl winner at home—has its own astrologer.

Buddhism teaches that each person is living out his or her karma in this world, so who you are is who you are supposed to be. This means that the king is revered, as are religious leaders, but the Western cult of celebrity doesn't exist—something that causes discomfort for hot-shot outsiders and some amusement for the Bhutanese.

"We don't have hero worship," the tourism official said. "We do not go out and ask, 'Can I have your autograph?'" Not even when it's Mick Jagger. You can be admired in Bhutan for doing something exemplary, the official explained, but for simply doing the job your karma gave you, no. And Mick Jagger's job was being Mick Jagger.

My job in Bhutan was being a tourist—and an audience. When the little girl spoke to me at the Paro *dzong*, it was an opportunity for her father to do a commercial for his homeland.

"I have been in Japan," he said in English, "I have been in Bangkok, I have been in Manila, I have been in India." His conclusion: "To be born a citizen of my country—it was the luckiest thing in my life. We are a small country, but we like it."

I liked it, too, and I envied people like the little girl and her father who will be part of its future. This is as close to Shangri-La as I am going to get, I thought. Maybe I could get a job teaching here ... But was it my karma to do that, I wondered, or my karma just to wish it? I could not tell.

Paro's festival was almost over, and the festival grounds were emptying. Tibetan traders were closing their stalls and slashing prices on incense, beads and prayer horns. Bhutanese parents were hoisting tired, brocade-covered little kids on their shoulders and heading down the hill to town. I took another wondering look around the *dzong* and joined them.

Eastern Europe with Palm Trees

1999

——

THE OLD CARS said as much about Cuba as the political slogans I was eagerly writing down on the way in from the Havana airport.

"Revolution always," said one billboard.

"Go forward with works and dreams," said another.

"Fifty-five Fairlane," said my friend. A red-and-black Ford was moving past; the finish appeared to be house-paint.

It's a myth that there are only old American cars in Cuba. Classics from the 1940s and '50s make up about one-fourth of what's on the roads, but you still see them everywhere, adding a majestic note to Cuban traffic.

They also added a comforting familiarity to an otherwise unexpected country. These were the sedans of our childhood, the jalopies of our adolescence. "What are you doing here?" I kept wanting to ask them. The simple answer is that they are surviving, just like Cubans themselves.

Maintained with love and ingenuity, coaxed into running as if they were geriatric greyhounds, each ancient Chevy or Buick or Caddy we saw was a reminder of the two central facts of Cuban life: Fidel Castro's revolution and the United States' embargo.

The two arrived almost simultaneously. The Revolution overthrew a corrupt dictator in 1959, and *el bloqueo*—the blockade—followed on its heels. Among other things, that meant no American imports, not even car parts. Forty years later, it still means the same thing.

On the map, Cuba looks like a hammerhead shark. Our plan was to drive from west to east—from Havana, on the shark's arched tail, all the way to its head, home of the U.S. naval base at Guantanamo Bay and the handsome Spanish-colonial city of Santiago, a UNESCO World Heritage site.

Because gas is expensive and parts hard to come by, nobody drives any car—especially not the old ones—very fast. That gives Cuban traffic a stately pace, unusual in a Latin country. Therefore we figured the driving would be easy and allotted nine days for the round trip. It wasn't enough.

Cuba is about 750 miles long, and by day two, we knew we couldn't drive fast enough to cover it. It wasn't because of our weak-engined rental car or the potholed roads. It was the people.

They were all over the roads, trying to hitch rides on anything with an internal combustion engine.

Mothers with babies, old people with buckets, security guards on their way to work—everybody—clustered around intersections on the edge of towns, waving at passing vehicles. Some even risked their lives to stand in the middle of the lanes on the *autopista*, the wide quasi-freeway that runs the length of the country.

In towns, if we paused to ask directions of one person, others would lean in our car windows and plead, *"me lleva?"* Will you take me? The people were living proof of Cuba's public transportation shortage.

We weren't out of the Havana suburbs the first afternoon before we felt sorry for a young woman walking up the road-side and gave her 20-minute lift to the town where she lived with her father.

Five hitchhikers later, we agreed that at this rate, there was no way we'd make it all the way to the eastern end of the island and back in nine days. We focused instead on the body of the shark, Cuba's middle third.

In the course of the trip, we stayed in family homes, ate in "secret" restaurants (ones that don't pay taxes), poked our heads into classrooms and stores, libraries and theaters, and talked to everyone we met—every hitchhiker, every hostel owner, every taxi driver, even the confident little kids who came up to talk to us in the parks. We always asked the same questions:

"Do you have enough?"—meaning food, clothing, goods? Invariably, the answer was no.

"Do you want democracy?" Usually the answer was yes.

"Do you want capitalism?" No. Always a no. Where Americans tend to blur the distinction between freedom and economics, Cubans understood the difference. Many said they wanted to keep the best of socialism but with full political freedom. Kind of like Sweden? Yes.

We also asked a question almost nobody would answer: "What do you think will happen after Fidel dies?" After all, *El Jefe Máximo*, the Maximum Leader, is in his 70s; sooner or later, someone else will have to take over.

Responses varied but usually included nervous smiles or shrugs and sometimes silence. "We can't talk of such things," one person said quietly. "It'll just be more of the same," said another. Just once, we got a wisecrack: Cubans don't think anybody will succeed Fidel, one young man said with a grin. "We think he's going to live forever."

Cuba isn't like other places, I decided as the country unfolded. It's like *pieces* of other places: Mexico, sometimes. Honduras, sometimes. And sometimes. . . .

"I keep thinking of this place as a tropical Eastern Europe," my friend said from behind the steering wheel of our tiny yellow rental. It was our second day on the road.

I agreed. Not Eastern Europe as it is now, but Eastern Europe as it was before the old regimes fell, before 1989, when Eastern Europe was still the Eastern Bloc.

Cuba has the same sort of run-down neighborhoods, the same shoddy goods and empty shelves, the same long queues of people waiting for meat or fresh vegetables or some mystery item that might run out before they get to the front of the line.

But unlike Eastern Europeans a decade ago, Cubans aren't grim. Poor, yes, but also exuberantly friendly—even to Americans, even despite the blockade. Not once did we experience anything but kindness. Not once. We weren't just pleased. We were humbled.

One afternoon, for example, I was exploring Old Havana— the city's magnificent 18th- and 19th-century core—and wandered into a strange, almost empty shop on the Plaza de Armas.

"Welcome to the House of Water!" a man boomed in Spanish. Another man and a girl stood with him, beaming, at a counter topped with old-fashioned ceramic water jars. "Have some water! See—it's filtered!"

More museum than shop, this was the last of many *casas de agua*, dating from the 1800s, when Havana had a shortage of clean drinking water. It was free, but a donation would be nice. The man filled a jelly-glass from one of the crocks; I drank it, and then we all talked, as if we were in a non-alcoholic neighborhood bar.

They asked where I was from, and when we got to my nationality, smiles broke out. "My father is in New Jersey!" the girl said. "Merry Chreesmas!" said the second man. And when I had to leave, the first man clasped my hand to his chest and wished me "a very happy New Year and a good trip to your home!"

Biased by the look of the old Soviet Union, I've always associated revolutions with austere ugliness. That wasn't true here, either. Cuba was gorgeous, and driving slowly gave us more time to savor it.

We went through town after small town with long streets of crumbling housefronts in pastel stucco, like old birthday cupcakes with the icing flaking off. In the town centers, there were Spanish-style squares and parks, built before the American Revolution and perfect as movie sets, preserved first by poverty, now by government decree.

Away from the towns, royal palms graced the rural landscape like oaks in American pastures. Miles and miles of soft sand beaches baked in the sun, empty of tourists. There were soft green mountains in the distances, and feathery stands of sugar cane in the valleys, and tiny white shacks, their sagging red-tiled roofs picturesque with age.

You can see quaint little shacks like that in many nearby countries, but in post-revolutionary Cuba, these quaint little shacks have power lines running to them. That's rural electrification, something most Central American and Caribbean countries haven't fully managed, and something that the United States didn't fully achieve until after World War II.

Another thing: The people in those shacks get free health care, delivered by cadres of well-trained doctors. And the people can read. It was this widespread literacy—estimates exceed 96 percent—that impressed me most.

In the nine days that we drove around Cuba—often lost because street and highway signs are few—we never encountered anyone, anywhere, who couldn't read our map and set us straight.

That may sound routine to literate Americans—but except for Costa Rica, I've never traveled anywhere in Latin America where that was true. It's not true in quite a few places in the United States, either.

There was something else, something we sensed but couldn't identify at first. Then it grew clear: Cuba is a multiracial country, whose people shade from African black through every shade of coffee to pale Spanish white. But Cuba didn't feel racist.

Racism is hard to kill anywhere, and people will tell you that it isn't dead here. But modern Cuba appears to have done a better job of beating it down than America has. Everywhere we looked, we saw a rainbow of Cubans, all shades mixed together—in schoolrooms, in stores, in groups of friends on street corners, in families.

As Cuba defines it now, "revolution" means maintaining the positive changes that the country has achieved since 1959. Literacy, health care, even the multi-hued population—all that is the Revolution now, and Cubans are justly proud of those achievements and of hanging onto them despite the economic disasters of the past decade.

Everybody we talked to cited those achievements—before they complained about what they didn't have.

The more we looked, the more it seemed as if Cuba were emerging from suspended animation, as if Part 2 of the 20th century hasn't started playing here yet. Everything is frozen in the amber of the 1950s.

That means no skyscrapers to break the profile of Havana, no Golden Arches, no neon strip malls in the suburbs. All over the country, hordes of beautiful buildings from the last century and even earlier are still in use, because there hasn't been enough money to tear them down. Even Varadero, the beach resort being developed east of Havana, is low-key compared with Miami.

The lack of glitz gives Cuba a peculiar sense of quiet, as if everything were running in slow-motion. Often, it really is.

In small towns, horse-drawn carts do the work of pick-up trucks, and eight-seater horse-drawn carriages take the place of buses. Hay, after all, is cheaper than imported gas. The fast clip-clop of horses' hooves is everywhere, as Cuban a sound as the ever-present rhythms of maracas and conga drums.

I found the working horses charming—and ultimately sad. If and when the embargo is lifted, and American money once again floods the country, the need for those horses is one of the first things that will evaporate. I expect the old cars will be next.

For most Cubans, the end of the embargo will probably make life easier. There'll be more goods to buy, and for some people, more money to buy them with. But easier and better aren't always the same.

Racism, for one thing, could flare again. Already, class distinctions are beginning to. "Cubans used to dress about the same," one young man said, almost wistfully. "Everybody had Cuban clothes. Now some people can afford to buy foreign clothes. And others can't."

Old ladies kept asking us for soap. "To wash myself with," they would say, miming a bath. Some wanted it for themselves, but we suspected some wanted it to sell. Another woman, much younger, scoffed at our gullibility. "Soap is *always* available," she sneered.

But a bar costs half a peso—which at first sounds like a bargain, because it's only a nickel. It isn't a bargain. That's because there are two economies at work: one peso-based, the other based on U.S. dollars. Any luxury item—and in Cuba that's everything from extra food to new clothing—is priced in Yankee greenbacks. But Cuban salaries and pensions are still paid in pesos. The exchange rate—of about 20 pesos to one dollar—makes peso salaries sound ridiculous when they're translated into American money.

"In my profession," a young engineer told us, "the average monthly salary is $8. A dentist gets $12." His retired father gets a monthly pension of about $5. Numbers like those make a nickel bar of soap loom large indeed.

Like elderly Russians selling their belongings at subway stops, some needy Cubans sell their goods at consignment shops. We stepped into one in Sancti Spiritus, a pleasant colonial town in the middle of the country, and were shocked. Clearly, the people didn't have much to consign—except hope.

Among goods ranging from old faucets to living-room furniture, I saw the most humble of all: two well-used diaper pins with blue plastic heads. Asking price: $1—an eighth of a month's salary for that engineer.

Our Cuban embargo has been in place for so many years that it's part of the background for Americans, like faded wallpaper in a house we moved out of. The Cubans are still living with it.

"I blame the blockade," one woman said, talking about the shortages that bedevil Cuban life. The state provides the basics, she and others said, but they're rationed.

"So how do you get a piece of meat?" I wondered.

"Oh, *mi amor*," she said, "you are such a child. There is supposed to be meat, but there is no meat. Do not even talk of meat. Talk of eggs."

OK, I said, how about eggs? Sorry, they're rationed too.

"Five eggs a month," the young engineer said. At the time, we were eating breakfast at his family's table. His mother had just served us two fried eggs apiece. I'd been picking at mine. I looked at the plate and felt guilty.

Ah, but those are tourist eggs, I rationalized, eggs bought for dollars from an independent entrepreneur. You can get other things that way, too, including meat—if you've got enough dollars. A woman who serves elaborate meals to foreigners but frugal ones to her family told us that her 6-year-old grandson recently asked, "Why can't I eat meat like the tourists?"

But meat is nothing compared to what she said were the real "forbidden fruits," foods reserved for tourists, foods that ordinary people aren't supposed to eat. People always lowered their voices when they mentioned them: "Shrimp," they would say, glancing around just in case there were spies, "and lobster," as if they were talking about cocaine and hashish instead of food.

Which leads to the flip side of this controlled society—the bright side: Drugs aren't a problem in Cuba. Sexual assaults are said to be virtually unknown. As for crime, our guidebooks said to watch out for pickpockets in rough parts of Havana and not to leave wallets on the beach when you go swimming. But violent crime—the U.S. sort—seems not to exist.

"How bad is the crime rate?" I asked a taxi driver. He didn't understand the question. I reworded it. He looked nonplussed and answered slowly, "I would say it is . . . zero."

Near the end of the trip, I was standing in front of an apartment house in central Havana, waiting for other tourists to pile into a tour van, when a ghastly screech ripped the air above me.

"*Faisan*," the tour driver said, reassuringly. Pheasant. "Someone is keeping a pheasant on his balcony."

As a pet, I asked, or to eat?

"Pet, I think. But that apartment"—he pointed to a third-floor balcony packed with crates—"I think they are keeping chickens." With impeccable timing, a rooster crowed on the balcony. A rooster in the center of a city of 2 million! It was like hearing a Holstein moo in Manhattan.

The driver grinned and added, "There are people in Havana who raise a pig in their bathtubs—and they get big! You have to take baths around it."

We'd heard other such stories. "Cubans are very inventive," someone explained. Economics made that essential. Before the Revolution, the U.S. was Cuba's biggest trading partner. We bought virtually all of its sugar harvest, the mainstay of the economy. When we broke off relations, Cuba had to look elsewhere to survive. It turned to the Soviet bloc.

But when that fell apart in the late 1980s and early '90s, Cuba's economy collapsed with it. Things were worst in 1993, one man said. "We had nothing. Nothing. There were no goods. There were no stores. There was no gas. Cars were just sitting around on the streets. Nothing."

Cuba scrambled desperately to make ends meet. One of the things it turned to was tourism. Given the scenery, the spectacular untouched beaches, the music, the pleasant people,

Cuba was a natural for it. But you can't build a tourism business overnight. Particularly when the biggest potential source of tourists has made it illegal for its citizens to come to your shores.

"We think it's interesting," a young museum guide told me, with a sly edge to his voice, "that the country that is always talking about its freedom forbids its citizens to visit this one." We thought that was interesting too. More than interesting.

No Place Like Nome

1999

—·—

S IPPING A SUMMER-MORNING latte in the Lucky Swede
Gift Shop on Nome's main street, I was wondering whether
I could find a real live gold miner to interview, when fate solved
the problem by sending one in—a trim guy in his 30s with
sandy hair, a good grin and enough self-gathered information
to qualify him as a gold encyclopedia. Even better, he was a
gold encyclopedia from Minnesota.

Like me, Bob Hafner was just stopping in for coffee before
starting work. Unlike me, he was working for himself. The
waitress steered him over. Did I need somebody to show me
around? he asked. Sure do, I said.

His adopted hometown is best known these days because
it's the finish line of the annual 1,100-mile Iditarod dog-sled
race. But it wasn't sled dogs that put Nome on the map. It was
gold. Gold is still what keeps it there.

For the rest of the day and into the long, sunny June night,
Hafner steered his red pickup as if it were a Land Rover, jolting over the pitted gravel roads of Greater Nome—population
4,000—to give me a close-up look at gold dredges, gold mining camps and more real live gold miners.

We even helped some of his friends shovel for the precious stuff on the long, windy beach—the famous "ruby sands of Nome," which drew 20,000 gold seekers to this isolated Alaskan dot at the dawn of the 20th century.

Along the way, he told me stories, starting with his own. Mining gives him a sense of pride, Hafner said: "I produce a durable good for the country. At the end of the day, I can look at it and say, 'I made that,' and I can take it to any country in the world and use it as money."

He got into gold mining in the early 1990s, after he'd come to Alaska for another job and decided to stay on. For the first six years he was in Nome, he kept trying to convince his family back in St. Paul that "this is what I do. This is who I am."

But the family kept asking, "When are you coming home?" Then one visit, Hafner brought back five ounces of gold that he'd mined himself, "and I had a check for it in my hands three days later." After that, his parents understood his commitment. "Now it's 'When are you coming home for vacation?'"

Nome's "ruby sands" really are pink—and intense enough to look rosy from the air—but what tints them isn't rubies, it's tiny garnets. Where you see pink sand like that, Hafner said, you're also likely to find gold. But you need a pink beach that drops an inch a foot. That's the ideal angle for letting the heavy gold settle out while lighter stuff gets washed away. It's the same angle that a goldminer's sluice box is built to have, the same angle at which you hold a goldpan.

In beach mining, however, you're relying on the ocean to do the panning. Basically, you just shovel and sluice. You can do it on land, shoveling sand into a sluice box while you stand on the beach. Or you can put on waders or a diving drysuit and go out in the water with a portable gold dredge and pump pay dirt off the bottom.

Because gold is so heavy—19 times the specific gravity of water—"it's on the bottom, and it's in the beach," Hafner said. "But a good storm will move a sandbar five feet." That could cover the pocket you're working, burying your chances. Or it could stir it up, move it off the bottom, make it easier for you to get at. The key, of course, is luck. Just the same as it always was, he said: "It's all a matter of inches."

The summer I was in Nome had been a good one for the ruby beaches, thanks to a couple of rough storms the previous fall that churned up the underwater sands. "Of all the years to be beach-mining, this is the one," Hafner said. Neither he nor anyone else I encountered would say just how good a year it was—partly because the answer was as personal as a bank balance, partly because nobody wanted to touch off another gold rush. But I heard it rumored that the luckiest and hardest-working of the beach miners might pull in as much as $2,000 a day.

Unfortunately, independent gold miners are a lot like gamblers. They don't take their winnings and leave the casino. "They'll invest it in more equipment," Hafner said. If they're typical, they'll also hoard some of it, converting it to cash bit by bit, only as needed. That keeps income taxes down.

This, too, is in the spirit of the original Gold Rush. The miners were taxed on their gold, according to a park ranger in Skagway, another old gold town. In the Klondike, "maybe half the gold was never declared," he said. "Maybe 80 percent."

The history of gold mining in Nome traces to "The Three Lucky Swedes"—hence the name of the coffee shop. In the Old Country, they were a tailor, a coal miner and a reindeer wrangler. As mining partners, they made a series of strikes here, late in 1898. The richest was Anvil Creek, which the Swedish gold seekers named after an anvil-shaped rock formation that overlooks it.

Hafner took me up there. It's not a very high hill, but because there aren't any trees around Nome, and because the rest of the shore is low, you can see several miles—up and down the straight coastline and far out to sea. The view got him talking about nature.

Back home, Hafner said, "I'm an environmentalist." So at first, his friends in Minnesota had wondered how he could participate in anything that brutalized the landscape as much as gold mining does. "This," he said, gesturing at the scene, "this is just a scratch." Below us, there was an ugly pond and tailings piles spread out around a big commercial gold dredge. He was right—distance did make the mess look insignificant.

I could just barely make out a few tents on the long pink beach south of town. Campers? I wondered. No, beach miners, Hafner said. His reply gave me one of those time-travel thrills: Just like the old days, I thought.

Except that back in 1900, when there were 20,000 gold seekers here, each was working a bit of beach barely wider than the stretch of their arms on either side of a sluice box. It looked like Coney Island and felt—well, it must have felt like a gold rush.

Then and now, the race was less to the strong than to the committed. To survive at beach mining, you have to be willing to shovel beach sand all day, and summer days last forever this far north. You don't get rich quick.

We drove down to the beach for a closer look. A couple of nylon dome tents and a makeshift hut of plastic sheeting were flapping in the chronically stiff winds off the Bering Sea. The treeless landscape made the virtually empty beach look even emptier.

Hafner stopped the truck where a couple of his friends were wrapping up a day's shoveling. They were about to start what miners still call "clean up"—one of many Gold Rush terms now so commonplace in English that we don't think about their roots anymore. A lot of them, like this one, contain hidden lessons. Next time you hear somebody say they "really cleaned up" on a stock market purchase, remember the greed that prompted other big rushes: the Klondike. Fairbanks. Nome.

Hafner's friends took a break to talk. Dan Mount, 39, was a self-described nomad who had gotten hooked on mining about five years before and had lived on the beach for three, enduring collapsed tents and 60-mile-per-hour winds. He and his mining partner, Rick Sanchez, 29, typically put in eight-hour days on the beach, meaning four hours of shoveling apiece.

"It's grueling work," Mount said. "You lose the romance real fast."

Mount and Sanchez let me shovel a few last pounds of beach sand into the sluice box before they began carefully rinsing out the mesh that lined it. Their day's work reduced to a single bucket of "cons," meaning concentrate, a dark slurry of heavy sand and water.

"It doesn't look like much in that form," Mount said, "but there's probably a couple of ounces of gold in there." Sure enough, when the pair panned out a sample, it left a smear of brilliant yellow on the bottom of the black rubber goldpan.

It didn't glitter, but it sure did gleam. And it didn't look anything like iron pyrites—the fool's gold that novices always fall for in Western movies. I felt a foolish pang of greed and forgot about how heavy those shovelfuls of beach sand had been.

What supports independent miners is largely "fines" like that—fine gold, literally gold dust, tiny flakes no bigger than dime-store glitter. "Nuggets sound romantic, but you're better off with fines," Hafner said. With fines, "I don't see gold any-more, I see green." That's because nuggets tend to be sold as nuggets, not melted down. It's easier to part with fines: "You send 'em to the refinery—and pay the bills."

It had gotten to be suppertime, and we both admitted to hunger. But there was this one more place to see—a deep open-pit operation in low hills well inland from the beach. The mine belonged to Betty Krutzsch, a youthful-looking Californian whose first husband owned some claims around Nome. After he died, she decided to mine on her own; with her then-teenage son, she broke ground in 1990.

"It was a challenge, a real challenge," she said, "and every-body said 'you can't do it because you're a woman.' Now I can't see doing anything else." She and her current husband, Tony Johnson, a retired meat-cutter, got married on her claim in 1992. "We got married in rubber boots and mining clothes," she said, smiling. "I had, as my bouquet, my gold pan and gloves."

I shot my last pictures at the Krutzsch mine, pleased with how golden Betty and Tony looked in the late afternoon sun. Then we let them get on with grilling their dinner and dis-cussed getting some food ourselves.

I glanced at my watch and was shocked, for about the hundredth time in Alaska. I'd been fooled by the midnight sun again. It looked like five in the evening, but it was after midnight. We'd missed real suppertime by hours. Even then, Hafner wasn't ready to quit. He'd thought of one more thing I just had to see.

Half an hour later, on the still-bright summer night, we were 15 feet down in another claim, at the bottom of a muddy cut, and Hafner was eagerly picking bits of dirt out of the damp walls and excitedly telling me what it meant. "See that? See the blue clay? That's a good sign! Clay's like a false bedrock—the gold could settle there and not get through. You follow that layer...."

It was one in the morning, we hadn't had supper, and Hafner was still going strong. A real prospector, I thought. A prospector to the core.

The next time I talked to him, a year had passed; I phoned him in Nome to see how he was doing. Hafner sounded as enthusiastic as ever—and a lot more positive about nuggets. He'd found two big ones while he was dredging offshore. That meant working in a drysuit, in 10 to 12 feet of frigid water, breathing compressed air through a tube from a pump on the surface while he pumped sand off the bottom for, oh, five to eight hours a day.

"It's called hookah diving," he said cheerfully. He was refining this technique for winter work on the sea ice. Well, not exactly *on* it. More like ice fishing, only you're down with the fish. "You mean you're *under* the ice?" I asked. That's right—the tube for the compressed air goes up through a hole in the ice to a compressor on top. The good news, he said, is that there is no wave action to contend with; the bad news is that you could feel "boxed in" down there.

That had to be an understatement. Beach mining still sounded outdoorsy and do-able, kind of like career camping, but under-ice dredging made me shudder. Hafner's dedication shouldn't have surprised me, though, given the pace of that endless day we'd spent on the ruby sands of Nome.

Epiphany in Sun and Smoke

1994

—

"THERE ARE MANY Annapurnas in the lives of men." I no longer remember who said that, but the quotation is one of my favorites. I kept it tacked to my bulletin board for years—though I mentally added "and women" every time I read it.

"There are many Annapurnas in the lives of men." That sums up for me the personal nature of challenge and risk, in travel as in life. And it doesn't matter that I've never seen Annapurna, or that the biggest mountain I've had to climb wasn't in the Himalayas. It was in me.

I bumped into my personal mountain in the old walled city of Dubrovnik, on a summer morning not long before Yugoslavia shattered into war and history.

I had driven there from Sarajevo the previous night and checked into the modernistic Hotel Argentina, built on the edge of a cliff overlooking the Adriatic. (Later, it would be used to house refugees when Dubrovnik was shelled during the Bosnian horror.)

From my balcony that morning, I could see the creamy

stone walls of the Old City shining in the sun, with bright blue sea beyond.

I was up early, with my favorite kind of day ahead: no interviews scheduled, no need to move on that night, nothing on the agenda but time to explore, to learn and to take pictures in that spectacular light.

So why was I lingering in the dimness of my room? Why was I combing my hair again, counting rolls of film, checking camera batteries, reading the guidebook? Why wasn't I out there?

The answer came gradually. I noticed that I was feeling a wisp of dread that morning, nothing heavy but awfully familiar, like a whiff of distant smoke.

I sat on the bed and stared at one of the modern white walls and felt the smoke thicken, coalesce. I realized, with dismay, that I was afraid. Realized that I had always been afraid like this, every morning, even at home—especially at home, where there weren't the lovely distractions of the road. I'd lived with that faint smoky fear for so long that it just felt normal.

OK, then, so I was afraid. But why? Everything was going well, I was safe, the day was perfect, and there was that great, great light. . . .

The reason was so simple it made me cry. I was dawdling that morning because once I went outside, I'd be committed to the day, and I didn't know how it might turn out. I was afraid of beginning because I was afraid of failing.

If you grow up, as I did, believing that everything you do has to be perfect and knowing in advance that it can't be, then starting anything is the same as starting to fail.

So that was why I'd been a procrastinator all my life! And that certainly was part of why I love journalism and its pressures:

Sooner or later, a deadline catches up to you, and even the worst procrastinator is pushed into delivering the goods. It's like having an external conscience, and I always feel better afterward.

I'd like to be able to say that after I figured all this out, I dried my tears and went forth into the Yugoslavian sunshine and shot the best pictures of my life.

I didn't.

But I shot *good enough* pictures, and—maybe for the first time in my life—not being perfect felt just fine.

I also left my room that morning with a new mantra. Forget Annapurna, I thought. Remember Dubrovnik. Every day is a new Dubrovnik.

Glass as Good as Gold

1995

I KNEW I HAD CROSSED into the former East Zone when the colors began draining from the landscape. The villages grew plainer, sterner, grayer, with dark gray stucco on old buildings, light gray on new. Then I turned into the narrow valley where Lauscha lies, and I thought the lights had gone out.

This was late on a rainy afternoon in December, and I was heading for the village that invented Christmas ornaments. I expected something colorful and cheery, like Christmas itself. Lauscha was anything but colorful. A dark town, it looked about as welcoming as a black-and-white photo—grim and forbidding, seeming worse in the rain. But that was before it took me in.

Lauscha's old houses are big three-story affairs, like antique apartment buildings, completely shingled, roofs and sides, in slabs of dark-gray slate, which the cold winter drizzle had wetted to the color of night.

In the depths of town, I found a brand-new hotel—black as the others outside but mercifully decorated like springtime inside. Then I went looking for a place to eat. I wasn't hopeful. The only choices were around the Hütteplatz, the tiny triangle

- 139 -

of cobblestones that is the heart of Lauscha—and, although I didn't know it yet, the spot where the town's original glassworks, its *glashütte*, had operated for 300 years.

Everything was closed except for one bierstube. Though the valley was as gloomy as a damp church basement, its windows glowed like a fairytale cottage. I opened the door, and a wave of warm air, cigarette smoke and singing flooded over me.

This was Lauscha's own gathering place, clearly for locals, not tourists. I settled at a table next to the silvery Christmas tree in the front window, ordered a platter of sauerbraten and dumplings and watched as half the village wandered by.

Every time somebody came in, different tables called out greetings and invitations, but usually the newcomers were pulled into the largest group—a local choir, still in the white shirts and dark pants that were their singing uniform, celebrating after a Christmas concert at an old-folks' home.

Eventually, primed by beer and good will, the choir table sent two emissaries over to me. Was I the person driving the white car with the Wiesbaden plates? Ja, they thought so; they'd noticed it in the Hütteplatz, and since I was the only stranger around, it had to be mine.

I explained that I was writing about Christmas ornaments. Could they, I wondered, help me find some glassmakers to talk to? This was like standing on the assembly line at the Ford plant and asking if anybody knew any auto workers. Their faces lit up, and I was borne back to their table, where—between choruses of folk songs and attempts to teach me to yodel—everybody had suggestions.

In Lauscha, everybody's a glass blower, a retired glass blower or a glass blower's child. A perfect example was sitting next to me: Traundel Bittner, a slender-faced, steel-haired woman whose rich contralto sustains the choir's higher notes. She is a retired maker of glass animal eyes for taxidermy; her father had been an animal-eye maker; her husband had made spun glass; all her siblings were glassmakers, and her grandfather had been an ornament maker—twisted glass icicles were his specialty.

Walter Muller, the stocky, sandy-haired tenor who was accompanying everybody on guitar, was not only Lauscha's city planner but a descendant of one of the town founders, a pair of glassmakers who opened the original *glashütte* in 1597.

And that man over there, the quiet man with silver hair, playing cards with friends in the corner, that was Rudolf Hoffmann, retired director of the Lauscha Museum of Glass Arts and a national expert on German glassmaking. I had come to the right place.

Before they finally sang "Arrivaderci, Hans," the German equivalent of "Good Night, Ladies," the choir had worked out my schedule. Herr Muller offered an interview at City Hall in the morning (and got teased for saying he'd be there early). Frau Bittner would guide me through the glass museum. And I had to talk to the people at the Krebs ornament factory and to Herr Hoffmann and. . . .

And then—small world—Mayor Fritz Kohler dropped in, and the choir told him he had to talk to me too, and—smaller world—I already knew his wife: One of Lauscha's proud new entrepreneurs, Frau Kohler owned the hotel where I was staying.

This was networking, small-town style, and I loved it. It made Lauscha seem like a village anywhere in the world, where everybody knows everybody else, for good or ill, and when they decide to take you in, you're in for good. For the first time in 30 years of travel here, the specter of World War II, which walks beside me whenever I'm in this country, receded a little into the shadows.

We were doing all this talking in German, and I loved that too. West Germans usually switch into impeccable English when they hear my accent, but no one did that in Lauscha, because in this part of unified Germany, the second language for most adults isn't English, it's Russian.

The networking continued next morning at City Hall, when Herr Muller tracked down a home workshop that hadn't closed for December—a real feat, given that that's the only time of the year when glassworkers can go on vacation: Orders for this Christmas had already been shipped, and the pressure to produce for next Christmas wouldn't start till January.

After phone calls to a half-dozen home workshops ("*Guten Morgen*—are you blowing?"), he reached Margaret Haberland, daughter, granddaughter and great-granddaughter of glass-makers, the mother of another one, and a glassmaker herself. She would show me every step of the process.

She also showed me some of the realities that Lauscha has lived with since reunification. "Would you like some tea?" she asked when I was settled at the broad pine table in her kitchen, in a corner of one of those big black houses.

When I said yes, she dispatched her grandson to buy a bottle of water at the grocer's. "Oh, no," I protested, "don't bother—tap water will be fine!"

Margaret gave me a pitying smile and shook her head: I clearly didn't get it. Tap water wouldn't be fine. Tap water in Lauscha is polluted, too polluted to drink even after boiling, and it was going to be polluted for a long time to come—until the town could afford to build a modern sewage treatment plant and replace 90-year-old pipes that the communists had done nothing to maintain.

Margaret Haberland's family illustrated both aspects of what Germans call *Die Wende*, the turning back of the communist page of their history: first pain, then success.

As the communist glass factories were privatized, their new owners stripped down for action. The town's old ornament factory, for example, went from 1,000 workers to about 160 when Krebs, West Germany's best-known ornament firm, took it over.

Across the economy, those who got laid off first were men too young and women too old—meaning age 35, Margaret and her daughter, Maritta, told me sarcastically over the teacups. Now 58, Margaret had lost her job at the local bank. Her young son, Michael, now 27, got laid off from an art-glass factory. Her daughter's husband still had work—he's a fourth-generation glass-eye maker, able to shape eyes to fit individual sockets—but Asian imports and plastic eyes from America were cutting into that market too.

This wasn't new for Margaret Haberland; she was used to struggle, and sadness drifted over her face as she remembered. She had lost her husband to a heart attack in his 30s and had had to raise the children alone. "I have had a hard life," she said quietly, staring out the kitchen window at the gray day. "My children are my joy."

Then she brightened, telling how Lauscha's traditions came to their rescue. Lauscha's huge houses tend to stay in families, generation after generation, so all of the Haberland clan was still living in the massive black-slate home that Margaret's parents built in 1929.

Decades of family castoffs were piled up in the storeroom—

including, she remembered, a trunkful of Christmas ornament molds that her father and grandfather had used. Too heavy for her to throw out, the trunk had sat there for a generation.

She and Michael dragged it out of storage, set up a workshop in a shed in the back yard and returned to their roots. "On Oct. 10, 1991, we jumped in the water," she said. "We did not know if we would go under or float."

Michael blew the ornaments, Mom finished them, and they found a jobber near Coburg—also from an old ornament family—to sell them to. Their business "floated," and within the first year they added another glassblower and five painters—all older women who had lost their jobs. By their third year in business, the Haberlands were shipping 600,000 ornaments in 140 styles.

"Those who started their own businesses after the change-over are doing OK," Margaret's daughter said. "Not millionaires, but also not beggars." Now their ornament business was so profitable that Michael wasn't just taking a break when I was there in December, he was on vacation with his fiancée in the Caribbean.

The process hasn't changed in more than a hundred years. Until I saw it, I couldn't picture it: Hard-edged, identically shaped, shiny as mirrors, a box of Christmas ornaments doesn't look like a handicraft. It looks like the product of a mechanized assembly line.

True, plain round glass balls usually are machine-done now. But anything with a complicated shape—a clown, a Santa, a little house, a Volkswagen, a trolley, Hansel and Gretel, whole bands of angels—these are still hand-made, which is to say mouth-blown.

They have always been blown *vor der Lampe*, literally "in

front of the lamp," though modern blowtorches have replaced heating lamps on everybody's workbench, whether at home or in the big Krebs factory up the hill.

The artisan takes a short glass tube, the kind you used in chemistry class, holds it in the blowtorch flame until it glows red-gold and sags like taffy, then clamps it inside a hand-carved mold and blows a quick short puff through the stem.

Instantly, the hot glass balloons to the form of the mold and cools enough to hold its shape. A factory artisan makes 600 in a normal workday, a Krebs spokesman told me; home-workers can make many more, limited only by how many hours they want to put in.

At this point, mouth-blown ornaments look like clear lollipops. The next step is silvering, another process that is out of place in a home setting—too chemical, too dangerous. But it's sure quick.

Margaret Haberland gathered a bouquet of clear glass teddy bears, held them upside down and poured a bit of liquid into each stem. Nothing happened. She beamed at me, knowing the surprise that was coming.

She added another solution, plunged the lollipops into hot water to speed up the reaction, and in less time than it takes to read this sentence, they were transformed from clear glass bubbles to mirror-bright ornaments.

It happened so fast, I didn't see the change: One second they were clear, the next second they were silver. It was astonishing, and I wanted to watch it over and over—not the first time on this trip that I had felt like an awestruck little kid at Christmastime.

The silver inside makes them shiny, Haberland explained; everything else—all the colors and glitter and trim—goes on the outside. She opened a can of yellow lacquer and dunked the little bears into it. They came out a sparkling golden-brown.

When they were dry—in moments, because the lacquer is as volatile as Duco cement—their eyes, noses, smiles and claws would be painted on. Next, their glass-tube stems would be trimmed off and a little metal cap and loop added so they could be hung on a tree. Then they'd go into bins in the garage, to await boxing and shipment for next year.

The chemical fumes were so strong in the Haberlands' shed that when a neighbor bounded in to demonstrate glass-blowing, I cringed as he struck a match to light the gas blow-torch on the workbench. The shed didn't explode, and in seconds he was blowing molten glass into a small mold and removing bubbles shaped like hummingbirds. They were enchanting, but I couldn't enjoy the show.

Safety standards in the former East are not yet up to Western European par. Lauscha's water pollution was one example. Home glassblowing workshops were another.

I'd been in the shed only 15 minutes and already my head ached. Whenever I took a breath to ask a question, the fumes caught in my throat, and I coughed before I could speak. I felt as if I were sniffing glue.

"Don't you get headaches?" I finally gasped to Frau Haberland. She smiled radiantly. "Not any more!" she trilled, waving a handful of silver bears.

Later, back at City Hall, Mayor Kohler, a gentle-voiced man with a black beard and tired-looking eyes, elaborated on Lauscha's problems. The old streets needed repairs, he said. So did the gas lines. The creek was undercutting some house foundations and ought to be rerouted.

And there was a real housing shortage, with multiple

families crammed into those big old houses. Impossible during the communist era, some people could now afford to build new ones—but they couldn't build yet because the communists stopped keeping track of property titles, and land ownership needed to be sorted out.

"What had been kept for centuries—*kaput!*" Kohler said sadly. "That makes for lots of anger."

The housing shortage had gotten suddenly worse while I was there, and the mayor apologized for not being able to talk longer because of it. One of the big slate houses had burned in the night, leaving five families homeless, and City Hall was scrambling to find temporary places for them to stay. (They would succeed, of course: "It's like a family here," Margaret Haberland had told me. "People help each other.")

Government aid for Lauscha would be a good while coming, the mayor said, because needs all over the former East were so great that the reunified German government had to practice a kind of triage: The town that squeaks the loudest gets the dough.

And Lauscha, despite its problems, was better off than many other Eastern villages. For example, the mayor said, it had great potential for tourism. I could see it: Lauscha lies deep in the romantic Thuringen Forest, still rich with such wildlife as wild boars, deer, foxes and rare falcons.

The low mountains around town are necklaced with trails that provide great hiking in summer and even better cross-country skiing in winter. And for summer sports, the mayor said, "my crazy idea is to dam the creek and make a lake farther down the valley."

More than anything, though, Lauscha had its glass, and glass still meant work for people in about half its 1,800 families.

There's a story, told with local pride, that back in the old days, when Lauscha's communist ornament factory didn't include a badly needed truck in its five-year plan, enterprising employees simply bought one on the black market.

They traded Christmas ornaments for it. "Lauscha *geld*," ornaments are called here: Lauscha money.

Travels with Freud

1986

———

PETER SELLERS CALLED my sister Jane the other night, long-distance from London. Yes, I know Peter Sellers is dead. Jane knows that too. This was in a dream.

"He was trying to get hold of you, but you weren't home," she told me afterward, adding so much detail that I was kind of sorry I hadn't been available.

This reminded me of travel dreams I've had or heard of over the years. They're probably just a variation on the ordinary anxiety dream, like the examination nightmare so many college students complain about.

That's the dream where you have to take a final exam in a course you never registered for. You don't know the name of the course, the professor, the textbook or any classmates you could borrow notes from. All you know is that you have to take the final.

To me, though, travel dreams are a special category and deserve equal billing with the ones that so intrigued Dr. Freud. Many involve fear about getting safely home again. Mine is one of those.

It takes place on a trip, somewhere in the Middle West,

on a nice day in summer or fall, just before sunset. I'm driving through farm land and woods on a gravel road that eventually runs into the edge of a flooded river.

There's no bridge, but that's not a problem. It's not a big river, and it's not badly flooded. There's a little water over the road, but you can tell where the road is because of the grassy ridge between the ruts.

Feeling confident, I edge the car into the water. After I've gone a little way, though, I notice that the river is somewhat wider than I thought. There is more water flowing across the road, and the grassy ridge ahead is beginning to look like a dotted line.

It's also gotten much darker. But the sunset has thrown a lot of light on the river, and the black lines of trees and the ridge of the road stand out as clear as charcoal streaks on shiny paper.

Now some of the road in the middle of the river appears to be completely underwater, but the broken line of ruts re-surfaces just beyond, and you can see where the road climbs out of the water near the other bank. Driving from here to there will be no more complicated than connecting the dots, so I push on.

As I near the middle, though, I realize that more like 30 or 40 feet of road is completely submerged. The river is now a half-mile wide or more—it's hard to tell, because the light is almost gone. The remains of the road are impossible to pick out from the deepening shadows on the surface and the dark-ness of the river bank beyond.

Then I feel the car sway a little, pushed by the moving water, and realize that it is losing its footing. I don't dare go forward.

There is no way to turn around, so I decide to back up. I put the car in reverse, look over my shoulder—and am shocked. The view behind is now the same as the view in front: smooth water, glassy gray, unbroken by any trace of road.

That's where the dream ends.

It may stem from actually riding through a shallow flood on a family trip in childhood—my father liked that sort of adventure—except that I don't remember being scared then.

Surely it was reinforced by the damp week I spent covering a hurricane on the north coast of Honduras in 1974. That time I hired a Volkswagen taxi, because I'd seen ads saying VWs had really good door seals, and asked the cabbie to take me as close to the flooded villages and washed-out bridges as he could. I figured to wade in from there. It worked great. The cabbie drove until the car practically floated, and I ended up with some good pictures. And this dream.

Personally, I think it symbolizes a tendency to get in over my head at least once on any long trip, but that's another story.

Whatever the original cause, at least I came by this dream honestly. It may even be hereditary. My father drove our family—five kids, our mother and our grandmother—all over North America for about 15 years' worth of summer camping trips, despite his recurrent dream that the car was falling apart.

His car dream always started out OK, he said—"It's a nice day; the car is running well"—but gradually, as he maneuvers the family station wagon over steep, twisting, narrow mountain roads, "Something starts to rattle in the back of the car. Then something loosens in the front."

A bumper falls off. Then a front fender goes. Then the other fender. The trunk lid. The roof. The left front door. Then all the doors.

It takes a long time, but finally only the frame and steering wheel are left, so the car looks like one of those cutaway models in an advertisement.

And all the people my father is responsible for are huddled together on the bare chassis while he keeps on driving: "The final thing is, I start to turn, and I realize that the steering wheel isn't attached to the car any more. . . ."

My mother elevated travel dreams to the global level. Consider her dream encounter with a KGB agent in Leningrad. She was on a bridge over the River Neva when she spotted him: "I was alone. I knew who he was. I knew I had to stop him. And then I remembered that I'd had a course in karate. . . ."

So she kicked him as hard as she could. That did it for the Russian agent. Also for the dream, since she slammed her foot into the bedroom wall so hard she woke up. She also broke her big toe. Probably because she hadn't had a course in karate.

Paradise Reconsidered

1991

———

"WE MUST GO," Raka urged. "The bull is already in the cemetery." That sounds like dramatic nonsense when I write it now, but then it gave me goose bumps. And it made us hurry.

Dressed in sarongs and temple scarves, two fellow tourists and I climbed into our new friend's Jeep and sped off for a nearby village.

A prominent local family was about to cremate the man who had been their husband, father and grandfather. His body would be stuffed inside a wood-and-paper statue of a bull and torched, and we didn't want to be late for the big show.

If that sounds ghoulish, well, welcome to Bali. This famous island is everything the Western mind imagines—and, unfortunately, a whole lot more. Yes, it is wildly beautiful—in places. But it is also overpopulated. Overbuilt. Dirty. And for a Westerner, all too often ghoulish.

It wasn't that I didn't like Bali. I was tormented by Bali. And disappointed that it didn't live up to the perfect-paradise image that has been promoted around the world for 70 years.

The problem is that Bali is a real place, full of real people.

That means it can't be perfect. Nothing human is. What's weird, though, is that it becomes whatever you want it to be. If you've always pictured an island paradise, that is what you find. And if you're a typical Westerner, who has paid a lot to get here, you'll make yourself believe you've found it.

Half the size of the Big Island of Hawaii, Bali has nearly 3 million people—more than 20 times the population of the Big Island. As a result, you can drive from Bali's international airport north through the capital of Denpasar and beyond that as far as Ubud—the foothills town considered quiet only because it's quieter than Denpasar—and see almost nothing but unbroken red-brick walls.

Walled houses connect to other houses, to walled temples, to shops. Villages run into villages like unpunctuated sentences. You remember the rare breaks in this urban wall precisely because they are rare: A farmer in a coolie hat, wading in a rice paddy beside the road. A handful of boys playing soccer in a grove of palms.

Oddly, tourists seldom regard any of this condensed urbanness as Balinese. In fact, they ignore it, the way they ignore Bali's dogs—dogs roaming the streets, dogs fighting over piles of garbage, dogs sleeping in the dust outside your guesthouse door, dogs everywhere.

Far inland, you can still find the views that Bali is renowned for: Hillside terraces so bright with new rice that they give off a green, unearthly light, as if they were lit from within. Or a beach-front village at Candidassa, palm trees silhouetted against a silver sea. Or the empty beach at Sanur just after dawn, with the tide far out and the waves booming on the distant reef, and tiny snails and hermit crabs crawling at the edge of clear, receding water.

Whenever we encountered one of these moments on our drives with Raka, my companions would sigh and murmur, "Ah, now that's the real Bali!"

No, I would think, the real Bali is back there on the road and in the crowded, dusty towns. But I stopped saying so, because it felt like talking about the emperor's clothes. And besides, I realized I'd been doing my own kind of denial every time I picked up my camera. I'd been making my pictures prettier, by zooming in and cropping out all the extraneous bits, the pieces of Bali that don't fit the dream, that aren't "real." Like the dirt. And all the people.

That lovely beach at Sanur was another example. In the silence of early morning, with the sun already turning wicked and foreigners still breakfasting in the shade beside hotel pools, I stood taking a picture of empty sand, shimmering in the rising heat. It made me remember the Noel Coward line, "Mad dogs and Englishmen go out in the noonday sun . . ." except it wasn't anywhere near noon.

Because I was the only tourist on the sand, I was the only target. Far in the distance, I spotted two tiny Balinese women, who spotted me and zeroed in. They had huge straw hats hiding their elfin faces and long-sleeved t-shirts over their sarongs, the sleeves hanging down to their delicate fingertips, the neckbands safety-pinned tight around their throats, protecting their complexions against the skin-darkening sun that tourists worship.

Their slim hips and legs were tightly wrapped in sarongs, garments that make everyone but hulking Westerners seem graceful, even when they are hurrying. The women took small, quick steps and closed in fast, smiling and waving. I waved back. When they got close enough to speak, it was not words of friendship, but of business.

Please? You see my shop? You want batik, madam? I plait your hair? Massage, madam, I give you massage? They followed me, ceaselessly pleading, until I ran for cover inside the grounds of my hotel. But that, too, was the real Bali. Commercialism was as ubiquitous as the dogs.

Even in Ubud, as picturesque as a Balinese town can get, the streets are gantlets of shops and vendors—all hawking shadow puppets, demon masks, cheap sarongs, temple scarves, batik bedspreads, tickets to performances of the Ramayana saga, tickets to the *kechak* chanting dance, tours to the volcanoes and the Mother Temple, anything you want, anything.

For respite in Ubud, tourists hang out by the private pools in their guest houses or seek solace in familiar food—spaghetti at the Lotus, American food at Murni's—and the whole place feels a lot like Katmandu, Nepal, in the waning days of hippiedom.

But time immunizes you against the things you don't want to see. As the days passed on Bali, I, too, began to believe that the nightly dance performances, the peaceful Hindu temples dotting the hills, the rice paddies and the plodding water buffalo were more "real" than the ugly things. I began to overlook the traffic and the pollution, the dirt and the run-on compound walls, the garbage dogs and the monkeys in the Monkey Forests who beg for bananas and bite your fingers if you don't hand them over fast enough.

In the end, what Bali gave me was a disturbing mix of memories. Yes, some were ugly. But some had been exquisite—like the magical peace I felt one evening beside the Dragon Temple in Ubud. I lingered there for half an hour, above the crashing Campuan River, under the temple's holy banyan tree, and watched sarong-clad families bring in bowls of offerings on their heads.

The offerings were part of the preparations for the Great Ceremony to Straighten the World. A very Balinese special event, it was an attempt to right the kiltered planet's many wrongs by setting it on its proper axis again.

Inside the temple, in the days leading up to the Great Ceremony, women had been arranging sculptural offerings of rainbow-colored rice-flour paste and bouquets of skewered pork rinds from sacrificed pigs. Now the temple looked like a Midwestern church the week before Christmas: full of busy women, bossing the men around, pointing out how they'd put this or that down in the wrong place and finally bustling over to do it themselves, just so.

All that effort was sincere, and the scope was daunting. "When we go to church, we pray for ourselves," one of my American companions said. "When they go to church, they pray for everybody."

That, too, was the real Bali—the soul of Bali, I came to think. Certainly the best of Bali. But the island's soul was in the cremation, too, and to my surprise, so was some of mine. The memory of that cremation will stay with me forever.

For days, local travel agencies in Ubud had been announcing tour packages with signs like this: "Don't leave Bali without see big cremation."

So much for privacy and the sanctity of local rituals. Our new buddy Raka said he knew the deceased's family, which made us invited guests. Raka, a folk-art exporter who enjoys taking tourists around the island, also coached us on how to behave so we wouldn't give offense. The other tourists didn't get that message.

On the day of the burning, the man's body was brought out of his house after a 17-day wake and a final morning of last respects. It was placed in "the tower," the Balinese equivalent of a hearse, a tall pagoda-like concoction of gilded paper on a framework of thick bamboo poles.

The tower was so heavy that it took 40 men, all from the dead man's neighborhood, to carry it on their shoulders. They bore not only the tower and the body, but also a priest and a family friend who rode along and called out directions and warnings. Other men ran ahead with long poles, to push power lines out of the way as the tower swayed along the road to the burning ground.

The first time the men lifted the tower, a strange cheer went up from the crowd—a great, sighing "ahhhhhh"—and I caught my breath and suddenly had to hold back tears. In Bali, Raka had said, the day of cremation is not supposed to be sad; once out in the street, it is an almost festive show. But that rising cheer sounded like death to me—like a pipe organ's inhalation of air before the first funeral hymn in any church at home.

Then the traditional gamelan orchestra started to hammer— PONG-pong, PONG-pong, PONG-pong, an eerie quick march on brass gongs and cymbals—and then everyone was hurrying, almost running, down the street to the burning ground.

Going so fast was hard work for the pallbearers, and their bodies quickly streamed with sweat. Every 100 yards or so, they would set the tower down and gratefully accept a sprinkle of water from a bystander with a hose. And then the pavement would steam like rocks in a sauna, sending waves of wet heat up our legs, past our chests, into our faces.

I remember it now in a blur: that strange heart-aching cheer, the steaming street, the clang of the gamelan gongs and the running. Something happens to you when you run.

It makes your reason for running seem urgent. Now it was important not to let the French tourists cut in front of me, important not to get hip-checked by the ponderous German with his videocam, important to keep up with the crowd. And vital to keep up with the tower.

Choking back tears, shooting pictures and changing film, I ran down the street with gamelan music clanging in my ears. It was death, death, all about death, the same as any death at home.

The pace changed when we reached the burning ground. Everything slowed down, and the action shifted from the tower to the life-sized figure of the bull, in which the dead man would be burned. The bull looked like a giant black pinata, too pretty for its purpose. Its shape, Raka said, indicated the man's high caste. Its color showed his marital status: Black meant he had had children; the bull for a bachelor would have been white.

Final preparations took a long time. Men had to saw and pry open a lid in the bull's back. Then they forced the shrouded body inside. Then ointments and oils were poured in; there was more fussing, then the lid went back on. Someone lit a handful of incense sticks, and a group of Indonesian Army veterans made speeches, honoring one of their own, and presented a wreath—like the skin of the bull, the flowers were paper.

In the midst of the tourists, still shoving and clicking and crowding, the dead man's relatives knelt for final prayers. Women with trays of offerings on their heads paraded around the bull, and then the family withdrew to the shade of a nearby palm grove and watched.

The funeral fire began subtly. In the brightness of the tropical afternoon, the flames were transparent, like pink-tinged air, and there was nothing ugly about them. They licked over the black velvet skin of the bull and curled the gold foil and green crepe paper of its harness. Then the bull's skin burned off, and the glitter disappeared; a rough framework of lumber and straw showed through, and then the straw caught fire.

Straw burns quickly, but wood does not, and neither do bodies. It was obvious that without help, the fire might go out. That explained the presence of an old, wiry man in a short sarong and a grubby T-shirt. The old man's job was to keep the fire going. He did it with big coiled tubes of rusty metal that sprawled in the grass near the pyre—flame-throwers fueled by red plastic hoses that drained from a gasoline can hoisted in a tree.

The old man in the T-shirt turned them on, and a roar like huge acetylene torches drowned out the crackle of the ordinary flames. He trained his beams of fire on the underbelly of the bull, where the body lay, and turned it into an inferno.

All this took hours. There seemed no good stopping point, no place to break away, so I just kept standing there, transfixed by the fire. Other tourists were also hanging around, almost the only people still out in the hot sun—except for the souvenir sellers, trying to tempt us with batik shirts, wood carvings and cold soda.

Tourists sneered at the vendors, as if their presence was in poor taste. But there was still our presence. What were we all waiting for? Horror? Thrills? The silhouette of a rib cage or a burning hand glimpsed through the screen of flame? Perhaps. Mercifully, that image never came.

Even with flame throwers, it takes a surprisingly long time for a body to burn. Too long for most tourists and all the tour buses. Too long, finally, even for Raka and my companions. They grew impatient. It was midafternoon, and they wanted lunch.

When we left, the bull was still burning, and the dead man's family was still waiting under the palm trees—and would wait until the whole contrivance was reduced to cinders, so they could take the ashes of their patriarch and scatter them at sea.

At least, that was what Raka told us, over hamburgers and milkshakes down at Murni's.

Riding the Chicken Bus

1994

⸺

I'VE JUST COME BACK from traveling in Central America again, and I'm suffering from reentry shock. I wander the air-conditioned aisles at Lunds, awed by that cool cathedral of food and wondering how I got born so lucky, when other people, whom I care about, did not.

Right now, their world seems more real to me than mine. It is certainly harsher, more intense, more vivid, more immediate. And so different from clean, bland, middle-class America that every image there—even something as minor as flies on fish in an open-air market—is branded on my memory.

I went looking for public stories to put in the paper. But the private ones, the ones I keep telling my family and my friends, are the ones I'd rather write—tiny portraits of other lives, like snapshots taken on the run.

My favorites kept riding into my life on country buses. A fellow traveler calls these vehicles "chicken buses" because there are usually a few live chickens aboard, adding their cackles to the din of blown muffler and bumpy road.

If you speak Spanish, there is no sitting in silence or isolation on a chicken bus anywhere south of the Texas border. On chicken buses, the other passengers are invariably short-distance riders, coming from home or going back, so a foreigner really stands out, raising curiosity. People want to talk to you, and if you understand and reply, they talk more. You don't get to take refuge in a book.

The farther south you go, the truer it is. I found it especially true in Honduras, if only because I've done so much chicken-busing there. Public transport in that poor, hot country is mostly on old U.S. school buses, mostly Blue Birds, mostly orange. I rode several of them on my recent trip, along the North Coast and into the mountains that border Guatemala. Every ride was like being in a movie without an ending, or an oddly edited collection of short stories.

Character after character boarded the bus, sat down beside me and started to talk. Each new character became an event, and I ended up stringing the events together like beads. I never got the necklace finished.

Joan Rivers rode next to me from Tela, Honduras, halfway down the coast toward La Ceiba. "Joan what?" I echoed when the lean old black woman told me her name. Joan Rivers. No mistake.

I wondered for a split second if she were crazy, if she'd seen our Joan Rivers on TV and liked her so much she'd adopted the star's name. No, she was just one of the Caribbean's many people of African descent who carry Anglo names.

She was 60, she said, which surprised me because that seemed too young. Her teeth were gone, her skin was wrinkled like antique leather, her limbs were bone and sinew.

"I have no house," she announced as the bus started to roll.

What happened? "It fell down." It was a house like that one. She pointed out the window at a square wooden shack with a metal roof.

Then where are you living? "In a box," she said. What about your husband? "He died." Your children? "I have no children."

Then she asked about me. I have no children either, I said, adding—because it was all I could think of to say—"That's how it is."

She seized my arm, gave me a sharp look and started to laugh. "That's how it is!" she repeated.

And then we were both laughing, holding hands and laughing and riding in an old bus down a road in Honduras. Joan Rivers got off the bus somewhere in the countryside, with no signs or houses or even boxes near, and set off down a path. That's how it was.

An old farmer got on, with a bundle of fresh vegetables in a plastic bag. He was taking them to his married daughters in the next village. He said he was 78, and I said he didn't look it. "A lot of people tell me that," he said.

Was I a foreigner? Yes. "Foreigners are mostly nice people— quiet, but that's because they don't speak Spanish. When they do speak, they're mostly nice." Was I an American? Yes. "Tell me, is Japan part of the United States?" No, it's a long way away. "Is Germany a part of the United States?" No, it's a long way in the other direction. "Israel isn't either, right?" Right.

This is pretty, I said, looking out the window at the variegated green that is the Honduran countryside. But I thought it had looked different on my earlier visits, almost 20 years before. Most hills wore cloaks of grassy pasture now, where I seemed to remember jungle.

The old man didn't think the land looked good at all and

made no bones about why. It was deforestation, he said, the loss of the rain forests, and even though he farmed himself, he didn't like it. "The trees are gone!" he said indignantly. "Fifty years ago, there used to be trees! Mountains of trees!" Fifty? Try 18.

"It's the government," he said. "They cut and cut, and they never plant anything. Now there are no trees, and the rains don't come anymore!"

Another farmer, a true *campesino*, got on in the middle of nowhere, boarding the bus from a backdrop of low green mountains. Young, small, wiry, he was dressed in Sunday-best Honduran-cowboy clothes: straw cowboy hat, pearl-buttoned cowboy shirt, ironed blue jeans, cowboy boots, a machete. He held a shoebox on his lap.

The box had holes the size of postage stamps punched in it, and it was tied shut with a strip of colored cloth, like a seam pulled from a woman's dress. Scratchy noises came from inside it—so many and so loud, I got worried. Tarantula, maybe? Snake?

What's in the box? I finally asked.

"A rat to catch mice," he said. Wow, I said, that must be some rat.

"CAT!" he corrected me, "CAT!"

He pried the lid open just enough so I could see. It was a kitten, barely bigger than a mouse—just stripey gray fur over tiny bones, and so young that its eyes were still milky blue.

"It was a present," the proud new owner said. The kitten scrambled back and forth, clawing to keep its balance, as he turned the box around and around, so I could get a peek at the frightened little thing. It would be a long time before the local mice were in any danger.

On the way into the interior of Honduras, the buses from the coast stop for half an hour at a big, dusty crossroads town called La Entrada. People with pans of homemade food swarm at the bus windows or clamber aboard to tempt passengers with corn steamed in the husk, small plastic bags of juice, sacks of hard dry cookies, lumps of caramel corn. In the wake of the hawkers come old ladies, hobbling on sticks up to the windows, to beg for money.

Well into the long wait, something rustled at my window, and I glanced out and saw a juice seller who'd been in the first wave. I'd noticed her then because she reminded me of the scrawny pup-worn female dogs that skulk around the bus stops, hoping for scraps.

She was maybe 35, but her thin face looked a generation older. She had only one front tooth, straggling hair, limp breasts and a seven-month pregnancy bulging under a dirty t-shirt. But she wasn't trying to sell me anything now. She just smiled and pointed at the window, and I jumped when I saw what had caught her attention: a bright green grasshopper poised on her side of the glass. As big as a praying mantis, as pretty as new grass, it looked like an emerald angel on the window.

Slowly, the woman reached out for the elegant insect, bringing dirty, calloused fingers closer and closer to its graceful tail. Just when she was about to pinch it, it escaped, dashing away, flying straight over her head.

She and I locked eyes, and she grinned and tapped her thin chest. "It would be good luck for me," she called through the window, and I thought, with a sudden jolt of sympathy, how much she must need it.

Morsels of France

1988

THE SPOKEN TONGUE is as pure, the perfume shops as well-stocked, the food as conscientiously superb as in any provincial town in mainland France. But step outside the restaurant door or onto the patisserie's porch, and you're in a foggy outpost off the coast of Newfoundland.

That's the biggest contradiction on St. Pierre and Mique-lon, but there are lots of other quirks, including beagles in al-most every yard and a 400-year history that includes a cameo appearance by Al Capone.

I'd wanted to see this strange little archipelago ever since I first read its name on stamps in my father's collection. Like most places a traveler spends a long time dreaming of, reality was un-expected, like the beagles, who had their own story to tell.

There's so little to do on these isolated islands that rabbit-hunting looms near the top of the list. But local law doesn't permit snaring rabbits, so people keep beagles to run them down. The sport is so popular, one resident said, that now "they even import the rabbits!"

As they do just about everything else, including food (mostly from Canada) and bureaucrats (from France). The policemen, the judges, the postal workers, even the doctors in the hospital at St. Pierre, the main town, come to the islands for three-year tours of duty under the French civil service system. They aren't wildly popular with locals.

"The French metropolitan people come over here as if they were coming to the colonies," one St. Pierrais said. "They look down on the local people, so there's always this rift." (Even so, at least one disgusted local woman would like to see the civil service fill another job: "We have no gynecologist on St. Pierre," she said, "but we have three vets!")

Another import is more obvious: house paint. There must be something about life at the ends of the earth that calls for riotous colors. It's true in Iceland; it's true in Tierra del Fuego, and it's true here: Houses in St. Pierre resemble blocks of sherbet—lime green, lemon yellow, cherry pink, raspberry red and a whole bushel of oranges from peach to nectarine. Some residents go in for stripes, wide bands of color that make the houses look Neapolitan: Chocolate and vanilla, for example, or blueberry and pistachio. The only flavor missing is grape.

Tourists are also largely missing. The short summer season brings in about 15,000 vacationers, said J.P. Andrieux, a hotel owner, a local historian, the head of the local tourism office and St. Pierre's honorary Canadian consul. One interview with him was like talking to four people anywhere else.

Although Andrieux and others are working to increase the number of tourists, one of the most refreshing things about this place is that they haven't yet succeeded. There still isn't much for tourists to do: boat trips, pleasant little restaurants, a few clubs and lots of fresh air. Sometimes there are performances of visiting musical groups and games of *zazpiak-bat*, a Basque sport. Even shopping is low-key. In addition to being tucked away on side streets, most of the shops don't have signs. "We know where they are," one man said.

Island life may be simple now, but there is nothing simple about its history. St. Pierre and Miquelon were first claimed for France by Jacques Cartier in 1536 and have been an official French overseas department, or state, since 1976. That makes these islands truly *"un morceau de France"*—a morsel of France—as the local tourist office describes it.

"Morsel" is accurate. This eight-island archipelago totals only 94 square miles—mostly stony hillocks dotted with lichens, mosses and trees not much bigger than bushes, when they occur at all—and about 6,300 people, most of them clustered around the narrow, picturesque harbor of St. Pierre.

The place was a pawn in the great tug-of-war between France and England over North America. Like most of the larger islands in this part of the Atlantic, including Newfoundland, they were important because they lie near the once-rich fishing banks of the continental shelf.

St. Pierre et Miquelon changed hands often, whenever France and England ended a war and signed a new treaty. The last round occurred in the early 1800s, when France resumed control of the islands. A boulder on the St. Pierre waterfront commemorates the return of 150 French residents in 1816.

The ancient English-French struggle hasn't completely died, just changed its form. The modern version is the 20th century's "cod war." Andrieux explained it: St. Pierre and its other islands lie within Canada's 200-mile off-shore fishing limit, established to prevent overfishing by international powers. But if France can't send fishing boats within 200 miles of the Canadian coast, then the French citizens of St. Pierre and Miquelon can't go fishing, either.

Geography is also complicated. There were originally three main islands, not two. The island of St. Pierre, though it's the smallest, has the best harbor and therefore became the center of population. About 5,700 people live on its ten barren square miles, most of them in the little town that is also called St. Pierre.

Miquelon, an hour's ferry ride away, has 600 people in a spread-out village along the water's edge between two low, treeless hills. When I visited, it was so uncommercial that if you wanted lunch, you went to local homes, and you had to let the housewife-restaurateurs know a couple of hours in advance, so they could start cooking.

Langlade, the third and largest island, used to be separate but is now connected to Miquelon by a narrow, seven-mile-long grassy neck called La Dune. With no permanent population, Langlade is a pretty place of summer homes, spruce forests (though the trees are seldom taller than 15 feet), soft, empty sand beaches. And shipwrecks. It wouldn't be attached to Miquelon if it weren't for the wrecks.

Originally, Miquelon and Langlade were separate islands with an underwater sandbar between them. But sailing ships kept running aground there, currents gathered sand around the wrecks, and gradually the sandbar rose above the waves. *Voilà*, la Dune.

Since 1800, more than 600 wrecks have piled up around these morsels of France, making salvage practically a local industry. A modern example took place in 1971, when a West German freighter, carrying a cargo of juke boxes and riding mowers, ran onto a rocky islet just beyond the St. Pierre breakwaters.

The night she was declared a total loss, Andrieux told me—he's also a shipwreck buff—about 70 dories full of men rowed up and unloaded her faster than any vessel in the history of the islands. But there wasn't a lawn in St. Pierre that could use a riding mower, "so the kids used them as go-karts." Eventually, Andrieux said, the fishermen sold them for next to nothing, and departing civil servants took them back to France.

Because of the dangerous rocks, lighthouses are still important here, and off-shore bells and warning horns provide a kind of background music for the rough-edged scenery. At the pretty cove called Savoyard on the west end of St. Pierre, where many people keep summer cottages (just a stiff walk from their winter homes), the sound of the neighborhood fog horn is more memorable than the waves. "Whoooo?" it wonders plaintively, every few seconds. "Whoo? Ohhhhh, whooooooooo?" Once, the answer might have been Al Capone.

St. Pierre today may be France in law and spirit, but during Prohibition, it was France on the rocks. Taxes on bootleg liquor built the islands' infrastructure, paving local roads and erecting the breakwaters in the St. Pierre harbor and providing plenty of local jobs. It may have been the only place in North America, in fact, that was truly sorry about Repeal. Even now, when old people talk about the halcyon years between 1920 and 1934, their eyes shine.

From their side, it was all legal. Prohibition was a matter only of North American laws. It didn't affect France or the rest of Europe or France's colonies. And while American distilleries shut down, Canadian distilleries were allowed to keep manufacturing liquor as long as it was for export. What handier place to export to than St. Pierre and Miquelon?

Led by an American named Bill McCoy—said to be the source of the phrase "the real McCoy" because he shipped only the finest—rum runners used these islands as a transfer point for millions of bottles of forbidden liquor, champagne and wine.

At peak, about 300,000 cases a month were being shipped

here by Canadian and European manufacturers, then secretly shuttled to rendezvous points off the East Coast, a stretch of the Atlantic known as Rum Row. Smaller rum-runners picked up shipments there and sneaked them past U.S. Coast Guard patrols and into the waiting cups and glasses of America's speakeasies.

Every now and then, American gangsters dropped in on the islands to which they owed so much. Andrieux proudly displays Al Capone's hat—a straw boater the gangster gave to his grandfather. Other souvenirs were bigger. One of the island's major tourist attractions is a small summer house on the road to Savoyard. It's called Cutty Sark Villa because that's the brand on the siding.

St. Pierre et Miquelon's other great claim to fame is less enchanting. This was the last place in North America—perhaps the only one—ever to have used a guillotine. That fact is made more peculiar by the islands' traditional lack of crime. Even today, my tour guide said, "If you rob, where can you run?"

But after a particularly ugly murder in the late 1800s, a local judge ordered the perpetrator's head chopped off. A guillotine was sent in from Martinique, in the French Caribbean, but it was old and didn't work well.

Andrieux's grandmother witnessed the public beheading as a child and told him about it. The result was so grisly, he said—the blade didn't cut clean, and somebody had to go in and work at the prisoner's neck with a knife—that the population was shocked, and the guillotine was never used again.

"The guillotine is still here," hidden in government storage, Andrieux said. "I've seen it. It kept me from eating lunch on the day I saw it."

Beirut Reborn

1999

——

I̶T WAS SPRING, and the jacaranda trees were blooming when a friend and I went back to Beirut, 36 years after we'd last seen it. The trees looked like clouds of periwinkle blue, and as our visit went on, the flowers dropped, and puddles of blue spread out on the sidewalks below the branches. The color was beautiful against the yellow stucco buildings that characterize older neighborhoods in this French-influenced city.

We had lived there in the summer of 1963, when we were teen-aged college students. We had never seen the trees in spring. I was surprised by their beauty. I hadn't expected it. I hadn't expected normalcy, either, but it was there, too.

For much of the time we'd been away, Lebanon had been convulsed by war—primarily among the country's many religious sects, intermittently with Israel. That's an oversimplification, but it has to be: The shortest list I've seen of key events in the Lebanese civil war ran to more than five pages.

The war destroyed the heart of the capital—the business district that we knew as the Bourj. Even eight years after the fighting stopped, and even with rebuilding underway, that wasteland is still one of the most shocking things I've ever seen.

But the rest of the city, despite bullet-pocks and occasional empty lots, was nevertheless the way I remembered it—exotic, exuberant, unpredictably friendly—and alive. My friend Jim and I were never scared. Despite its wounds, Beirut felt—I am not exaggerating—normal.

Officially, the war lasted from 1975 into 1991, but everywhere people still talked about it. "We all have war fatigue," one middle-aged woman told me, "which we're probably not going to get over."

Once I stopped at a tiny grocery to buy tomatoes, and because I was a tourist, a rare thing these days, the proprietor—a white-haired man named Ahmed Nazim—invited me to share a beer. "Was there fighting around here?" I asked as he poured. A dumb question: I could see bullet holes in the facades across the street.

Yes, he said, in excellent English. "I have seen the highwaymen. And the bandits. And the ringleaders." He smiled ruefully. "But that is life. We come into this world by accident. No one knows the consequences."

Then he said something I've carried around ever since. It was the core of his philosophy: "Everybody is the architect of his fortune."

If I were mayor of Beirut, I'd put that on the city crest.

Two blocks away, I asked directions at a beauty parlor and stayed to get a quick haircut. At my hairdresser's back home, you talk about shape and cut and the men in your life. At the hairdresser's in Beirut, you talk about shape and cut and the men in power.

"Do you think the peace will hold?" the energetic stylist, Maurice Chala, asked in American English, scissors snipping near my ears. I said I had no idea, but I hoped so—"maybe with this new man in Israel." [A few days earlier, Ehud Barak had been elected Israeli Prime Minister.]

"Yes!" the hairdresser agreed. "Maybe now we have a chance. It has to stop, I hope, for my children's future." Then he told me his life story, or rather the story of his life in the war. He had left Beirut and gone into voluntary exile, working three years in Paris and two in America—Manhattan, California, Philadelphia, Boston.

He came back to Beirut about a year before the fighting stopped, because the rest of his family was there. "You cannot live without your family," Chala said.

Beirut looked most normal on the Corniche, the Mediterranean promenade that has always been one of the city's great pleasures. As before, I loved walking there.

True, most of the palm trees were gone—shredded in the fighting. And occasionally I passed sentry posts where a soldier with a submachine gun watched the crowd from behind a few strands of barbed wire. But the soldiers looked out of place now, like mourners at a sunny block party.

All along the seafront, there were families strolling and friends walking arm in arm, kids on trikes and two-wheelers, teens gliding in and out on inline skates and skateboards, young lovers embracing, old people on benches watching the passing show.

A snack vendor pedaled past with a rack of ring-shaped sesame breads on his bike. A coffee man set up two enormous silver pots and half a dozen tiny cups on the sidewalk. On the wet, weedy rocks below the seawall, people were fishing, flicking long, supple poles in and out of the surf, not catching much, just having a good time.

From the Corniche, I could see two wartime landmarks

that the whole TV-watching world would recognize—two hotels reduced to hollow ruins by fighting among the myriad militias. "They discovered they could aim anti-aircraft guns sideways," one Beiruti noted cynically.

Both the white tower of the Holiday Inn and the shorter, equally damaged Phoenicia Hotel—the name honors the ancient Phoenicians who inhabited this coast—were being rehabbed. The pink-and-white Phoenicia was almost finished. Again.

In 1963, it was the newest hotel in town, and seeing it brand-new twice in my life was unsettling. Soon the Phoenicia would look exactly the way it did when my friends and I used to spend languid afternoons by its pool, taking breaks from studying or interviewing or, in my case, digging at an archaeological site in the Bekaa, Lebanon's central valley.

Jim and the others lived around the American University of Beirut; I joined them from the dig on weekends. Our old neighborhood had changed very little, especially the quiet, seaside campus and the bookshops and eateries across from it on Rue Bliss, named not for happiness, as I preferred to think, but for a university founder.

What had changed, of course, was downtown. I knew that almost everything in the central business district had been blown to bits. But knowing and believing are not the same.

On our first day in the city, we took a taxi to the Place des Martyrs, once the palm-dotted center of town. The cab dropped us off where the buildings stopped. In front of us lay what looked like a level beach. For blocks and blocks, the buildings were gone. I mean gone.

An occasional old building rose here and there like a

snaggle tooth—wrapped in scaffolding and plastic sheeting, or still raw and ragged and waiting for the rehabbers.

When I got over the shock, I could see that there had been a lot of progress. There were no rubble piles—those had been bulldozed into the sea to build a new coastline. And around the edges of this no man's land stood whole blocks of pristine, butter-yellow limestone structures. They were copies of what had stood there before, clones as new as tomorrow, with new sidewalks, new fire hydrants, new infant trees, new everything.

"It is the biggest preservation project in the world . . . and the biggest urban rebuilding project since Berlin," said a spokeswoman for Solidere, the government-authorized corporation that is midwife to Beirut's rebirth.

Although the city lost more than 600 buildings, nearly 300 "heritage structures" were being saved, including churches, mosques, Beirut's city hall and the Lebanese Parliament. New buildings in compatible styles would go up around them.

Ultimately, the multi-billion-dollar effort will provide housing for 40,000 people and office space for 100,000, with two new marinas and a new stretch of Corniche.

The effect was Beirut-by-Disney—everything spanking clean, with corners and windowsills sharp as knife blades, and none of the skeins of telephone and electrical wires that swoop above the streets in authentically old neighborhoods.

Not everybody likes it—too new, some say. But the city's best-known archaeologist just smiled when I asked her about that. "You can't rebuild it *old*," said Helga Seeden. "Give it 10 or 20 or 30 years. It will be old."

I had known Seeden when I was a student. Now a professor

of archaeology at the American University, she had been assistant director of the dig I worked on. After the war, she headed one of the largest archaeological excavations ever undertaken anywhere: a three-year marathon dig in the devastated heart of the city.

"The only good thing that came out of the war is the archaeology of Beirut," she told me in a cafe near the university. "Beirut is going to be the best-known city in the Mediterranean."

Supported by Solidere, archaeology teams cut through 5,000 years of history, from the 20th century down through the Ottomans, the Mamelukes, the Romans, the Phoenicians. "We went down to bedrock—then the developers took over," Seeden said. Key discoveries are being left uncovered, like tiny archaeological parks.

That triumph helps offset the archaeological losses Lebanon suffered in the fighting. Without a strong government to enforce the laws, "It was a free-for-all for antiquities dealers," she said. Precious objects vanished by the container-load; "I doubt they'll find the real culprits."

I asked her about the country's chances for a normal future. "Things are picking up," she said. "Nobody wants further disruption. But nothing will change until Lebanon is accepted in the world as a country that wants peace."

Seeden, who was born in Germany, has spent virtually all of her adult life in Lebanon. She left only once during the war, in a lull in 1982, but fighting resumed within days, and she felt stranded outside. Leaving your family and friends and then listening to the news, she said, was more horrible than staying behind. She didn't leave again.

I wanted to see the infamous Green Line. During the civil

war, world media always described it as the division between "predominately Muslim West Beirut" and "predominately Christian East Beirut."

It had run mainly along the Damascus Road, but nobody I asked could trace it precisely, not even the concierge at my hotel. People were either too young to remember, or they'd begun to forget. Either way, their vagueness seemed healthy.

I walked east across the city for a couple of miles—I felt perfectly safe doing that—but I never got to the old Green Line because I found a new one.

"Green Line" now denoted an environmental education group, founded by university students in 1991, the year the civil war ended. "That term back then was destroying our country," the group's spokesperson explained. "We turned this term into a useful one . . . . Green means 'hope' after the war."

So was she hopeful? Yes, said Nessrine Nassereddine. She was 24—born "the same year the first trigger of war was pulled" and, like the rest of her generation, she'd grown up with war.

"I remember terrible things," she said. "We used to sit in the shelters, and the windows would start to crack, and we would feel like the bombs were going to hit our heads.

"We the people didn't ask for this war. It is ridiculous to kill each other because of religion. . . . I think all people, they don't like war. They like peace. They want a better life for themselves and their children. It's time to rest."

Once, Jim and I were exploring a partially rebuilt mosque downtown when a tall young man in a polo shirt stopped us and asked, in English, "Excuse me, what nationality? British?"

No, we said, "American." Giving that answer in the Middle East always makes me a little uneasy: Except in Israel, being a Yankee isn't the greatest thing to admit to. The man looked surprised—Americans are very rare in Beirut—and then smiled warmly.

"You are welcome in Lebanon," he said.

It was like that everywhere we went, in stores, in restaurants, on the street. Beirutis had been friendly when I was a student, but not this friendly. We speculated: The Lebanese had been cut off from international tourism, particularly American tourism, for a long, long time. Our presence, then, must have been another sign of healing. It made us part of their normal.

Humor is a part of normal, too, and Beirutis have a reputation for it; it helped them get through. So when I asked, "Are there any Syrian jokes?" I was pretty sure of the answer. Our two newest friends, Fadia and Khaled, laughed and nodded.

Syria still had thousands of troops in Lebanon [they wouldn't be withdrawn until 2005], and the Beirutis we met regarded them as yokels. So, of course, there are Syrian jokes, and they are always on the Syrians. Like this one:

There's a long delay at a Syrian checkpoint. Drivers are getting impatient. Somebody leans on a horn.

A Syrian soldier walks over to the first car in line and harasses the driver: "What's the matter? Can't you wait your turn?"

"I didn't do it," the driver protests, "it was somebody behind me."

So the Syrian opens the back door and slugs the passenger. "Don't do it again," he says.

Fadia and Khaled wanted to take us someplace special for dinner on our last night in Lebanon. They promised food that was "Oriental" and a place that was "in the mountains"— always Beirutis' favorite destination. I braced for chow mein with a view.

What we got was paradise—literally, because the restaurant's name, Jana, means paradise in Arabic. We also got another lesson in the realities of Beirut life. To get to paradise, we had to drive through hell.

I remembered the road. It was the one I used to take through the mountains to get to my dig in the Bekaa, riding in old school buses. I remembered the pretty houses that had stood along it—cream stone, red roofs, peeking through clumps of pines.

There were still pine trees, but the houses were bleak shells, their roofs gone, their doors blasted, rubble around their feet. Our friends drove us past without a glance. To them, it was old, old news.

Paradise itself was part garden, part restaurant, its tables on switchback paths under tiny lights at the top of a wooded cliff. The decor, the music and the lavish menus were straight out of the Arabian Nights. There was even a man in satin robes whose job was to freshen the burning charcoal in the men's hubble-bubble pipes.

From the boiled almonds that began the meal, through the platter of oranges, apples and kiwis that ended it, we were served 28 different dishes; some, buried under the avalanche of plates, we didn't discover until we were already full.

The timing was very Beirut: We started into the mountains at 10:30 at night, began eating about midnight and didn't get back till 4 a.m. Other revelers were still dancing and eating when we said we had to leave.

Three weeks later, after I was home, Hezbollah launched an attack on Israel from southern Lebanon, and the Israelis bombed Beirut in retaliation. Now I got a bitter taste of what Helga Seeden had talked about—how it was worse to "go out" during the war than to stay behind.

For the first time in three decades, I had friends in Beirut, and the city itself was a friend again, and I could find out no details. It felt like a fist around the heart, a tightness akin to choking, the way you feel when a child darts into the street before you can yell "Stop!" and you hold your breath until you see they're safe.

Khaled and Fadia had e-mailed immediately, but to my office; an entire weekend of worry went by before I found their message. "Terrible Night in Beirut," the subject line read. They said they had been afraid Lebanon was going to "be like Kosovo." But they were fine, and their families were fine, and there hadn't been many deaths. The chief target had been a powerplant above the city, apparently on a hillside not unlike one where we'd stopped on the way back from Jana.

I pictured the view again—lights like diamonds around Jounieh Bay with Beirut beyond, diamonds in the sky and brighter ones below. I couldn't believe we were talking about the same city. It was like trying to imagine bombers over St. Paul. Everything had been so normal, I kept thinking. It had all been so normal.

How, um, Picturesque

1996

———

EVERY SO OFTEN, I get to thinking about how quaint we could be in the middle of this country if we really tried. You know—if we hooked our thumbs under our overall straps and started salting our talk with colorful, folksy phrases like "I reckon" and "purty near" and giving advice like "Red sky at night, sailor's delight. Red sky at morning, sailor take warning."

My grandmother used to say that whenever we happened to see a sunset together. It never occurred to me to wonder where a woman who'd spent all her life in the center of the continent could have picked up such coastal wisdom.

That was also the woman who once described another's hair as "straighter'n a yard of pump water." Sounded right normal to me.

Maybe we wouldn't have to try all that hard to assume a mantle of quaintness. At least I wouldn't. Calling a big thunderstorm "a real gullywasher" came purty natural to me after I'd lived a year in a Deep Midwestern village where I'd heard people say that—and where we had a lot of storms to say it about. Unfortunately, I accidentally dropped it into a phone conversation with a friend back in Minneapolis.

"Gullywasher?" she said, incredulous. "*Gully*washer???" In her mind, I'd been away from civilization far too long.

But the veneer is thin, even here in the cultural capital of the Upper Midwest. I had a clear glimpse of our innate quaintness on an autumn Sunday, while driving a visiting journalist from Holland around Minneapolis.

It was her first visit to the United States, and unlike most international tourists, she had not seen New York, Miami, L.A. or anyplace else before she got to us. For her, the Minneapple *was* America.

We'd driven along the Mississippi, gone around a couple of lakes and were heading for downtown when we spotted a crowd outside the Basilica. As we got closer, we could see that the crowd included big dogs as well as people.

When I noticed little dogs and blanket-wrapped cats in people's arms, it dawned on me: "They're blessing the animals! I've always wanted to see that!" My new friend wanted to see it too, so we ditched the car and raced into the church just as the service was starting.

There were pets everywhere: cats peeking over shoulders, little dogs on laps, big dogs on pews, more dogs lying on the floor, a few wagging dog-butts extending into the aisles, guinea pigs in cages, even bowls of goldfish.

The clergy had their own pets with them, up beside the altar. A dog accompanied the lay reader to the lectern, and there was a red-tailed hawk looking regal on a perch near the choir.

The whole scene made me happy, and I glanced at my companion to see if she felt the same way. From the look on her face, she was happy, too, but I knew we weren't seeing the same Minneapolis.

I recognized that look. It's a journalist-turned-tourist look, slightly greedy around the edges. It means, "Where's my note-book?" or "Drat, I forgot the camera!"

It's the same look I've worn whenever I'm in a place so re-mote, so different, so *foreign* that I can't believe it's real.

It reminded me of how I felt watching Tibetan pilgrims circling the Jokhang temple in central Lhasa, in traditional costumes, with prayer beads in hand and saint-like smiles on their faces.

Or the enchantment of stepping out of a Chinese restau-rant in Popayan, Colombia, into the candlelit midst of a Holy Week procession, the air thick with incense as figures of saints were borne along head-high by men in black robes and tall pointed hoods.

Or the time in Luxembourg when the annual Jumping Fes-tival of St. Wilibrod came dancing right past me, commemo-rating the saving of the town from a medieval plague, and I got so caught up in it that I jumped too—through the church doors and right down to the crypt to the shrine of the saint.

Now I saw that same look on my Dutch companion's face, and I suddenly felt like a foreigner myself. A quaint foreigner at that.

I've felt out of place often overseas—including in front of the Jokhang—but until that moment I'd never felt pictur-esque. That, of course, is how people I photograph in foreign countries must feel in front of my lens. After all these years, I could finally, fully empathize, and it wasn't comfortable.

The pet-blessing service was short, in human terms, though it probably ran half a day in dog time and a couple of years for the goldfish. Then the barking, panting, sniffing, scratch-ing congregation adjourned to the back of the church for dog biscuits, cat treats and animal-shaped sugar cookies.

It had been a success. Not only were all the owners smiling, but—as my mother used to say with relief after any big family celebration—"nobody fought."

Still, all the way through, I felt at pains to explain it to my companion. We don't normally do this, I stressed. Not all churches here do this. This is special. This is like, like—I reached for European comparisons—"like blessing the fleet!"

"I've heard of that," she said, nodding, but the "Oh, wow!" look never left her face.

Rafting the Himalayas

1996

——•——

W<small>E MADE CAMP</small> beside the River Bheri just before dark on Halloween. There was a small rapids shushing in the background, late sun shining on a yellow cliff across the river and the aroma of corn popping over the campfire—a tea-time snack for my friend Jim and me.

I draped my wet rafting clothes over several boulders, propped my wet shoes and myself against another near the fire, warmed my hands around a tin mug of Indian tea and pondered events so far.

Some things were clearly the same as on an American river trip:

The anticipatory fear before the first big rapids. The raft's sudden rush forward. The shock of a wall of cold white water crashing over the bow. The benison of dry clothes at day's end. And the sickening grate of fine sand in the barrel of a telephoto lens.

Some things weren't the same at all:

On the Salmon or the Colorado, for example, you don't raft past women in saris beating laundry on the rocks. Or see a body being cremated on a stack of logs at the riverside. Or make camp to the distant throbbing of funeral drums. And you sure don't get to rescue any sacred cows.

Yes, it had been quite a day.

It grew dark in the canyon while I was thinking all this, and our two boatmen, Jerry Thapa and Cadji Lama, turned their efforts from making popcorn to full-fledged dinner. They were stocky, good-looking young Nepalis, both in their late 20s, well-muscled from working on the river, with dark hair and deep eyes and unfailing cheerfulness.

Suddenly, Jerry, grim-faced, jogged across the beach and began heaving rocks at something in the river. I stood up to see. It was only a log—a charred log—eddying into shore. But it meant that the cremation was over upstream, and the wood of the funeral pyre had been shoved into the river, along with whatever remained of the body.

For Jerry, this wasn't just target practice. If you're a devout Hindu, you don't want such grisly reminders of mortality anywhere near you. He was throwing rocks to drive the log away from where we would eat and sleep that night, so our camp would not be polluted by death.

Eventually, the current caught the log again and carried it off. A fitting touch, I thought, for Halloween.

———

Jim and I have been friends since college. We went on to jobs that required us to travel, usually alone. But occasionally I get a postcard from him, mailed from some exotic corner of the globe, inviting me to join him on some other exotic adventure. Did I, in this instance, want to go white-water rafting in Nepal? You bet.

We rendezvoused in Katmandu, made arrangements with

an outfitter and caught a late-afternoon plane to the grungy town of Nepalganj in southwestern Nepal.

The adventure began on that plane, as we chased the sunset westward along the Himalayas. The great peaks marched beside us for almost two hours, like a snowy wall, like an angel army, like the white spine of the world.

In Nepalganj, we met our boatmen and crawled with them into an old dark-blue van, along with our duffels, rations, tents, sleeping bags, oars and even the raft, rolled up like a giant silver sausage and wedged behind the seats.

For the next few days, there would be just the four of us; Jerry and Cadji would be our guides, caretakers, porters, cooks, steersmen and ultimately friends.

We barely spoke on the dusty, teeth-jarring, four-hour night drive to our put-in point, but if I'd had any doubts about the company or the trip, the boatmen's energy soon erased them. In midnight darkness, at a sandy campsite under a bridge across a narrow gorge, they built a fire, pitched our tents and whipped up a hefty stew spiced with ginger and curry, while Jim and I stood near the fire, staggeringly tired and doing nothing.

The next day went just fine until it was time to get on the water. Then we got a scary safety lecture from Jerry. Standing by our 18-foot, inflatable raft, with our orange life vests feeling tight and hot in the sun, Jim and I listened and got nervous.

Point one: "Sometime, by mistake, raft hit a hole and go over," Jerry said. "Don't panic." Don't try to swim out from under it, either, or you'll get pinned by the raft—"like a sandwich." Instead, we were to grab a lifeline and push up on the raft while pulling ourselves out from under it, backward. Huh?

"How often does this happen?" I asked, confused by the directions.

"Very often," Jerry said, smiling.

(My heart started to beat faster. "That's it," I thought. "I'm gonna die.")

Point two: "Sometime, by mistake, you fall out. Don't panic." Don't float on your stomach, and don't fend off rocks with your hands. Float on your back, fend with your feet. OK. . . .

"How often does this happen?" I asked.

"Very often," Jerry said, still smiling.

("Yup, I'm gonna die.")

Point three: "Sometime, by mistake, I fall out. Hang on very tight. Don't panic." Cadji would come forward from the stern of the raft and take the oars, then we'd rescue Jerry.

"And how often does *this* happen?" I was feeling small and far from home.

"Very often."

("Gonna die. Gonna die.")

About then, it dawned on me that while Jerry's English was generally wonderful, he thought "often" meant "seldom." Ah, that explained why he kept smiling so reassuringly. I exchanged a glance with Jim, relaxed and got in the boat.

The Bheri comes down from the Himalayas, opaque with rock flour scraped up on its journey and still intensely cold, even where we were, in the semi-tropical lowlands called the Terai. Setting out in the raft that morning was like embarking on a river of icy blue jade.

We hit the two biggest rapids on the lower Bheri in the first hour and a half. We could hear them coming.

Rapids roar in the distance the way whirlpools are said to do in myths, and the advance notice jump-starts your adrenaline. I've always imagined Scylla and Charybdis sounding like this, and the real song of the Lorelei must have been the sinister, distant music of mountain white water.

First Rapid—the name was tamer than the thing itself—was as rough as a giant washing machine, and it bounced us and the raft around as if we were a clump of rags. Instantly cold rags: I gasped when the frigid water slammed into us. It felt like being punched.

Our wet clothes were still plastered to our skin when Jerry and Cadji steered into shore, leaped out of the raft and scrambled over huge boulders so they could get a view of Second Rapid and decide how to run it. It was rough anyway.

Even bigger boulders were hidden in the river, the granddaddies of the ones on the banks, and they were sending a wall of water into the air like a cresting ocean wave. The raft hit the wave nose-on and shot up, then sideways and down the crest, ending where you don't want to be—in the hole, the swirling downriver pit where all the disturbed water smashes back together. I shrieked.

Seconds later, we emerged safe—blinking and sputtering but safe—as gallons of icy water drained off us, coursing down our necks and under our clothes and flooding the floor of the raft calf-deep.

After those two thrills, the Bheri's white water became increasingly pastel, and it grew quiet enough to hear Cadji singing at the oars—soft, lilting Hindi melodies whose rhythms I could never manage to duplicate. Jerry translated all the lyrics merely as "love song."

Now what was on the river banks became more interesting

than the river itself. Lazing on the front tubes, letting the sun dry us off, Jim and I shore-watched.

And I reached, almost instantly, the point in a trip that normally comes only after weeks on the road—the point when I can imagine no other life but this. It felt like a personal summer, and I wanted it to last. I wanted to stretch time. I wanted the river to go on forever. But rivers never do.

Over the next few days, ours was going to widen, flatten, grow tame, split itself into shallow channels, twine its channels back together, and we would drift to journey's end in a kind of slough, with elephant grass on the banks waving its plumes above our heads. Between now and then, there would be more rapids, blue foothills and an ark-load of jungle creatures from black cormorants and white-necked storks to the man-eating crocodiles charmingly nicknamed "marsh muggers."

—·—

But it was Halloween that made the trip for me—a day and a night that I am still savoring.

After the big rapids that morning, we had lunch on a rocky beach, gobbling the Nepali version of Cornish pasties—pie crust stuffed with curried vegetables.

The instant our tin plates were stowed away, an upset Jerry power-rowed us across the current to some trouble he'd spotted on the opposite bank.

As we got closer, the mass of tan boulders on shore sorted themselves into many tan rocks and a single tan cow. Jerry estimated it had been there perhaps a week, trapped in chest-deep mud. It was going to die unless we could free it.

How the cow had gotten there—onto a tiny scrap of beach at the foot of cliffs—none of us could tell. Somehow it had picked its way down through the boulders to the water to drink, and its own weight had driven its front legs deep into the slurry of silt at the river's edge.

The cow's struggles had only worked its legs deeper, and now it was exhausted. It looked as if it were resting, but in truth it had given up.

Cows are sacred to Hindus and treasured in this part of the world. The animal had to be saved. In urgent silence, Jerry and Cadji jumped into the mud beside the cow and tried to pull it free. No luck. It struggled once, gave up again, then put its head down, almost into the water.

Its front legs were locked in mud to the shoulders. Cadji dug with his hands, and Jerry pulled until they had one leg free, but the cow wouldn't try to move. More frantic digging and pulling at the other leg; still no good.

They tried pushing at the cow's hindquarters and encouraging it with cries of "Ut! Ut!" No luck.

Jim and I grabbed a rope from the raft and jumped into the water too. The boatmen noosed the rope around the cow's neck and yanked, trying to drag it onto solid ground, but it only cut into the cow's creamy hide.

"It'll choke!" I yelled.

"Put it around the horns!" Jim shouted.

They looped it around the horns then, and I pulled while Jim joined Jerry and Cadji in pushing on the cow's flanks. Nothing. We could have pulled its head off before the heavy body budged.

By now, the cow's eyeballs had rolled back in its head, and its eyes were blankly white between their open lids. I was afraid the cow would die as we watched or, worse, that we'd have to give up and leave it to continue to suffer.

Then the boatmen had a brainstorm: Maybe we could *roll* the cow up the steep slope to solid ground.

The men tucked the animal's legs close to its body, and we all got in the murky water and helped push it over: onto its side, onto its back, finally—one more push—onto its belly again.

This worked. It helped that the cow didn't fight. (In the process, we observed that our cow was a steer, which may have compromised its official sacredness. No matter: By now the animal was sacred to us, too.)

The first roll got it out of the muck, but it lay limp, with its head on the ground and its eyes still turned to white. We had to roll it over two more times until it was up on fully dry sand. Still, it just lay there.

Now Cadji wrestled big cobblestones over to the cow and worked them under its hindquarters, exactly the way you'd chock a car's wheels on a steep slope. Then he began tearing branches off saplings and pulling up armfuls of grass, to pile in front of the cow's nose.

At the smell of food, it put its head up, looking a little bleary, then stretched out its neck to reach the greenery and began to nibble. We all smiled with relief.

The cow was still munching when our raft struck the current. A pessimist, I wanted to get out of sight fast. I figured that once the cow regained its strength, it would stagger right back into the muck, and I didn't want to watch.

"If it goes back in," Jim said, "then that's its karma."

———

Our karma was to steer around a steep headland with a primary school on top. As we hove into view, a horde of little kids burst out and ran to the cliff edge, laughing and screaming and waving.

"Bye-bye!" they yelled, "bye-bye!" Apparently rafts don't stay in sight long enough on the Bheri for "hello" to catch on.

Around another headland, six men stared at us from a waterside ledge. Jerry held the raft against the current while Cadji shouted a long speech to them about the stranded cow, complete with urgent gestures. The men understood and began moving up the bank. Good, I thought; maybe they could save it from its karma.

By the time we met those men, we were used to seeing people along the Bheri. The wooded riverbanks looked like wilderness, but they were occupied. There were people everywhere—in riverside villages, on beaches, in pastures, on footbridges over-head. They made us curious, but we were the real curiosities. And always great diversions.

Every morning, gangs of little kids managed to find our camp and would hang around till we shoved off, solemnly watching us comb our hair, brush our teeth, pack our water-proof duffels and stow our cameras. The kids always hoped—but never begged—for novelties: our used plastic bags, an empty bottle of mustard oil, a ride on the raft, photos from Jerry's last raft trip.

On the night of Halloween, in what I thought of as Crema-tion Camp, we were alone again. Cadji cooked enough chicken curry to feed 20 men, and we wolfed it by the light of the fire and the makeshift luminaria—candles in plastic bags weighted with sand—that the boatmen planted every night near the food and at the doors to our tents.

The funeral log had long since drifted downstream, but something else about this place made Jerry uneasy. All through dinner, he kept glancing over his shoulder at the woods behind us and nervously shining his flashlight into the trees. Finally he explained: He was scanning for jackals.

"Anubis," said Jim sagely, supplying the name of the ancient Egyptians' jackal-headed god, the one that presided over the process of embalming. I smiled; Anubis was creepy, but real jackals would be downright thrilling.

"Please, do not leave outside your leather shoes," Jerry said earnestly. Jackals might steal them to eat. Sometimes, he added, they had even run off with the camp tablecloth because it smelled like food. This was another nice Halloween touch, but I was too comfortable to take it seriously.

Thus warned, we lingered by the campfire after dinner, sipping tea and staring into the flames as Jim told the South Asian equivalent of ghost stories. "There were two tigers who escaped from the Delhi zoo . . ." he began.

"Royal Bengal tigers?" Jerry wondered sweetly, asking a question straight out of Kipling.

"Yes," said Jim, "Royal Bengal tigers. . . ."

Now, *there* was something worth worrying about, I thought. Never mind the jackals.

I stayed up very late that night, meaning till about 9:30, but it was long after the boatmen had sought their sleeping bags and Jim his tent.

Satisfied in body and mind, I sat there alone until it felt like midnight—until the fire died down, and the air chilled, and the metal mug grew cold in my hands. Then I turned in, too, my heart full of the day's strange happenings.

Imaginary jackals lurking behind us, a burned corpse floating down the river in front, sacred cows stranded in our memories, tigers in the air. It was the most perfect Halloween I ever had or ever want to have.

Before I fell asleep, I made myself fetch my still-soggy shoes from among the boulders. A good thing, as it turned out. There were jackal tracks all over the beach next morning. Jerry hadn't been kidding.

Reliving Living History

2003

———

WHENEVER THE ACTION swept toward me, the cavalry came so close that I could hear the clang of saber on saber and see the sweat shining on the horses' sides. Big cannons were blasting nearby, their explosions so loud that my lungs shuddered, and the air was tangy with gunsmoke. It lingered over the field like sulfurous fog.

This was time travel, pure and simple, a painting of the Civil War come to life, a Mathew Brady photograph in living—thankfully not dying—color.

Even watching from the sidelines, I found it thrilling. For my comrades on horseback that weekend, the battle of Gettysburg had to be spectacular. They were Confederates—reenactors whose hobby is living and breathing the Civil War. A few months earlier, they'd invited me to camp with them at the huge reenactment scheduled for Gettysburg's 140th anniversary.

The invitation had been irresistible: I've always been interested in the Civil War, and I'd always wanted to try reenacting. But I never imagined I'd be wearing gray. Or that I'd be impersonating a man. Now, in the sweet rolling farmland of southern Pennsylvania, I was doing both.

I was a dismounted but duly registered member of the 35th Battalion Virginia Cavalry. I was living in their camp, sleeping in one of their white canvas tents, drinking black coffee from a tin cup beside their cookfire in the mornings and listening as they rehashed old battles in the cricket-filled evenings, while their picketed horses nickered in the woods nearby.

We weren't on hallowed ground. The National Park Service doesn't permit such activity on the actual battlefield, so the reenactment was taking place on rented farmland about three miles north of Gettysburg National Military Park.

We weren't there on the right dates, either. That was a matter of weather. The real battle of Gettysburg took place the first three days of July in 1863, and anniversary reenactments are normally held on the nearest weekend.

But heavy rains had left the fields too wet to handle thousands of soldiers and spectators, let alone heavy artillery and hundreds of horses. So the reenactment was postponed to early August.

The original battle was one of the pivotal events in American history. It was a turning point for both armies, the last time Robert E. Lee attempted to invade the North and the place where his forces reached the now-legendary "High Water Mark of the Confederacy."

Counting both North and South, about 170,000 Americans fought at Gettysburg, and more than 50,000 were wounded or killed. Far fewer than that—about 14,000 reenactors—were registered for Gettysburg's 140th. But there is a limit to what the mind can comprehend, and the ranks of soldiers at this modern battle looked like the entire world to me.

On the Confederate side, hundreds of small white A-line tents had been pitched on hilly high ground. In the distance, on flat land at the bottom of the wide, sloping battlefield, hundreds of Union tents were laid out in neatly gridded rows.

On both sides, cars were parked out of sight, and in the evenings, when spectators had gone home and the lemonade and hot-dog concessions had closed, the only light came from the moon and from candles in lanterns along the quiet rows of tents.

At such times, the camp looked and felt real, and even though I knew nobody was going to die in battle the next day, it kept bringing tears to my eyes.

What is it, anyway, about the Civil War? Why does it have such a hold on so many people? There have been so many wars. Why can't we let this one go?

Maybe it's because the nation came so shockingly close to destroying itself. Or that so many lives were lost in the four-year struggle. Or that they were all Americans.

I don't know. All I know is that it tugs at my heart, more than any other war America has had. Gazing over the moonlit camp, I was pretty sure everybody in those tents felt the same way I did about it.

Motto on a reenactor's T-shirt: "I sleep. I work. I reenact. Life is simple." Except it isn't. Reenactment is an expensive hobby, and most of the hobbyists are not rich—they're just ordinary people, like the ones who did the original fighting, like the ones who fight all wars.

These days, it costs at least $1,000 to outfit and arm yourself properly as a foot soldier—more if your whole family gets into reenacting and needs period clothing, much more if you're in the cavalry and have to buy and care for a horse as well.

"As reenactment has gotten more authentic, it's also gotten

more expensive," said Ken Wilt, colonel of the 35th. People with young families often can't afford it, so "there are a lot of reenactors with gray hair. The good thing is, we live a lot longer than they did then."

That's good for another reason. Reenacting demands a big time commitment. Of the twenty-five members of my unit who camped at Gettysburg, most stayed all four days, and many said they do reenactments every chance they get, usually every other weekend from spring through fall.

Reenacting may also be the hardest work of any hobby I've ever encountered—like heavy, heavy camping *now*, because that's how it would have been *then*:

In addition to horses, tack and weapons, the 35th brought iron fire grates to cook on, full-size coffee pots, black cast-iron skillets and ponderous Dutch ovens, wooden folding chairs and tables, sturdy wooden cots, even small carpets to put on the tent floors.

Wilt, always referred to in camp as "Colonel," and his wife, Vonda, brought gear befitting a high-ranking officer—a wall tent and a full-sized bedstead with a patchwork quilt.

All of this was authentic, though the enlisted men wouldn't have used tents in summer. "If this was then," said Jim Shank, the 35th's quartermaster, "we'd'a been sleepin' on the ground. Your saddle'd be your pillow."

The Gettysburg reenactment, titled "Three Days of Destiny," ran Friday, Saturday and Sunday. But we "went into period"—meaning clothes, camp, everything—on Thursday morning. From then on, everything modern was out of sight. That meant no plastic mustard or ketchup bottles on the tables, no walking around with bags of potato chips, no chugging soda from a can. You could consume all that stuff, but it had to be in 1860s-style cups or bowls or kept well hidden inside your tent.

I stashed a Styrofoam cooler behind a wooden crate, parked plastic jugs of drinking water under my cot and fretted that my jeans were too "farby"—incorrect, in reenactor lingo—because they had a zipper instead of a button fly. Colonel made an exception for my camera, notebook and felt-tip pen. Nobody mentioned the jeans.

Strict as it sounds, the 35th is a "mainstream" unit, not "hard-core." Really hard-core reenactors want every detail perfect, right down to the correct number of stitches on a buttonhole. "We call 'em 'stitch Nazis,'" said Bill Buser, the 35th's bugler.

We had a few modern conveniences—portable potties were tucked into corners of the grounds, and a solar shower was rigged up in the woods. But the illusion of the past was still uncanny.

"Why can't we *live* here?" Doug Nalls, the first lieutenant, said to the group after supper one evening. It surprised me, because the illusion was so good, I'd forgotten they didn't.

It extended even to conversations. In most social gatherings, people talk about their jobs and houses and kids. But real life seldom came up in camp. Neither did politics, whether of 1863 or 2003.

What the 35th did talk about were saddles, sabers, how to keep the horses hydrated in the steamy summer heat, differences between Federal and Rebel bugle calls, their favorite battlegrounds and funny things that happened in fights.

Do you really fight? I asked. Yes, they said. It's like playing touch football, Nalls explained: "They're your friends, and you play, but you play *hard*."

Reenactors swing sabers with enough force to nick the edges, to break off the hand guards, to bend modern blades—which is why some in the 35th prefer using original Civil War sabers: They're tougher.

For safety, you're supposed to fight with sabers pointed up, not horizontal. Firearms are loaded only with black powder, and you're not supposed to aim at anybody's face. But reenactors can get carried away. "We've all been hurt," one of my new buddies told me. "We've all been shot in the face. We've all had powder burns."

But it's still so much fun that I heard one commander order his troops not to smile when they were fighting close to spectators: It wouldn't look authentic.

After a while, especially if they do this a lot, cavalry reenactors start running into each other on the battlefield. It's common, guys said, to be in the midst of a fight and hear the enemy say something like, "Haven't seen you since Antietam! How are the wife and kids?"

The battles themselves—there were two a day at Gettysburg this time—are compressed history, Cliff's Notes versions of the real thing. In most cases, the outcome is known. Pickett's Charge, for instance, is not going to end in a Confederate victory.

But even in scripted battles, there can be surprises. Commanders are ordering men around, and sometimes—amid the popcorn rattle of musket volleys and the boom of cannon and mortars—the soldiers can't hear the commands and get confused. Just like then.

"It becomes real," Wilt said. "Contact sports? There's nothing like this."

Between battles, I did what nearly 20,000 other spectators and a lot of reenactors were doing. I wandered the camp, talking to people and checking out the sutlers' tents.

Sutlers are the purveyors of authentic everything. Regulation uniforms, period hats, hoop skirts and corsets, brass buttons and hardtack—you name it, if it existed at the time of the Civil War, there's a sutler you can buy it from.

And if it didn't exist then but needs to now, you can find that, too, right down to clip-on ringlets for short-haired ladies and gruesomely bloody plastic body parts for surgical depictions.

Everywhere, I kept asking reenactors the same question: Why do you do this? Everyone—North and South, soldier and civilian—talked about how reenacting is so much fun, how it educates others, how it ties in with genealogy, how it's a great family activity, how you meet such nice people.

Once we got past that, everyone invariably said there is more to it. Just *what* was all over the map.

"Politically," a corseted, hoop-skirted, parasol-carrying Southern belle said in a New Jersey accent, "it's so we can tell people never, ever, ever again fight your brothers."

"Did you ever see the TV show 'Fantasy Island'?" a sutler said. "This is a miniature version."

A woman dressed entirely in black—from the hem of her hoopskirt to the feather in her hat—explained that she depicts a Civil War widow, even though her reenactor husband is very much alive, "because everybody has had losses."

Doug Nalls, of my unit, had a more personal incentive. "I do this for two reasons," he said. "One, I love history. And two, I want to remember my fallen."

Like many in the unit, he had Confederate ancestors, including one who died at Gettysburg and another who survived the battle and drew a veteran's pension from the state of Virginia till his death in 1934. It was $12.50 a month. Nalls also had living ancestors in camp: his mother and his father, the 35th's first sergeant, were there, along with his wife, teenaged son and nine-year-old daughter.

Reenactors also say there's a sense of respect in what they do. "It kind of puts you in awe when you think of what those men went through—what a human being can really accomplish if he believes it's right," said John Tompkins, who rides with the 35th. He had Civil War ancestors "on both sides of the coin," Union as well as Confederate.

Reenactors "read about the battles, and it's not quite enough for them," said a knowledgeable-looking gentleman in a brocade vest, white coat and straw hat. He was Bill Holschuh, publisher of the reenacting magazine, Camp Chase Gazette, and a reenactor himself.

"They want to see if they can live it," Holschuh said. "They want to feel the whole experience—the taste and smells and all of it. Short of actually shooting at each other, this is as close as they can get."

But some reenactors say they get much closer. "Here's the truth," said Don Hotchkiss, a civil engineer from Las Vegas who depicts a Union officer. "I'm not a touchy-feely guy. But I swear there is a force out there, as if the ghosts of these guys are reaching out and want their stories told."

All weekend, there were moments when I was sure Hotchkiss was right, moments when I felt past and present ricocheting around me.

I felt it most intensely when it came time to say goodbye. It was Sunday morning, right before the 35th rode into battle for the last time. The bugler sounded the command to mount up, but just before they did, Nalls gave me a bear hug and said, "If we don't see you again. . . ."

In any other context, he'd have finished by saying "stay in touch" or "nice meeting you" or "have a good trip back." And he might have.

But I didn't catch what he said next, because for an instant all I could picture was my guys riding into a killing hail of grapeshot and musket fire. I gasped and almost wept. For that split second, Gettysburg felt too real to bear.

The White Continent

1994

—–—

YOU ARE NOT supposed to walk up to wildlife in Antarctica, but nothing stops the wildlife from walking up to you. That meant the Gentoo penguin chick was within its rights when it bit me.

The half-grown chick, a one-foot-tall clump of gray fluff, waddled up to my feet, pecked at my black rubber boots and flapped its downy wings. I knelt down beside it, took off my glove and held out my fingers.

The little penguin didn't need enticement. It opened its orange bill and clamped down, hard enough to hurt.

On any other trip, that encounter would have been the crystallizing moment—the instant when something becomes a symbol, the first thing you'll think of whenever you remember that journey. In Antarctica, though, the penguin that bit me was only one of many rich moments, all strange, all crystallizing:

There was the blue light of icebergs and the wild glance of seals. The constant slap-slap of trudging penguin feet. The fresh taste of meltwater from the face of a glacier. Shrieking skuas that dive-bombed my head when I came too close to their hidden nest. Three Minke whales that played around our raft like cavorting trout. The napping Weddell seal I nearly tripped over. . . .

I filled a journal with moments like those.

Antarctica has been called the most beautiful place on earth. Until I saw it, I would not have believed that. Now I do. And I miss it. At first, I wouldn't have believed that, either.

On day one, mere steps into the first landfall of the trip, I was down on all fours on a rough edge of Joinville Island, off the Antarctic Peninsula. Glasses greasy with sea spray, feet slipping on sharp ridges of black rock, I was stuck, physically and emotionally.

"Is this what it's going to be like?" I thought with something approaching panic. "Is this *it* for the next week?"

While I was struggling to find a foothold and stand up, two fellow passengers suddenly screamed for help: a woman who had gotten her foot wedged between rocks and a man who had stepped onto what he thought was solid ice and was now floundering up to his chest in slush.

We had been taken off our cruise ship in Zodiacs, inflatable rubber boats that look like silver bugs and carry about a dozen people, jolting over the steely waves in a real-life amusement-park ride.

On that first, frigid run, I hadn't understood how stable a loaded Zodiac is, and I clambered onto shore feeling scared and trembly and promptly slipped. The screaming of my companions didn't help.

But everything got better after that, the way things usually do on trips. I managed to stand up and take pictures, even though I couldn't see well enough through the dried salt to focus; the woman got her foot unstuck, and the man crawled out of the ice-water ditch on his own.

It got better still when we were warm and dry and back on our ship again, and the trip director admitted that the landing had been "an experiment" he wouldn't try again. At least, he added, we were probably the first human beings ever to set foot on that rocky beach. We passengers sat up straighter and smiled at each other. Antarctica is still a place where a statement like that could be true.

From that point on, we were Antarctic veterans, hopping in and out of the Zodiacs with aplomb, scrambling comfortably over rocks for closer looks at wildlife and managing to laugh at the mess that ever-present penguin excrement made of our boots and trousers.

Going to the tip of the Antarctic Peninsula and trying to talk about the seventh continent is like going to Key West and saying you've seen North America. You can't do it. It is too big.

At 5.4 million square miles, Antarctica is nearly twice as large as Australia, and its area doubles in winter when sea ice forms around its margins. It is a place of superlatives, higher, colder and drier than any other continent. The permanent ice cap stands two miles thick at its deepest and contains 70 percent of the planet's fresh water. All this ice and the frigid currents that flow outward from it affect weather around the globe.

It's also the emptiest continent. Unless you count mosses and lichens, nothing lives on the white continent, except along the shore.

The surrounding Southern Ocean teems with life—seabirds, fish, squid, penguins, seals, whales and krill, particularly krill, the tiny shrimp-like creatures on which everything else, directly or indirectly, depends.

But there are no polar bears (wrong pole). No other land

predators. And no people, though some of the scientific stations, inhabited all year, might as well be little indoor towns. About as messy, too.

We visited several defunct stations—including a British base on Deception Island that was ruined when its volcano erupted in 1967—and three active stations: Argentina's Almirante Brown on the Antarctic Peninsula, and Brazil's Comandante Ferraz and Poland's Henryk Arctowski, both on King George Island.

With housing that looked like a cross between barracks and semi-trailers, the stations were embedded in the detritus of the outside world—gas tanks, wires, cords, PVC conduits, even road graders at the Brazilian base—a concentrated ugliness in the name of science, even though the nations of the Antarctic Treaty have agreed to clean up their collective act.

But away from the stations and the guano-smeared penguin rookeries, the white-and-black land was clean and pure, and the water was liquid crystal, so clear you could have read through it.

We made more than a dozen landings—often in battering winds and stinging sleet—in the seven days we spent along the Antarctic Peninsula, getting as far south as 65 degrees 12 minutes Southern latitude. Each landing was different and intensely interesting, demanding that we live completely in the moment, which made the time both stand still and race by.

What we saw quickly became predictable, though it never stopped being a source of wonder: Ice, rock and penguins—a recipe spiced occasionally by elephant seals, living glaciers, spouting whales, nesting petrels and abandoned huts, legacies of one or another scientific expedition.

Because places that are good for people are also good for penguins—reliable rock beaches, mainly—penguin rookeries have extended into many old research stations. The penguins look out of place standing around among the derelict buildings—like squatters trying to act natural or a dog caught sleeping on the good chair.

Once, approaching a rookery of Gentoo penguins on Petermann Island, we were astonished to see a man in a dinghy rowing across the harbor. We were so accustomed to the absence of people by then that he seemed like an apparition.

The explanation was equally astonishing: A Frenchman and his wife had sailed south from Tasmania on their custom-built aluminum-hulled sailboat to spend the Antarctic summer cruising the peninsula and its islands.

Our own ship was a 500-foot-long scientific research vessel, the *Akademik Sergei Vavilov*, owned by the Russian Academy of Science and chartered for tourist groups of about 75 people—small by Antarctic cruise standards but plenty big. The French sailboat was 36 feet long, with a crew of two. We were impressed by their nerve. And I don't think I have ever been more envious of a lifestyle.

Once you've mastered getting ashore from a Zodiac—you sit on the front pontoon, swing your legs over the side and hop down into the shallows—the toughest thing about an Antarctic landing is getting dressed for it.

It was always a big production. In order, from the inside out, I put on regular undies, long underwear, a thermal turtle-neck, polar-fleece pants, windproof pants, a fleece vest, a down sweater, a fleece hat, polypro sock liners, two pairs of heavy socks, a plastic rain suit, black rubber wading boots, a life vest, my daypack with camera and film, wool gloves and, oh, yes, don't forget to grab the sunglasses and the oversized rubber gloves to keep penguin guano off the good ones.

We saw five types of penguins in Antarctica: Adelies, Gentoos, Chinstraps, a few Macaronis and one juvenile King penguin, about 1,000 miles from its home. Penguins not old enough to breed—adolescents, in other words—often do some cruising on their own, we'd been told; this youngster was clear proof.

I found it impossible to regard the penguins as birds. They looked too much like tired little men in dirty tuxedos, their white fronts splotched with pink guano, like boozy party-goers on the morning after.

They raise their young in rookeries, age-old penguin home-lands so stained by their droppings that the sites are visible on satellite images from space. Rookeries are raucous places. They also smell bad, with a stinging ammoniac stench worse than an unemptied cat box behind a bad seafood restaurant—and I mean a really bad one. Even so, they're fascinating.

Partway through a morning among the Gentoos on Cuver-ville Island, standing in stinky penguin muck under gray clouds and a light drizzle, the miracle of it all hit me. In less than two hours I had seen, with my own eyes and no effort, every pen-guin behavior I'd ever heard of: Nest-building, stone-stealing, egg-incubating, chick-rearing—it was all happening literally at my feet.

In the heart of the rookery, penguins crowed, their throats pulsing in and out like bagpipes. Older chicks were "creching"— huddling together in groups, called creches, for safety. Others were following adults on the "feeding chase" as parents tried to separate their offspring from unrelated greedy babies.

Chicks tapped their bills in an orange staccato against their parents' bills, begging them to open up. Parents' throats swelled as they hawked up a good cud for their little ones. Babies poked their heads halfway into the adults' mouths, crossways, as they gulped down dinner.

By the shore, penguins were leaping into the slushy mixture called brash ice, or popping back out as if shot from underwater cannon, bouncing onto their feet and waddling inland, feet slapping on guano-spattered rocks.

It was 30 degrees above zero, hot for Antarctica in its midsummer—far warmer than Minnesota at the time—and the adult penguins were feeling it. Everywhere, adults flapped their stubby wings, nibbled bits of ice, drank ice water at the shore—all attempts to keep themselves cool.

Not so the chicks. They wanted warmth. Unlike adult feathers, their down is not waterproof, and they suffered in the chill rain. I saw a bedraggled one shivering like a human child and could not forget the image. In the first phase of hypothermia, it could not live if the rain kept on. The rain kept on.

All over the colony, penguins squawked and lashed out with their bills as they passed each other, each an interloper from the other's point of view. One had claimed the whole ocean. Each time it stooped to sip ice water, another penguin or two would get the same idea, and the first one would stop and noisily chase them away. It made me laugh: There was the whole Southern Ocean, and here was a single small penguin saying "Get away! This water's mine!"

Behavior like that is what makes them seem so human. So cute. So endearing. If you can be objective with other forms of wildlife, maybe you could pull it off with penguins, too, but I doubt it. I couldn't.

By mid-February, it was already too late for nest-building, too late for the eggs still being incubated, too late for the littlest chicks still trying to crowd in under their mothers' warm tummies. There wouldn't be enough time for these late babies to grow up before winter came; the advancing cold would kill them before they could fledge. That makes a penguin rookery a sad place in late summer: You know so many of the cutest ones will die.

But the birds don't know that, and they keep busy. For half an hour on Cuverville, I watched as a young adult—a non-breeder, just practicing this year—built a nest of stolen stones. Stone after stone after stone, he'd pick one up in his bill at somebody else's abandoned nest site, waddle over to his own and drop it into place. Then back for another. And back again. With no competition at this time of the year, he had constructed the biggest nest in the place—two feet across and growing. He strutted around it, acting proud.

"He's forgotten just one thing," a young English researcher said. "A mate."

The sea beyond the rookeries, the sea everywhere, was full of icebergs, the constant backdrop of the voyage. Their plain name does icebergs no justice: They deserve better. They are ice sculptures, ice fantasies, ice dreams. Together they become flotillas of ice, armadas of it. They make Antarctica a world of ice.

But these bergs are not our ice—not sleet-white or slush-gray. They are old ice, heavy ice, so compressed by the weight of their parent glaciers that only blue light travels within them.

Late one afternoon off Pleneau Island, we rode Zodiacs into a city of ice—a realm filled with bergs the size of armories, the size of cathedrals. Meltwater had honed their edges into thin white blades and carved out crests and hollows, windows

and pylons and natural bridges. All around we heard the dripping sounds of a cave, but this cave was open to the sky and
no stalactites formed.

Underwater, icebergs are the color people their paint swimming pools—a brilliant turquoise, bright as Acapulco. Above,
they give off a surreal glow—as if blue Christmas-tree lights
shone inside them. Yes, they are that blue, and other blues, all
blues: sapphire, cobalt, Caribbean, sky.

Even on a drab day, nearing dusk, when sunlight is all but
gone, they still glow blue. You can lean out of a Zodiac and put
your hands on a berg's cold, wet flank, and it will still be blue.
It is no distant illusion, this color.

Once we saw them form. We had often heard them calving—
breaking off from the fronts of sea-coast glaciers and making
explosive booms in the distance. But one afternoon on Paradise Bay, we saw the equivalent of a block of city skyscrapers
shatter into huge blue fragments, as if detonated, and collapse
into the sea.

The new bergs dove deep down and then shot upward, out
of the water, like blue whales breeching, then fell belly-first
onto the sea and began to cruise away from the cliffs on their
own shock wave. The ripples rocked our Zodiac, half a mile
away.

Several times, cruising in the Zodiacs, we came upon swimming seals and accidentally cornered them for a moment against
the icebergs. They would stare at us for a few seconds, startled,
before sinking into the safety of the deep. They had familiar
eyes, big and brown, a white edge showing as they glanced
sideways at us. Eyes like my dog's, I thought. Mammal eyes,
our eyes. Kin in the water.

That is the great wonder of this place. I know of no other

where human beings can approach wildlife so closely, or with so little between us. No underbrush, no civilization, no middlemen, no barriers.

Even the food chain is short here—plankton, krill, seals. Plankton, krill, penguins. Plankton, krill, whales. That simple. Except that nothing in Antarctica is really simple, and it is getting more complicated. An estimated 60,000 people have visited it, arriving at the rate of 5,000 a year; about 2,000 are scientists, the rest tourists.

Tours are getting more complicated, too. There is even one that will take you to a nesting site of Emperor penguins, deep inland, in the dead night of the Antarctic winter, an experience that explorers risked their lives for as recently as the early 1900s.

Five thousand people on a continent bigger than Australia doesn't sound like much, but the numbers are high enough to cause concern. We heard about it from a team of young researchers who sailed back from Antarctica aboard our ship. They had been on Cuverville Island, studying the impact of tourism on the penguin rookery there: 3,000 visitors to one small beach in three months.

The questions they were asking weren't simple, and the answers aren't yet known. How long, for example, does it take for moss and lichen to recover after being trampled? Even if tourists keep their distance, do they still distract the penguins? Does being distracted make penguins or their young more vulnerable to attack by predatory birds?

Aboard ship, bound for their home base at Scott Polar Research Institute in Cambridge, England, the researchers talked about the future. Every tourist they had surveyed, they said, comes back from Antarctica wanting to preserve it.

But the tourists tell their friends, as I am telling you, and the friends want to see for themselves. Too many tourists, even with the best ecological manners, will have an impact, and the balance of life on the great white continent is more fragile than it looks.

Antarctica, I think, is the strangest place on Earth and surely the last pure place, the only one humanity hasn't managed to wreck. Keeping it that way is the puzzle.

So far, what protects it is the 1959 Antarctic Treaty, now supported by 40 nations. The core group of 12 has agreed to ban weapons, military bases, nuclear testing and nuclear waste below 60 S. latitude. More recent agreements aim at protecting the environment—limiting mineral prospecting, conserving Antarctic seals and protecting whales. Given that level of international concern, it is not surprising that there's talk of controling tourism. As visitor numbers grow, some sort of change is bound to come.

I believe in Antarctic preservation, so this may sound contradictory. But if it's in your heart to see Antarctica, my advice is go there now.

Go before somebody thinks of building viewing platforms above the penguin rookeries or landing ramps on the beaches. Go while the seals still pause to look at you before they dive. Go while a penguin chick can still walk up and bite you.

Kingdom of the Dead

1996

T HE ROYAL TOMBS were hyphens, punctuating a tense day of oven-heat and arguments. Even inside, they were hot; it is only their shadows that trick my memory into thinking they were cool.

I had been waiting to see those tombs since I was old enough to read and just strong enough to carry a set of heavy archaeology books, one by one, from a bookshelf to our dining-room table.

I spent my childhood dreaming about them, mesmerized by mummies, by the blank eyes of painted queens and pharaohs and—above all—by the wondrous story of Howard Carter and Lord Carnarvon and how they found the treasure-filled tomb of King Tutankhamen.

More than anything in my life, those books—and that tomb—shaped my interest in distant places. I would go there, I promised my child-self, someday I would go there. As with most dreams, reality was what I didn't expect.

I didn't expect the searing heat, I didn't expect to get sick (and I had), I didn't expect the constant hassle of traveling alone as a woman in Egypt. Even with a guide and driver—hired because I thought they would ease the way—I felt burdened, limited, slowed down, as if I were walking in boots of lead.

I also didn't expect that when the journey was done, none of that would matter.

The town of Luxor has two things going for it. One is its breathtaking light, the sun falling through air so clear and dry that there was never any haze, even over the river, and twilights and dawns barely existed.

No wonder the sun was worshipped as a god here. When it rose over the town each morning, it was so instantly, piercingly bright that I expected the air to chime.

The other boon is the town's setting: on the eastern bank of the Nile, between the ancient Egyptian temples of Luxor and Karnak, with the river like a blue ribbon beside it and creamy sand reaching to the horizons beyond.

In between the temples, modern Luxor is a worn, dusty little place, its center just a few long streets paralleling the water. Everything that serves visitors—hotels, restaurants, souvenir shops, sightseeing boats and the city's elegant small museum—clusters there.

Tourism has been big business in Luxor for more than 200 years. European visitors were carving their names on the monuments even in the late 1700s, and their graffiti are now old enough to qualify as antiquities themselves.

But for a tourist town, Luxor was surprisingly empty when I was there. A few feluccas, the traditional wooden sailboats of the Nile, fluttered over the sleek river like moths, but most were bobbing at the wharf, their sails furled and their masters clamoring for passengers.

Dozens of horse-drawn carriages, another Luxor tradition, were patroling for clients along the Corniche, the riverfront boulevard. Taxis were idle too, parked in flocks outside the hotels.

Everything seemed to be waiting for tourists—and that may not change soon. Fears of terrorism and strife in the Middle East have diminished Egypt's flow of foreign visitors; I saw few Americans, one busload of French tourists, perhaps three of Germans, and only a smattering of intrepid young backpackers.

Empty or busy, Luxor is mainly a jumping-off point, a gateway to greater things. It always has been—though for travelers on a different journey.

Anciently, this was Thebes, the ruling city of Egypt during the New Kingdom, 1550 to 1069 B.C. Perhaps as many as a million people lived on the eastern bank.

Only the dead dwelt on the western bank, the place where the sun went down and the journey into the afterlife began. That was where the royal mummies were prepared and buried—and where I needed to go.

Because I'd lost time to illness, I had to compress what should have been a three-day tomb tour into one. Guides like to take things easier in Luxor, following a set itinerary and including long lunches, and this hurricane pace irritated my guide.

It exhausted me and made everything I saw rush together into a kind of tomb video played on fast-forward. Two places stood out, sites so wonderful I didn't mind how everything else blurred.

You need tickets to see any of the tombs—and tips for the tomb guards if you expect to see them in peace. Tickets are cheap and abundant, with one exception: The Tomb of Queen Nefertari, one of the greatest art treasures in the world.

Closed for 40 years and under restoration for six, it had

reopened less than a week before I got to Luxor. To protect its new jewel, the Egyptian government was allowing only 150 visitors a day, for no more than 15 minutes each, and the tickets were so pricey—$30 U.S., about six times normal—that guides and taxi drivers shook their heads in sympathy over the expense.

I wanted to go anyway, over the protests of my guide, a heavy-bodied guy in his late 20s, who wore jeans, a white sweatshirt, dark sunglasses and a couldn't-be-bothered attitude. There wouldn't be any tickets, he insisted. Tour companies were sending flunkies to wait in line before dawn each morning to snap up the day's tickets as soon as they went on sale. I wasn't on a group tour, so I didn't stand a chance.

Still, my guide agreed to try. He went into the ticket office and stayed a long time—long enough for my hopes to rise. No. He came out empty-handed. Some things aren't meant to be, I told myself, and we went on to see other tombs in the Valley of the Queens. Royal wives and some princes were buried there, while pharaohs were buried in its more famous neighbor, the Valley of the Kings.

Both valleys are twisting defiles of beige sand and buff-colored rock that cut into the base of a low, pyramid-shaped mountain peak, called the Horn. Sandy paths connect the tomb entrances, like tracks in a prairie-dog town.

Royal tombs have similar floor plans: They're usually long and narrow, with a ramp leading down from the entrance and a central hallway running through a series of rooms to the burial chamber at the back. The ramps made it possible to slide the heavy stone sarcophagi into place.

Mid-morning, I was just emerging from one when my guide announced that he had good news. Did I still want to see the tomb of Nefertari? I nodded. "One of my friends, another guide," he explained carefully, "had an extra ticket," and that guide had sold it to my guide while I was underground.

My guide took the precious ticket from his pocket, held it in two fingers and waved it back and forth as he spoke. I squinted at it in the glare, feeling both delighted and tricked.

I was certain there was no friend; we had encountered no other tour group that morning. I was certain my guide had actually bought the ticket for $30 before we started, secreted it in a pocket until it was nearly time to leave and . . . .

"There is only one thing," he said, and I braced myself. "This ticket costs $40." Of course it does, I thought. Of course he would keep the extra $10. Of course I'd pay it. He knew it, and I knew it.

"We have an English word for this," I said, as I counted out the cash from my dwindling supply of U.S. dollars. "It's called 'scalping.'" My guide grinned, liking the word, and repeated it a few times for practice.

In truth, I would have paid $50, $100 or even more to see Nefertari's Tomb—and paid it happily. Hers is not the largest tomb in the valleys. But it is the most beautifully painted, as befitted the favorite wife of the powerful pharaoh, Rameses II. It looks as it would have when the 45-year-old queen was laid to rest—though in 1224 B.C. it would have been lighted by torches, not fluorescent tubes.

The walls are snowy white, the colors intense—rust-reds, deep turquoise, black, green, indigo, tawny gold. But it is the figures of the gods and goddesses that stun, and Nefertari is the most stunning of all, seeming to float on the walls that were painted for her.

She wears a full-length, starched dress of white linen so sheer that her slim arms and legs show through the fabric. And she smiles. The effect is disarming—and it puts the Mona Lisa's little smirk to shame.

As in most royal tombs, the paintings show the deceased on her soul's journey, the journey all beings make, into the realm of the dead. Hieroglyphics surround the figures like flocks of birds, giving guidelines, signposts, directions: Do this just so, the walls instruct; say this at this point, tell this to that god, follow these rules, and you'll come through safe.

Through it all, Nefertari goes, sometimes with a god or goddess leading her by the hand, sometimes alone, her eyes calm, her smile serene, her body graceful as a girl's. There is a touch of bravery in the poses. She makes death look good— and peaceful.

"Oh, she's so pretty!" an American woman gasped to a companion, as they gazed at the figured walls. The queen would have been pleased by that. To be thought beautiful, 3,200 years after death, is exactly what ancient Egyptians hoped for: immortality.

There is nothing in her tomb now. The sarcophagus is in a museum in Italy, but her mummy was already missing when archaeologists opened the tomb in 1904; probably it was destroyed by ancient grave robbers. Most of them were.

I was standing where it would have been when suddenly the lights went out. I thought this was the signal to leave, and I resented it. I wasn't done.

The tomb was pitch black. A guard I couldn't see materialized next to me, murmuring, "Please, madam. Please, madam." He took my hand and started pulling me through the darkness.

I pulled back. He put his arm around my waist and drew my arm around his shoulders; I pulled back harder, trying to wriggle free of this unexpected bond.

Finally, I realized that the lights weren't supposed to be off and that the guard really was trying to help me get out. I complied then, and we shuffled forward, me feeling for the steps with my toes as we edged toward the entry.

Just then, the fluorescent lights began to flicker on and off, blinking in different parts of the tomb, so that the painted figures flashed in and out of darkness. Pale Osiris in his mummy bandages; jackal-headed Anubis; Khepri, the sun-god, whose face was a huge beetle—the macabre gods jumped and danced on the walls like characters in an old-time movie.

When we were close enough to see the steps, the guard let go of me. I looked back for an instant and was shocked at the utter blackness of the tomb below. I thought of how it must have felt when the people who loved Nefertari climbed back into the realm of the living and left her in this permanent night. It must have made their hearts ache.

Nearby, in the Valley of the Kings, only one of the 62 tombs found so far still holds a royal mummy, and it is the pharoah I least expected to encounter outside a museum: Tutankhamen, the young king whose burial treasure electrified the world when it was discovered in 1922.

Tut had been buried in a hurry, in a compact tomb much smaller and simpler than a pharaoh deserved, and his grave goods—everything from his sandals to his gold-and-ivory furniture—were jammed into spaces not designed to hold them.

The other royal tombs had all been ransacked, usually not long after they were sealed, and archaeologists had gotten used to digging their way into chambers that contained broken statuary, fragments of pottery and ravaged or missing mummies. Tutankhamen's tomb changed all that.

Ironically, although Tutankhamen's tomb remained unplundered for more than 3,000 years, it has been plundered now. His religion held that the body would be needed in the afterlife, as a home for the soul—hence the meticulous care given to preserving it and providing it with foods to eat, clothes to wear, beds to sleep on, even an army of pretty doll-like figures called *shawabti* to do its work.

But everything that Tutankhamen took to his grave, everything that defined him, everything intended to make his journey into the afterlife successful and safe—everything—has been taken to Cairo and put on view at the Museum of Egyptian Antiquities.

Cases of his exquisitely crafted jewelry are there—rings, bracelets and necklaces like small, perfect monuments in gold. So are his three golden sarcophagus covers, which had fitted over him like a glittering series of nesting boxes. And finally his full-length inner coffin of pure gold, and his splendid burial mask, the solid-gold helmet that was used as a symbol when some of his treasures toured the United States in the late 1970s.

Stripped now, what's left of Tutankhamen's body lies in a bare stone sarcophagus that nearly fills the floor of his burial chamber, surrounded only by poster-like wall paintings and tourists.

It was late in the afternoon by the time we got there. Shadows were cooling the sand and rock outside, and most tourists had left the valley. My guide was bored and tired. He had led me into so many other tombs that he was sitting this one out.

"It is a very small tomb," he said. "It will not take you long." He waved me on alone, to my relief.

I was tired, too—tired of hurrying, tired of listening to him, tired of having to follow the beam of his flashlight along lines of hieroglyphics when what I wanted was just to feel the places themselves. This was my chance.

The tomb was very small, but its smallness made it intimate. No one else was inside, except for the body that lay hidden in the sarcophagus: King Tut, all by himself in the Valley of the Kings. I was touched by that. And by a sense of ancient loneliness.

The Egyptian cult of death that the West finds fascinating—witness our mummy movies, mummy curses, all that creepy mummy stuff—was a real religion, practiced for some 50 centuries. It struck me as sad that Tut was there without the comforts, talismans and guardians that he had died believing in.

I tend to personify inanimate objects anyway, and this one was human, so it was not much of a reach to start thinking of the dead king as a person instead of a relic. In a way, I'd known him since I was a little girl.

"Thank you," I whispered to him, "for being such an influence on my life and a part of it for so long."

Freed by that, it occurred to me I could also pray for him. It did not matter that his gods weren't the same as mine. I stood there in his tomb and called down blessings on Tutankhamen, from all our gods—something that couldn't have happened very often over the 3,300 years he'd been lying there. It was about time he had a few prayers.

Then a young French couple clanged down the ladder-like stairs, breaking the silence and the mood, and I turned to leave. I was climbing out, up steps that rose almost vertically as I neared the top, when something moved on the next-to-last tread.

It was a huge beetle, a living scarab, one of the beetle symbols that ancient Egyptians associated with resurrection.

Counting its long trailing back legs, this one was about three inches long, charcoal gray and slightly dusty, and it was moving slowly just in front of my eyes. It had not been there when I came down the stairs, and it could not been there when the young French couple did, or they'd have stepped on it.

I'd never seen a live scarab before, only those carved on monuments, modeled on jewelry or drawn in hieroglyphics. Drawn, in fact, on King Tut's very walls. I'd just seen many of them, in the ovals called cartouches that represent human names. A creature like this was part of Tut's own name.

That pleased me, and I smiled. Perhaps the dead king was not entirely bereft of his old guardians, after all. I stepped carefully over the crawling beetle and back out into the light.

ENGLAND

Great Expectations

1993

"GO TO HELMSLEY," my uncle, the professor, advised my mother and me before a trip to England. "Have a drink at the Three Feathers."

So we did. We made a special effort to get there, in fact, arriving late in the evening when we could have stayed somewhere else, because my uncle's taste in foreign places was superb.

What I remember about Helmsley is that there was a nice church looming over a small brook, a ruined castle and some guy in the Three Feathers pub who bought us each a Scotch.

He accompanied this with a long lecture about how tricky Scotch whiskey is to create—lots of care in the selection of wood for the barrels, for example—to ensure just the right flavor. I was prepared to sip it neat, to get the full tang of all that aged oak, but he dumped half a bottle of lemon soda into each of our glasses before we could get them to our lips. My mother didn't like it either.

Helmsley was my uncle's town; it clearly wasn't ours. By the time we'd figured that out, I had developed a bad cold and was confined to my bed, where I read three Brontë novels and avoided Scotch. My mother was simply confined to Helmsley.

In the course of our enforced sojourn, we speculated on what made this town so special to my uncle. "He must," my mother said carefully, "have had a really great conversation with somebody."

He must, indeed.

Now, whenever someone recommends a place I just *have* to go, I think of Helmsley. That is, when I don't think of Loches.

Before a European trip a few years ago, I mentioned to a friend that my husband and I would be driving in southern France. Her face lit up. "Loches!" she said. It was her family's favorite town from their own French visit. "Go to Loches!"

We did, figuring to stay overnight there. As we drew near, the sky, which had been sunny and clear, turned angry, and as we passed the signpost announcing the village, the clouds broke. We drove into the main square, barely able to see for the torrents of rain rippling across the windshield.

What we found were utterly empty streets that we couldn't quite blame on the rain. Empty streets, darkened shops, shuttered windows—Loches looked like a ghost town. Except for a couple of men who emerged from their doorways and stood, hatless, in the pouring rain, smiling at us oddly. They made me think of zombies. We had the creepy sense that they didn't get many tourists in Loches, and perhaps the ones they got never managed to get out.

Only one building approached normal. The ground floor of the hotel on the square was lighted, and we could see people in the dining room. But all the floors above it were empty. The windows were broken, and the wind had teased their thin white curtains out into the rain, where they whipped back and forth like captive wraiths. Behind them, the rooms were as black as the eye sockets of a skull.

"Want to eat here?" my husband wondered, sounding innocent, knowing what I'd say.

A mile out of town, the rain stopped, and a couple of miles farther on, the sun came out again. Really.

I had to be careful not to hurt my friend's feelings when she asked me later how I'd liked Loches. I said "Fine." I meant, "Your town is cursed."

It's the Helmsley effect: You have to consider the source. And the moment in time that the source was there. In other words, you had to be there. With them. Then.

Special places often become special for reasons that don't make the guidebooks. So it isn't the place itself that counts. It's what happened there. Or even what didn't happen.

I remember a restaurant-hotel under the walls of the Old City in Korčula, on the Adriatic. I'd intended to drive farther up the coast, but I was tired, and the food smelled good, and the terrace was pretty.

So I lingered over an early supper, surrounded by oleander blossoms, and watched sailboats drift across a tiny silken harbor in front of the huge orange setting sun. I was there alone, but it was so pleasant and I was so happy, that I tend to forget that. I feel as if I had company. "This is perfect," I thought—and still think whenever the topic of favorite places comes up.

It's possible—likely, even—that Korčula has cloudy evenings, that food at "my" restaurant can be bad, that the harbor looks like satin merely because it's polluted.

Which is why I've held back whenever I've been tempted to recommend it. I'm afraid that anybody I sent there would come back saying, "It was fine," but thinking, "She must have had a really great conversation. . . ."

Rewriting Life on the Plains

1997

———

O URS IS A FAMILY of record-keepers. For us, a blank
page is a challenge, and a black felt-tip pen left on our
cabin's coffee table is as imperative as a flung gauntlet. My
nephew William, age 7, spending Memorial Day up north,
reaches for the pen and starts to write.

Last summer—possibly influenced by email addresses—
William was into periods, lots of them, always between words,
never at the end. For example: "We. rentad. a. bot"

This year, he's working on cursive. He knows the letters are
supposed to connect, so all of them do. He writes his name:
"willoreilly." Then he writes his mother's name: "momoreilly."
His Ys have impressive curly tails that swoop across the page,
like busy snakes. He draws a few snakes, too, just to make the
difference clear.

But this is mere warm-up. "Can I write in the guest book
now?" he asks.

Of course. It's one of our cabin traditions. The guest book
is as old as the cabin itself. Four generations have signed it
during the past 60 years, the entries getting longer and more
detailed as time passes.

That figures. In this family, guest books invariably become journals, and journals become full-fledged memoirs. Even our charades scores have headlines and attitude: "Us Boys vs. Them Girls," reads the top of this weekend's tally, already pasted in the guest book.

We're attracted to other people's records too. I was pleased to find one at the first flea market of the summer: a thin, battered blue volume with red leatherette corners and the words "Record Book" stamped in black on the cover.

The pages were full of pretty handwriting—the old-fashioned Palmer Method cursive that William admires—so at first, I thought it was a journal.

It was just the opposite: It was the minutes of the twice-monthly meetings of the Ladies Aid Society of the Methodist Episcopal Church of Arthur, N.D.—kept faithfully from 1910 to 1925.

Fifteen years in the life of a small town, and the dealer wanted only $2.75. For me, an artifact like this is an invitation to travel through time, and I find it as irresistible as any trip on land or ocean.

I paid the money and took the book back to the cabin, where my sister—"momoreilly"—and I leafed through it. Then, thinking we'd missed something, we went through it again, more carefully. Finally, we read it page by page, line by line, hoping for something—anything—more than what we found.

We were looking for defiance or at least deviation—any attempted escape from Robert's Rules of Order, any clue to the nature of the town or the personalities of the ladies. And in vain.

"Nothing ever happens," I said, amazed, when I reached the last page again.

"Nothing ever happens," my sister agreed. Nothing.

And yet everything happens. World War I fell into those 15 years. So did the great influenza epidemic of 1918. So did—must have—births, marriages, deaths, new jobs, lost jobs, droughts, floods, failed crops, boom years, family squabbles and national feuds.

And in between those events would have been myriad little ones: Whole lifetimes of cooking meals. Of children roused for school, washed, dressed, fed, sent off to the world. Quilts. Curtains. The Monday wash. Thanksgiving turkeys and Christmas trees. Apple pies. Birthday cakes. Weeding the tomato plants, thinning the lettuce, hoping for flowers. Killing the chickens, sewing the clothes, baking the bread, putting up the beets and the pole beans.

Woven through all that, the Ladies' Aid Society would have been a part of every member's household, and the regular schedule of its meetings would have beaten like a slow pulse in their daily lives. Even the kids would have felt its quiet influence. I could almost hear the mothers' voices: "Don't touch those doughnuts! Those are for Ladies Aid tomorrow!"

The record book mentions none of that. Reading it was like trying to eat the holes in a piece of Swiss cheese: Real life was everything around it.

The missing parts fascinated me. I looked up Arthur, N.D., in an atlas and learned that it still exists, that it's 25 miles northwest of Fargo, has a population of 400, has a bank and a still-working post office, is near but not on the Burlington Northern rail line.

From that and the things the book didn't mention, I started piecing together a composite picture, until Arthur took on a sort of life. But it's no more accurate than if I'd seen the town in a rearview mirror—just a chain of eye-blink impressions as it receded into the distance. I only guessed at what lay behind the reflections.

The record book told me that the Arthur M.E. Ladies Aid met every other Thursday afternoon, sometimes for a late luncheon, sometimes an early supper. The women took turns preparing the food. They didn't like anyone to show off, let alone show anyone else up. An early entry states that no more than four courses could ever be served; any lady serving more courses would pay a fine of $1. They voted on that.

The town was probably bigger then than it is now, judging by the names of stores that show up in treasurer's reports. There was a drugstore, which also sold flowers; a meat market; a grocery; a laundry and the multifaceted Arthur Mercantile, which supplied the Ladies Aid with everything from new chairs for the church basement to new eaves for the church itself.

Reading between the lines, I surmised that electricity was new to Arthur in 1915, because that year the ladies raised the funds to electrify the church—about $30.

The Methodist Episcopal minister wasn't very expensive either. One of the ladies' on-going good deeds was to pay his salary: $60 covered nearly half a year. (But did they like the pastor? Did that even matter? They never hinted.)

They raised the money they needed the same way, year after year—by holding suppers in the church basement, an ice-cream social in the summer and, in late fall, an annual church bazaar. They always sold the same things, and each type of item had a table of its own: work aprons, fancy aprons and fancy work (which meant a year of evenings spent making lace doilies, embroidered table runners and crocheted collars) plus homemade candy and a mysterious product called "The Peerless Stain

Remover," which didn't sell as well as the handicrafts. Sometimes they added a guess-the-weight-of-the-cake contest; they didn't record the winners.

I tried to picture the women and got only as far as their clothing. They must have dressed up for their meetings. Where else in a small town would you wear nice clothes and your good hat if not to church and Ladies Aid?

But the women themselves remained as shadowy and stiff as the sepia images in old photographs, the ones without names on the back, the ones that turn up, like refugees with amnesia, on flea-market tables next to old record books like this.

Vague as the ladies were, I began to be fond of them. But I kept wondering: In all those years, why didn't any of the secretaries ever crack? Wasn't anyone tempted to use a direct quotation? To note the weather? Or what people were talking about when the meeting was called to order? Didn't anyone, ever, want to break down and tell a tale or reveal a feeling? More important, how could they resist?

But resist they did. Robert's Rules of Order held them in a death grip. So there were no stories here, no quotes, no anecdotes, just the same mandatory litany, like this one from June 29, 1916:

"The Ladies Aid was entertained by Mesdames Ralph Parkhouse, Chas. Parkhouse and Lee Kamp at Mrs. Kamp's home. . . . It was decided to have a supper at the church basement, the proceeds to go towards repairing the parsonage . . . A lovely lunch was served by the hostesses."

Very rarely, a tiny detail sneaked past the reigning secretary like a mouse shooting across the church sanctuary to hide under a pew. "Aprons were 75 cents," my sister noticed in a report from an early church bazaar.

A decade farther on, I found an entry that, compared with the others, fairly sparkled with color: "Miss Edith Farnum favored the company with two solos: 'Roses of Picardy' and 'Little Mother of Mine.'"

Twice in the 15 years, someone revealed what the ladies actually ate: doughnuts and lemonade at one lunch; doughnuts, brown bread and coffee at another. No main courses. No salads. No mention of cakes, bars, cookies, pies. Were the menus left out because they were so dull? Or were lemonade and doughnuts all the hostesses dared to serve?

In fairness, the old record book did exactly what it was supposed to do: It reported on the business of those well-behaved twice-monthly meetings. Nothing more. When it ends, it simply ends. Period. The stop is so abrupt, so stark, so plain that it makes "Our Town" look like an epic, turns "Spoon River" into "The Iliad."

Only heroes realize that they're making history, and then only when they're involved in great events. But all of us are making history, all the time, for somebody, somewhere. We just don't think our ordinary kind will matter.

Closing the record book, I wished there'd been a way to tell that to the vanished scribes of Arthur, North Dakota. Ladies, I wanted to tell them, there will be a future, and your record book will be in it, and people you cannot imagine will read it and want to know what else happened.

It's too late to say that to the Arthur Ladies Aid, but it's not too late to warn folks wielding the secretary's pen today: If you are keeping the minutes of the PTA or the church fellowship or the Eastern Star, please, oh, please, break Robert's Rules every now and then, and put in a clue about life or love or how the kids are doing or how deep the snow is or at least Madame President's first name.

Someone, long years from now, will be grateful.

———

(Epilog: After this article appeared in the *Star Tribune*, the Ladies Aid of the Methodist Episcopal Church of Arthur, N.D., got in touch with me. They had all their other books of minutes, a spokeswoman said, and nobody knew how this one had ended up in Minnesota. Would I be willing to send it back? Of course, I said, and asked what I most wanted to know. Yes, she replied, Arthur is still a nice place to live.)

Babysitting Whales

2003

—·—

"RUBBER," the man next to me said, grinning. "Wet, cold rubber." A woman farther up the boat disagreed. "Egg-plant," she said.

I'd been busy taking pictures when the whales came close, so I didn't know who was right. I didn't find out for myself till the next day, when a baby whale thrust its weird, lumpy face out of the water in front of me and practically begged to be petted. I screamed just like everybody else, forgot about my camera and plunged my arms into the chilly sea.

Both fellow travelers had been right: The baby felt like a cold, wet, overinflated innertube, the kind kids play with at the lake. Or a cold, wet, humongous eggplant. With whiskers.

In the distance around us, whales appeared and disappeared like temporary islands—rising, spouting, diving, rising again—more whales than in any other bay in the eastern Pacific.

These were gray whales, and I had joined them in a wide, shallow saltwater lagoon that twists inland midway down Baja California, the skinny peninsula stretching 1,000 miles along Mexico's west coast. Plentiful as the whales were, it was still a mighty thin broth. The lagoon holds so much seawater that its 1,100 whales were more diluted than vegetables in cheap soup. They could disappear whenever they wanted. We were lucky that they hung around.

I was on a small tour run by Keith Jones, a structural engineer from California who is an ardent whale buff. "My mission in life is to teach people about gray whales," Jones told us as we left San Diego. His enthusiasm was contagious, but we hardly needed revving up: The eleven people in the group had laid out nearly $1,700 apiece and come from as far away as New York, Pennsylvania, Washington, D.C., and Minnesota, just to see whales in the wild.

We drove south from San Diego for about nine hours to a stretch of water called Ojo de Liebre—Eye of the Jackrabbit. It used to be called Scammon's Lagoon, after the captain of the first whaling ship to exploit it. That was in the 1850s, when gray whales were being slaughtered for their oil like every other kind of whale that Europeans and Americans could stick a harpoon into. Jones told us the whole ugly story.

The grays were the easiest to kill because their habits bunched them up: Each winter, they migrate from the Bering Sea down to Baja. At about 12,000 miles round-trip, it's the longest migration of any mammal.

The whales mate in Baja's shallow, protected, relatively warm lagoons, and the females who mated there the previous year return to give birth. They keep their babies by their side for months, like any human mom.

Harpooning the big, gentle creatures in the lagoon would truly have been like shooting fish in a barrel. Probably easier, since the whalers could count on motherly love. They would pursue a baby, knowing the frantic mother would rush to save it, putting her within range of their harpoons. The orphaned babies, too small and lean for the hunters to bother with, were left to starve. The gray whales in Ojo de Liebre were decimated so fast that even Capt. Scammon felt bad about it.

And yet, once whaling stopped, the gray whales rebounded from the edge of extinction. By the end of the millennium, their numbers were up to 26,000 in the eastern Pacific—possibly as many as there were before whaling. But experts say the grays have dwindled again, to about 17,000. They cite many reasons, but the fact is—and Jones stressed this about nearly every aspect of gray whale life—nobody's sure. Whales are like icebergs, he said: Most of what they do is underwater. Humans get to see only what the whales choose to share.

What they chose to share with us was themselves. Over and over, mother whales and their babies came up to our boat, swam around it, dove under it, did barrel rolls beside it or merely breathed next to it, in explosions of mist so fine they left rainbows in the air and droplets on our camera lenses.

Jones had promised the whales would be gentle, and they were. But when the first mother and child aimed themselves straight at our 22-foot boat, I felt a pang of dread. Maybe it came from reading "Moby-Dick," but I couldn't believe that the whales had forgotten our shared history of slaughter.

Whales are long-lived mammals, after all, and they're smart. They pass on a kind of culture to their young—starting with teaching them how to swim. Why couldn't they also pass on some Ur-memory about the bloody centuries of human persecution?

The whales' bumpy black backs broke the water like submarines. They were enormous. Female gray whales average

46 feet, and by March, when I was there, even the youngsters were 18 feet long.

But the whales that plowed toward our boat didn't crash into us. Didn't flip us in the air the way wounded whales did in old engravings. Didn't thrash us with their powerful tails. They just nuzzled up to the motor—set on idle, so the propeller wouldn't hurt them. Jones thinks they like the sound. The grays don't sing, he said. They just make glug-glug or thonk-thonk sounds, like an empty bottle when you tap it or—perhaps—an outboard that needs a tuneup.

What awed me is that they didn't just take a peek at us and leave. They lingered. Sometimes, they blew huge explosions of bubbles, always next to or under the boat. Tourists always scream when that happens, and Jones believes the whales do it on purpose because they find the screams entertaining.

True, the whales' presence felt like more than mere curiosity. They interacted with us. They seemed to like being touched and stroked, and they kept sliding along the boat, up one side and down the other, passing slowly along our hands, around and around the boat. Each time they presented their long, rubbery faces for petting, I felt relieved. And forgiven.

Lots of whale-watching groups, brought to Baja by other companies, camp on shore farther south, near the lagoons of San Ignacio and Magdalena Bay. But Ojo de Liebre, in an official whale count taken a week before we got there, had four times as many whales as either of those. It also had fewer tourists.

There are two main reasons: It's not as well-publicized as the other spots, and, except for the whales, it's not very scenic. The dry, flat landscape is patchy with sand and desert plants, and the coast is paved with huge white-crusted pools— evaporating ponds that belong to the area's biggest employer, a salt-making company co-owned by Mitsubishi and the government of Mexico. You drive between the ponds to get to the whale-watching piers.

Our group stayed in the small town nearest to the lagoon: Guerrero Negro, which means "black warrior," after a whaling ship that sank there. The Mexican government once attempted to change its name to something with nicer overtones, the way Scammon's became Ojo de Liebre, and the Sea of Cortez, named for the Spanish conquistador, became the Gulf of California.

But Guerrero Negro stuck. It isn't a typical Mexican town: There's no central plaza where people of all classes mingle and stroll. Instead, it straggles beside a very long main street, with a few motels, spots to park an RV overnight, cheap restaurants and open-air taco stalls.

This, plus rapid growth and largely unpaved streets, gives it the raw look of an Old West frontier town. It's not pretty, but we weren't there to see buildings.

We went out on the lagoon in *pangas*, long, stable wooden boats with enormous outboard motors, steered by local men. The pangas zoomed across water that was too shallow for whales, then slowed down when the water deepened. When a driver spotted a whale nearby, he shifted to idle, and we waited.

Nobody chases the whales in Ojo de Liebre. And nobody baits them. It wouldn't work anyway. The babies are still nursing, and the adults don't eat while they're here. Babies are born in late December and early January and spend the next couple of months bulking up. They can gain 100 pounds a day, Jones said, thanks to mother's milk that is more than 50 percent fat.

About the end of March, the mothers start taking the little

ones north to the Bering Straits, where the adults' food supply is. Gray whales are bottom feeders who survive on tiny
creatures in the Arctic mud. These whales don't have teeth.
Instead, their upper jaw is lined with giant brushes of baleen,
better known as whalebone because of its plastic-like tough-
ness and flexibility. (Whales were hunted for that, too; it was
used to make, among other things, umbrella ribs and the stays
for corsets.)

With jaws like steam shovels, the gray whales scoop up huge
mouthfuls of mud and squirt the water out through the baleen,
which acts as a strainer; the crustaceans get caught inside.

But you won't see this in Baja. The mothers swim south,
give birth, nurse their infants and swim north again, fueled just
by stored fat. In the process, it's estimated a typical mother loses
15,000 pounds—a quarter of her body weight.

Out on the water one morning, somebody called a baby
whale "a calf." The term has been in use for centuries, but Jones
winced. "That's another word I can't stand," he said. "Calf. Cow
and calf. It's a food-motivated term, and I can't stand thinking
of them as a crop." None of us uttered that word again.

All the time the whales are in the lagoon, the whale mothers were training the babies, getting them to swim against the
tidal currents, to build up their muscles and endurance. Jones
said he'd even seen mother whales teaching their infants to leap
into the air and dive deep down—fun for the babies but also
escape techniques they'll need as soon as they hit open sea.

That's because of the orcas, Jones said. Better known as
killer whales, they are the biggest predators on earth, and at this
time of the year, they lurk outside the lagoons, like wolf packs,
waiting for a chance at the prey that will be easiest to catch.

"The babies!" several people said, in horror. Our babies.

Whether from instinct or experience, the mother whales seemed to know that. But none of the babies did. Not yet. For them, the world was still a safe and loving place—just that big, protected blue pond, with mom swimming right alongside, rich milk to get fat on, water to jump and romp and dive in, and every so often those funny, noisy things going by, full of little creatures who squeal so happily when a whale comes close.

Inside Istanbul

1986

—·—

W HEN I FIRST SAW Istanbul, on a working trip early
in a chilly spring, it looked so appallingly shabby that I
wondered—despite years of roughing it through Central and
South America and other fragments of the Third World—I
wondered whether I could endure it for a week.

When I think of the city now, I remember the cockroaches
in my hotel room, the sultan's diamonds glittering in the Top-
kapi museum and the great rewards of enduring discomforts.

The city was like a great beauty turned bag lady, a once-
elegant grande dame needing badly to wash her hair and pare
her fingernails. Streets were grimy and noisy; the traffic im-
penetrable. Power lines and antique telephone wires hung in
bunches from cracked and peeling buildings. The famous Blue
Mosque looked like gray cement, more nuclear power plant
than architectural wonder.

What I thought were alleyways, too narrow and dismal to
be streets, my guidebook called thoroughfares. Changing the
label made no difference—I was still scared to walk down them.
People, muffled against the lingering winter damp, seemed sul-
len in their dark coats, even sinister.

The hotel I had counted on was the marble-encrusted Pera Palas, which once housed passengers from the original Orient Express, but it was closed by a strike. Other hotels in my guidebook were either closed or full.

I ended up at a hotel that a taxi driver recommended. I have always believed that is the worst way in the world to choose a hotel; Istanbul proved it to me.

The room was grimly decorated and dirty; the ceiling bulb was no brighter than a night light, and the bed had known too many guests. I wondered mildly about bedbugs until I saw the cockroaches that lived in the drain of the sink at one end of the room.

This is just for tonight, I promised myself; I'll look for another place tomorrow. But I never could: The days were too busy; there was never time to look for a better hotel and get back to my bad one before check-out time.

So every morning for a week, I pulled on my heaviest shoes and clomped around the room, trying to scare the roaches back toward the sink. More noise and running water eventually herded them down the drain. Then I washed and dressed and went out to interview and take pictures.

In the evening, I dragged back to my awful digs, promising myself yet again that this would be the last night, absolutely the last night. And then I would step into the room—and be instantly transfixed by the beauty of the view.

When I left each morning, my grimy windows showed nothing but fog and a scrap of dingy water and an army of gray apartment buildings. But night erased the wretched architecture, leaving only lighted windows like squares of amber on a ground of charcoal and violet.

Lights sparkled on distant hills and glinted from the masts

and rigging of the freighters and ferries and fishing boats ply-ing the Bosporus. Their wakes chiseled lines of silver and gold into the black water.

Where I stood was the last of Europe. Those hills over there were Asia. I felt like Marco Polo, gazing at the fabled East.

As the week passed, that view transformed my relationship with the city. I continued my cockroach rodeo, but it didn't bother me as much. I noticed hazy light at the foot of those alleyway-streets and began to regard them as charming. Over and over, when I asked for directions, sinister-looking strang-ers smiled and went out of their way to lead me where I needed to go, always with a hearty, no-strings-attached friendliness. I stopped being afraid.

But I didn't really start to love Istanbul until I went inside the Blue Mosque and saw its indigo tiles light up the walls. It was a good symbol for the city: What mattered was on the inside, not the surface.

Paris and Florence and Barcelona are pretty on the outside and easy to love; that may be why they belong to us all. But Istanbul is an interior city. It has to be worked at, and the re-wards are all the greater for having been hard-won.

After the Fall

1997

———

WHEN THE OLD MAN spoke to me, I was making a lunch out of the most amusing item on the menu at a fast-food outlet in the GUM store on Moscow's Red Square.

Written in Cyrillic, the first syllable looked like XOT, the second more like DOK. When I sounded it out, it turned into a hot dog, Russian style.

A funny hot dog, but not a very good one. I put the last third of it back into its ruffled paper tray and was concentrating on the dregs of my KOKA-KOLA when I heard a soft male voice at my side.

He was about 70, neatly dressed in a dark gray coat and black fur hat; I took him for a retired teacher or perhaps a former office worker. He was saying something, very politely. I don't speak Russian and imagined, wrongly, that I was being greeted. I said hello.

He repeated his words, now clearly a question and a bit more urgent. He glanced at the tabletop, and then I understood. He was hungry. He wanted to eat what I was throwing away.

Appalled, I slid the scrap of hot dog toward him, and he picked it up, nodded a thank you and disappeared into the crowd of shoppers.

The man was no ordinary beggar; he didn't have the style or the aggression for it. He'd become a beggar under the same new system that had given GUM its branch of France's Galeries Lafayette, its Christian Dior Boutique, its Benetton shop and the series of big pink banners over the main aisles, advertising Barbie dolls.

The encounter made me feel a little sick. Welcome to the new Russia, where there is finally the freedom to buy a hotdog and Coke. The freedom to shop your heart out, even for Barbies. And the freedom to starve.

The last time I'd been here was the spring of 1979, and I was riding the Trans-Siberian Railroad. In every town and village on the route, red flags were flying for May Day, but everything—houses, countryside, people—looked shabby and sad, as dreary as Minnesota in March.

Communism's leveling philosophy really had made people equal, I wrote at the time: "Everybody walks in the mud."

When I went back 20 years later, Russia had changed so much that it felt like a different country. In many ways, it was.

I noticed changes everywhere, in everything. Color, for starters. Where the old Soviet Union was drab and gray, there was color everywhere—color in people's clothes, color in the shop windows, color on newly restored buildings.

And there were cars. Moscow had about 2 million now, a tour guide said proudly. And the Western-style traffic jams to go with them.

Other things were conspicuous by their absence: There was

no line snaking around Lenin's tomb on Red Square, no ritualized changing of the guard in front of it—in fact, almost no guards to change.

The biggest difference, though, was things. Material goods. Stuff. Impromptu street markets all across Moscow had piles of brand-new TVs and VCRs for sale. Where stores had been virtually empty in 1979, now they were full, and there were no lines of people queued up to buy bread or meat or clothing. There was enough to go around. If you had the money to pay for it.

Clearly, capitalism was going full-tilt. But as at home, it had its casualties. There were grafitti all over public walls, and pickpockets worked the subway crowds—realities that did not exist under the old regime.

The beggars hadn't existed either. Now I saw them everywhere in Moscow and St. Petersburg, and I could not ignore the looks in their eyes or the pain in their voices. They were almost always old women.

They stood, eyes down, in the subway tunnels, holding their hands out toward the crowds. Or they waited, murmuring blessings, at church gates—because the churches are open again, and the devout are better bets than young businessmen with cell phones at their ears.

Other elderly poor were working, doing marginal jobs to stretch their pensions. Stoic in the cold, aged women sold lottery tickets on windy street corners or gathered in half-circles around Metro exits, offering homemade pickles, home-baked bread, a few fresh vegetables, lots of bottled vodka.

Younger, more vigorous people sold things more aggressively: At every major sightseeing stop, I was beseiged by sellers pushing fake lacquered boxes, nesting wooden dolls, leftover communist medals and big fur hats.

And so many names—of buildings, streets, whole cities—
had changed. Of the many bitter jokes that were circulating secretly the first time I was in Russia, this was my favorite, a double
jab at Soviet life and the regime's reverence for its heroes:

An old man goes to apply for his pension. The government
clerk behind the counter doesn't even look up. "Where were
you born?" she asks.

"St. Petersburg," he replies.

"Where did you go to school?"

"Petrograd," he says.

"Where do you live now?"

"Leningrad," he says.

"Where do you want to live?"

"Oh," the old man says, his face lighting up with remembered joy, "St. Petersburg!"

The joke came true, I kept thinking. Now the old man
could live in St. Petersburg, after all. The city had gotten its
name back.

But the new-old names caused me moments of confusion. I had a ticket to the Kirov Ballet in Leningr ... sorry,
St. Petersburg, but when I went to the concierge's desk to
check the time, the Kirov wasn't listed. That ticket had cost
$40, and I panicked: "Isn't it tonight?" I asked. Of course, she
said, it just wasn't the Kirov anymore. Now it was the Marin-
sky—again.

Renaming has bigger ramifications, of course. Changing
the name of the country's second-largest city back to what it
was before the 1917 revolution denies part of Russia's history,
and some Russians objected vehemently.

"It wasn't the Seige of St. Petersburg!" a Russian-American
protested to a tour guide, who had just mentioned the 900-day

seige that killed 700,000 people in World War II. "It was the Seige of *Leningrad!*"

And it always will be.

One snowy day in Moscow, another guide, a former English teacher who makes more money steering tourists around, took me to an elephants' graveyard of communist statues, behind an art school across from Gorky Park.

The most striking was a streamlined, red-granite effigy of Stalin, broken at the base. In the statue dump, it lay on its side, looking like an ancient relic. All it needed was the line from "Ozymandias"—"Look on my works, ye mighty, and despair!"

Where the statues had come down, other things were going up. A day later, I set out for a sight that hadn't been on the Moscow skyline in 60 years: Christ the Saviour Cathedral, now being reborn on the banks of the Moscow River.

The original was built in the early 1800s to commemorate Russia's victory over Napoleon. Stalin ordered it torn down in the 1930s; what went into its place was a gargantuan swimming pool. Now the huge church was back from the dead.

Another result of the collapse of communism had already been rebuilt on Red Square: The double-towered Resurrection Gate, complete with a tiny chapel, had rejoined the red-brick ramparts.

"They had taken it down so they could get their tanks in," my guide sneered, disgust tinting his words. No need to ask who "they" were.

These architectural rebirths were impressive. But when I talked about them back home, friends often pointed out that if Russia weren't rebuilding gates and cathedrals, the government would have more money to spend on such social problems as its impoverished elderly.

I agree, but it's strange talk to hear in rich, free America, where some of our own poor are living under bridges and panhandling on street corners.

The dilemma is compounded, I think, by our confusion about freedom, democracy and capitalism. The terms aren't interchangeable, and "freedom" doesn't mean the same thing to everybody. I'd learned that in 1979.

"In your country, you have freedom *to*," a Russian aboard the Trans-Siberian had said. In the USSR, "we have freedom *from*."

Freedom from want was the example he'd used. But wherever I looked in now-free Russia, want was there, lurking in the shadows behind the new business bustle.

Even my Moscow guide, who said he preferred the new system, admitted there were trade-offs, especially for the aged. Before, he said, "We had an imitation of freedom. Everybody had a very symbolic salary. We had no homelessness. Everybody had a place to live. We had no begging. No starving. We were poor, but we had theaters. We had ballet. We had music."

I could not shake the haunting certainty that, whatever the failings of the previous regime—and they were ghastly—life for many of Russia's ordinary citizens would never be as good under capitalism as it had been under communism.

Under capitalism, as Americans ought to know, the race is to the swift, and those who are too old or sick or weak to run get left behind. Or, in the Russian case, they end up standing outside the Bolshoi Ballet, pleading for pocket change instead of being able to pay a few cents to attend, as they could have in the old days.

"Please," a frail elderly woman murmured to me as I walked into the theater one night, "I must eat!"

Inside the Bolshoi, half the seats were empty—too expensive now for anyone but tourists and the rich. Another change startled me even more. Late in "Swan Lake," as Tchaikovsky's music reached a familiar crescendo, what was on the stage wasn't familiar at all. I leaned forward in the gilded, velvet-trimmed box and stared at the ballet dancers in disbelief.

This ballet has had several endings, but all the ones I'd ever seen were tragic. In this new staging, the swan was radiantly alive, and the happy prince was parading her around on his shoulders. When the audience broke into final applause, I clapped too, but I was in shock. "My God," I kept thinking, "they changed 'Swan Lake'! The Russians gave 'Swan Lake' a happy ending!"

It was like . . . I struggled to find an Anglo equivalent. Like . . . like . . . like having Romeo and Juliet get married, move to Fridley and join the PTA.

I located an English-language program and devoured its explanations—explanations that couldn't have been published under communism, let alone defended.

"I am confident that in a world of evil, violence and wrath, only love, sincerity and humanism can withstand and be the moving force in one's soul," the conductor of the Bolshoi orchestra had written.

"It is a divine matter," wrote the librettist. "The victory of high spirituality over ruling evil—is not that the eternal dream of the best minds of Russia?"

Yes, and it's also a tidy summary of Russia's history. Once again, the society had changed to its core. The past was gone, the present painful, the future unpredictable. Wanting a happy ending for "Swan Lake" made sudden sense.

Breakfast with Skinwalkers

1996

———

MORNING SUNLIGHT was flooding the front porch of the old sandstone house at the crossroads trading post of Nageezi, New Mexico, warming the four people having breakfast there. I was one of them, and I was happy. But that was before the skinwalker showed up and put a chill on things.

The porch is part of a tiny bed-and-breakfast, the only place to stay within 40 miles of Chaco Canyon, one of the greatest collections of prehistoric buildings on the continent.

I'd lucked out the night before, snagging the last of its three rooms. Now I was feeling even luckier: Nageezi's trader/innkeeper/postmaster had come out on the porch to chat with his guests. In blue jeans and plaid shirt, Don Batchelor, 40, looked like an icon of the Old West.

As we savored French toast and coffee, he told us that he came from a trading post family. His father had run one in Chaco Canyon when he was growing up; in 1972, the operation moved to Nageezi; Batchelor took over from his dad about five years ago.

"I like it out here," he said. "I like the lifestyle—room to stretch."

I had driven toward Nageezi—the placename on the map nearest to Chaco Culture National Historical Park—expecting a real town and planning on staying in a motel there. Thanks to that expectation, I shot right past Nageezi and had to double back.

Nageezi consists of two stone houses—one where Batchelor and his family live, one where his guests stay—plus the trading post building, a new post office, a gas pump and a red shed. That's it.

Posts like Nageezi are disappearing. There used to be seven or eight serving the Nageezi area's 3,000 people, Batchelor said; now there's only his.

Trading posts are basically general stores, with cans and boxes of food on the shelves, ranching supplies in the corners, and a few handwoven rugs or silver bracelets for sale to the occasional tourist.

Old-style trade—for corn, flour and other staples—"that's gone," Batchelor said. But Navajo people still trade their striking handicrafts for more valuable goods. "I've traded for a car," he said.

Trading posts are also gathering points for local people, though not big enough to justify the town-sized dots that indicate them on maps.

Batchelor said he likes the people he deals with—Navajo who live in widely scattered households throughout the area. They're still very traditional. Even down to beliefs and customs? Yes, he said, their religion has survived, though "those old ways are slowly but surely changing."

Until recently, in fact, local Navajo people would not take jobs at Chaco Canyon, the trader said. Their beliefs kept them away from the ruins because of the dead bodies buried within. Navajo culture is intensely death-avoidant: Even a deceased loved one leaves behind an angry ghost, and the builders of Chaco were unknown strangers.

Suddenly, Batchelor ducked back into the stone house—there was something he wanted to show us. He returned with a foot-high statuette, a wood carving of a grim-faced Indian man with blackened lips, a black mask painted around his eyes, zig- zag lighting patterns on his arms, pointed wolfish ears and a gray coyote skin over his head and shoulders.

The lower half of the figure wasn't human. Its torso stood on the legs of a horse. Batchelor set the carving on the table next to me. "Do you know what a skinwalker is?" he asked.

I nearly choked. Yes, I know what a skinwalker is. Anybody who reads Tony Hillerman's mysteries knows what a skinwalker is.

It's a Navajo witch—a human being capable of transforming itself into other creatures, even creatures that fly. It goes about at night, fomenting evil and armed with a bag of corpse powder—something derived from dead bodies. There aren't any good skinwalkers.

According to the Hillerman books, all set on the vast Navajo Reservation, the Navajo people don't even like to talk about these witches. That was true, the trader said.

I didn't like talking about them, either. That's because I am geographically superstitious: If something scares the locals, it scares me. So I don't believe in ghosts unless some proud innkeeper informs me my room is haunted. I'm not afraid of skinwalkers unless I'm in Navajo country.

Of course, I *was* in Navajo country. Out here, the whole idea of skinwalkers gave me the creeps. Now I was having breakfast with one. Just south of the kiwi-fruit, a little east of the French toast, it dominated the table.

"Turn it so I can see it," another woman at the table asked me reasonably.

"No," I said, surprising myself and feeling embarrassed. "I'm not touching it."

Traditionally, the Navajo don't carve kachina figures; the Hopi do. Kachinas are part of Hopi religious tradition. But kachina figures are popular as artworks, and some Navajo artists are also beginning to carve similar representations of their own culture's gods and dancers.

The carver who'd made the skinwalker was at work in the red shed at Nageezi. "You can go talk to him," Batchelor suggested.

Lawrence Jacquez, a shy-voiced young man with long black hair, was just finishing an exquisitely detailed *yei bichei* dancer, accurate down to the needles on the spruce ruff around its neck and to the soft curves of its moccasin soles.

This was a dancer from the Night Way, the carver explained, a curing ceremony that lasts nine days. How much would it sell for? About $1,200, wholesale, Jacquez said; he planned to use the carving to cover a few payments on his truck.

"They call what I do 'folk art,'" he said. "It used to bug me, but now I don't mind." Now 29, he got into carving five years ago "for the enjoyment of it." He quickly became known, winning major awards at the Intertribal Indian Ceremonial in Gallup and the Indian Market in Santa Fe. Collectors are starting to amass his work. But the reason he carves hasn't changed: "To this day, it is still the enjoyment of it."

Jacquez said he based his skinwalker carving partly on traditional belief and partly on "the one I saw."

Uh . . . you saw one?

Yes, he said. It happened about 2 a.m. when he was out one night with friends. A man appeared in the headlights—a man with a face painted red-and-white and a coyote skin over his head. The occupants of the car recognized what he was.

"And he was smiling," Jacquez recalled. "He was actually grinning. You could see his teeth."

Bad luck followed immediately. "We had a full tank of gas, and we ran out. We got shot at later that same morning. Could have been a coincidence . . ."

When Jacquez carved the skinwalker for Batchelor, he touched off controversy in the Navajo community. Among other reactions, "I've been accused of being one," Jacquez said.

But he knew, before he did the carving, that traditional people would object to his portraying the witch. "As long as you fear something," he said, "it will have power over you."

I stopped thinking about skinwalkers when I left Nageezi. Didn't think of them again until a week later, when I was down near Zuni, New Mexico.

Over dinner in a small town on my way back to Albuquerque, I talked about the skinwalker carving with a local couple and the restaurant owner. (I can't remember why I brought the topic up. Perhaps my breakfast with a skinwalker made me associate them with food?)

My audience was not only intrigued, it was prompted to tell skinwalker stories of its own. With darkness coming on and a several-hour night drive ahead of me, they weren't stories I wanted to hear.

"I saw one once," the wife said. It had terrified her, and she grimaced, remembering it.

"I saw one too, but I didn't feel afraid," said the restarant owner. She was 17 when it happened, and it was her turn to drive during a family move to Shiprock, in Navajo country.

She still remembers how her headlights caught the strange figure at the side of the road—a wolf-like shape with a human face. She kept quiet about it, figuring her parents would think she was punchy and take over the driving.

The woman finished high school in Shiprock and made many Navajo friends; they told her about their beliefs, and she realized that what she'd seen was a skinwalker.

One time her friends took her to a ceremony "where they had a shaker"—a Navajo elder who could read people's souls by shaking their hands. When she arrived, he took her hands as gently as if they were tender leaves. "Welcome, daughter," he murmured. "You have seen The Walker. . . . Do not be afraid."

The strange thing was, she had never told anyone—not her parents, not even her Navajo friends—about what she saw that night. So how had the old man known?

When her story ended, I hastened to my car. The last of the orange and purple sunset was fading to the west, and I was heading east, where the sky was already night.

I had a couple of hours to go—through a stretch of lonely forest, then more empty piñon-dotted desert—before I could pick up the interstate at Grants, New Mexico, and it would be another hour from there to Albuquerque. I locked the doors, checked the back seat, put the headlights on high and restrained myself from flooring it.

I tried not to watch the roadsides, not to stare too hard at shadows, and I chanted silently—just in case there were any skinwalkers in the neighborhood—"Don't show up. Don't show up. I don't want to see you."

This was magical thinking, of course, and the analytical

part of my brain thought it was silly. But the rest of my mind kept coming back to the old man who knew that the girl had seen "The Walker."

At the cluster of shiny-bright gas stations and motels that marks Grants, I pulled onto the interstate and relaxed; there had been nothing in my headlights, and now I was back in the real world.

Maybe a quarter of an hour later, something suddenly drifted down over the top of the windshield—a kind of charcoal-brown shadow that briefly hovered there. It was like seeing a soft rug being shaken out above me, and I was mesmerized, looking upward instead of at the road—a dangerous thing to do at freeway speed.

What was it? The shadow was too big for a bat. And not as jittery. Could it have been an owl? An owl hunting for prey along the highway?

Of course. It had to be an owl, and what transfixed me was the rhythmic throb of its wings. That's what I thought for the next four months. Now, writing about it, I wonder: How could an owl have kept pace with a car going 60 miles an hour?

To the Top of Africa

1997

——

As the cold African night wore on, and the going got tougher, I kept expecting—hoping?—to hear a familiar parental voice: "What do you think you're doing up there? You get down off that mountain right this minute!"

Believe me, Mom, I would have listened.

All I could see, in the frigid darkness, was a pale circle of light—a gray bobbing circle, dented occasionally by the toes of my boots. The circle came from the flashlight my guide held, pointing it downward so that I, climbing behind him, would not stumble on the rocks buried in the steep gravel slope.

The circle was the sole earthly light I could see on Mount Kilimanjaro, and for hours I trudged toward it and sometimes in it, mesmerized by its shape.

There was nothing else to look at. Not while I was moving, anyway. When I stopped for breath, which was more and more often as we got higher, I could turn and look back down the way we had come and see the tiny lights of towns in two countries—Tanzania to the south, Kenya to the north.

They sparkled as brightly as stars, until I looked up into the unpolluted sky, where the real stars put them to shame.

The sky arched above—clear, navy blue and so thickly spangled that it was hard to identify familiar constellations. But one was unmistakeable. For me, it is always magical, because I see it only on the longest of trips: the Southern Cross, burning small, compact and steady, like a fiery charm.

All night, it rode the sky just above my left shoulder. Even while moving, I could catch glimpses of it from the corner of my eye, and I looked to it for reassurance. Gazing at it was like praying, and when I put the prayer into words, it became the mantra of the climb:

Dear God, if I can't do this, let it be because my body couldn't, not because my spirit gave up. Let me not quit for lack of spirit. . . .

Officially, the climb had begun four days earlier, at the gates of Mount Kilimanjaro National Park in northern Tanzania, where I met my guide and watched three porters trot off up the trail with six days' worth of food, a case of bottled water and my duffel bag balanced on their heads.

My guide's name was Livingstone Frank Kisamo, known on the mountain only as Livingstone, age 28, good-natured and as tall and skinny as a young Abe Lincoln. His salary and tips from guiding support his wife, two small daughters and his mother, who live together in a village adjoining the park. The climbing season was winding down, he told me early on— the spring rains were due, which meant snow on the peak and "hungry time" for his family.

He didn't talk much, but he had patience and a sense of humor. And he gave me constant permission to walk slowly, telling me *"pole-pole"*—"slow-slow" in Swahili—over and over again. Pronounced "po-lay, po-lay," the phrase is the most common utterance on Kilimanjaro.

Unofficially, however, the climb had begun nearly 50 years before, in a couple of back yards in south Minneapolis, where my best friend, Karen, and I had spent our childhoods acting out adventure stories.

Most took place in Africa and involved our favorite hero, Tarzan of the Apes. Karen always got to play Tarzan because she dared to go barefoot in summer and could throw a knife better than I could. I always played Jane, which was considerably less interesting. I told her recently that if I'd gotten to play Tarzan more, maybe I wouldn't have to keep doing stuff like trying to climb Mount Kilimanjaro. She just laughed.

So: I'd been expecting to climb this mountain ever since I was seven years old. Not planning for it. Just expecting it, the way little kids expect to grow up and be astronauts. Somehow, it would just happen.

Then I got a chance to join a safari to northern Tanzania, which would put me on Kili's doorstep. To be that close and not go for it was unthinkable. Such a chance might not come along for another 50-odd years, by which time I wouldn't be climbing anything.

At first, the idea of the climb felt like keeping a rendezvous. Then I began to dread it. Kilimanjaro isn't an Everest—you don't need ropes, ice axes or technical experience—but it's a mighty big hill, and I am no mountain climber. I didn't have time to become one, either. In the weeks preceding the trip, I spent some time every day on a Stairmaster, but I was hardly prepared for hardship.

My loved ones worried, and so did I. At nearly 20,000 feet, the mountain is tall enough to cause altitude sickness, and some of its climbers have died. The reason is that the climb is done too fast for your body to adapt to the thin air.

I looked up the symptoms of altitude sickness—severe headache, vomiting, a gurgling chest, confusion. If I developed any of them, I promised family and friends, I would quit climbing and go back down.

"Even if it's the first day?" a close friend demanded, foreseeing correctly that I'd "get into some macho thing" about it. Yes, even then, I conceded, but I kept my mental fingers crossed when I said it.

Secretly, I was afraid of two things: getting sick, a fear that made sense, and failing to get to the top, which didn't. There wasn't any shame in a partial climb—or so everyone kept telling me. I wrote that down in my journal the day before the trip began; I knew I'd need reminding.

From a distance, in morning light, Kilimanjaro looks like a tilted blue tabletop. It's an extinct volcano, a cone with the top lopped off, so it doesn't come to a point.

The trail starts high—at 6,000 feet—in a lush rain forest, rich with the smell of eucalyptus and the noise of monkeys rustling in the trees. Rising gradually, it runs for nearly 30 miles to the cinder cone of the volcano and then shoots steeply upward to the crater's rim, emerging at 18,640 feet at a place called Gilman's Point, on top of the mountain.

You can go still higher, only you go sideways to do it: About a third of the way around the rim lies Uhuru Peak, 19,340 feet high, the highest point in Africa. Its name means "independence," and it's where every climber hopes to go, me included.

There are several routes up Kilimanjaro; I was on the most popular one, where the climbing is virtually choreographed. You have to have a guide, you have to have a permit, and you have to climb in fixed stages, one day each. You have to sleep in specific places too, at three permanent waystations built by the Norwegian government as a gift to Tanzania: first, Mandara Huts, at 9,000 feet; then Horombo Huts, at 12,500 feet, and finally Kibo Hut, at 15,500. The first two are villages of tiny A-frame cabins, but Kibo is a single stone bunker that serves as a base camp for the final push. It's where the trail turns steep and heads sharply up the cinder cone to the rim.

The trail rises through lovely country, its beauty stratified by climate zones: rain forest first, green and sweaty-hot; then moorland, complete with heather; then alpine terrain, and finally moonscape—as sere as a desert but on top of the world. All the layers are beautiful—or would be, if you had the physical and psychic ability to appreciate them.

"Thank God for the Norwegians," I would think every afternoon, when the next cluster of hut roofs hove into view. By then I'd have been going uphill all day, on a trail as rutted and stony as a dry trout stream, for a vertical gain of about half a mile. The effort exhausted me and made the unheated huts feel like mansions. It also meant I wasn't enjoying the eternally changing scenery.

Along with the air, plants grew sparser as we climbed. Animals were already scarce; Livingstone blamed poachers, local people who don't understand that if you eat all the animals, there won't be any more. Except for climbers and a few birds, the most numerous creatures we saw were gopherlike striped mice scurrying under the tables of the camp dining halls, hoping for scraps.

There are only two groups of people on the trail: those on their way up and those coming down. The first group always asks the second group the same questions: Did you make it? How hard was it?

Unasked is the question no one can answer—the secret question: Will I make it? This made climbing Kilimanjaro like reading a mystery novel, only you couldn't sneak ahead and peek at the ending.

The climbers were a multinational mix. On the mountain with me, there were—in descending numbers—Germans, Japanese, Italians, Brits, Dutch, Australians, New Zealanders and a couple of other Yanks.

We were bonded to each other by accident, but bonded strangely: People told scraps of their life stories, but you never found out the endings. Everyone was so focused on what was coming that nobody mentioned professions, private lives or— in most cases—even their names. We were all just raw people, pushing toward the same goal.

My own goal kept shifting, until my feelings about the mountain had twisted themselves into a thick braid of fear and yearning. I wanted to get to the top, but I was scared I wouldn't get through the next day.

I wasn't the only one. Many climbers mentioned being afraid on the way up. It was a normal fear of the unknown, of course, but no one could quite make it go away. Or at least keep it away for long.

Two days and 20 breathless miles into the trek, wheezing even at rest, nursing a sore knee and knowing the next day would be even worse, I gave in to depression. "How can I possibly do this?" I wrote in my journal. If I made it to the final hut at Kibo, I would be amazed.

Mercifully, reality gobbles fear. The next morning, the sun was bright, the air was crisp and clean, my wheeze was gone, the knee didn't hurt, and I pulled on my boots, joined Livingstone and began taking it step by step again.

Now, on the third day of climbing, we passed Mawenzi, a smaller volcanic cone that rises like a second head from Kili's broad shoulder. Beyond it lay a desolate sweep of sand and rock called the Saddle, a place as barren of life as the face of the moon.

That was where the last traces of green disappeared. It was like a silence falling—as if the mountain had suddenly gotten serious, shedding a disguise and letting its hidden harshness show.

In the middle of that wasteland lay the last hut, and I really was amazed. Of the climbers who'd started out that morning, I arrived at Kibo Hut dead last, but I had no headache, no nausea, no symptoms at all except a slight cough if I took too deep a breath. It seemed miraculous. Anything beyond Kibo would be gravy.

So of course I upped the ante: If only I could get up to Gilman's Point, I told myself, I'd be happy. And if I could get to Uhuru, a seductive inner voice whispered, I'd be ecstatic.

That was my culture talking, the old American go-for-it voice that I always succumb to.

———

Graffito carved by a climber from Glasgow on a wooden bunk in Kibo Hut: "Hell is just around the corner."

The Scot was right. Here begins the worst of the climb: the least air, the steepest trail. And Kibo is a lousy place to try to prepare your mind. Grim and wretched, it's an unheated blockhouse framed by boulders, where climbers sleep dorm-style, a dozen bunks per room.

Or try to sleep. Kibo is three miles above sea level. The air feels nonexistent, it's freezing cold, and few people are comfortable enough to do anything more than doze. You eat an early supper, crawl into your sleeping bag for a few hours—fully dressed, for warmth—then get up in the middle of the night and climb upward in darkness as far as you are able.

People dealt with their pre-climb jitters in different ways that night. A husky Dutchman in my room kept leaping in and out of bed, zipping and unzipping his sleeping bag, packing and repacking his gear. He was trying to be quiet, but the rustling nylon and crinkling plastic bags sounded like a thunderstorm in the silence of that isolated place.

The Canadian boy in the bunk next to mine was more troubling. He admitted to a bad headache but said defiantly that he was going to climb anyway. Long into the night, he twisted and turned and moaned. I worried about him: He was 20, too young to listen to his body's clear warning.

Kibo's alarm clock was a flashlight that one of the porters blasted into my face. Midnight. Time for tea and coconut cookies. Time to put on gaiters and boots, rain gear and Gore-Tex mittens. Time to find out how it would end. Time to climb.

Outside, it was Minnesota cold—familiar but not comforting. Livingstone snapped on his flashlight, and we started up. The mountainside was a gravel nightmare. If there had been rain, the gravel, called scree, would have frozen together at night, making our footing solid. But the rains were late, so the scree was still dry, dusty and loose, and every step forward meant a skid back. I walked as if on a slow-motion treadmill, getting nowhere.

Night covered Livingstone and me like a tent. I couldn't see his head, let alone how steep the mountain really was, or how big. That was a mercy.

We climbed on switchbacks, shuffling back and forth across the fall line, crunching through the gravel. Our footsteps sounded like spoons digging into sand, over and over and over.

Sixteen people started up from Kibo Hut that night. Within the first hour, some began to straggle back down—too cold to go on, too short of breath, too tired. "Good luck to you," an Australian woman in her 20s said, reaching out of the darkness to squeeze my mittened hand as she passed. I was astonished to be on my feet, still moving upward.

The hours passed. The night passed. By about 3 a.m., I could not have said why I was doing this. I just was. The slow shuffling pace and the noise of the scree were hypnotic. If it hadn't been so hard to breathe, I realized, the repetition would have been boring.

Physical challenges are supposed to sharpen your mind, focus your thoughts. I've seldom found that true. The harder it is for my body, the sillier it gets for my mind. Thoughts skitter around, slide and bounce like the stones we kicked loose on the mountainside.

That night, I kept thinking of a cheery Australian I'd encountered the day before. He'd decided not to try for the top— "thought I'd croak at Kibo!"—but offered this bit of encouragement: "The only thing that's hard about climbing Mount Kilimanjaro is the lack of oxygen."

That was like saying the only bad thing about being poor is not having any money. It also recalled a used car I'd bought in the '70s—a big white Chevy with a lot of weight but no power steering. "You only need it for parking," the owner promised me. True. But when you need it, you really need it.

Now, climbing in darkness, I thought about Chevys instead of the mountain. I also got scientific. This was the first time I'd seen my body work like a furnace: Get a little hungry or thirsty, and it would slow down. Toss in a Rice Krispies bar and a few sips of water, and it would speed up. The effect was obvious and nearly instant.

I was fascinated by this and fed myself morsels as if I were some kind of zoo animal. Watch the woman climb the mountain. Please do not throw peanuts. . . .

Actually, I wished somebody would throw smoked almonds. I'd left a pack of them on my bunk at Kibo. Too salty, I figured: They'd make me drink too much water, too fast. Because they were unreachable, they now became an obsession: "Smoked almonds," I thought. "Smoked almonds. Smoked almonds."

And so it went, all night: Prayers. Smoked almonds. Gray circles. The Southern Cross. Rice Krispies bars. White Chevys. Ernest Hemingway's short story, "The Snows of Kilimanjaro." Water. More prayers. And always that flashlight beam bobbing over the gray gravel at my feet.

Just before sunrise, Livingstone and I reached Hans Meyer Cave. My oxygen-deprived brain turned that into Han Solo Cave, but it didn't matter. The cave is at 17,000 feet. In four and a half hours, we had gained only 1,500 feet in altitude; we had more than that to go. All that work, and we weren't far enough! I nibbled a bar, sipped water and felt hopeless.

We were running late. According to Kilimanjaro's schedule, you're supposed to be at Gilman's Point by sunrise, so you can continue laterally around the rim to Uhuru before the clouds rise from the warming lowlands and hide the views.

We rested longer than we had so far, gazing down over the surreal landscape of the Saddle as the blue-black sky behind

Mawenzi Peak streaked with peach, then orange, then rose and pink and pale blue.

Then the sun broke free of the clouds, and the night was gone. So was the worst of the cold. I peeled off my down jacket and felt lighter. In the new, scaldingly bright light, the colorless rocks turned tan and ocher, but the gravel underfoot stayed gray.

The sun was well up by the time Gilman's Point stood out from the rest of the rocks on the rim. A sharp triangle on the escarpment above us, it looked like the head of a giant iguana.

I could see tiny specks of people standing near it. Two of them suddenly began speeding downhill, dust exploding behind them like thick smoke. It was the Canadian boy, the one who'd had the headache, being half-marched, half-dragged by his guide.

When they reached us, the guide paused to explain the situation to Livingstone, and the boy crumpled to his knees, then sagged backward, his head lolling, semi-conscious. The guide jerked him to his feet, and they started down again, fast, cutting straight through the switchbacks.

"I think, ten more minutes, maybe kaput," Livingstone said quietly. He wasn't kidding.

The youth survived; I saw him the next morning back at Horombo. He'd nearly made it to the top, he said wistfully: "I was ten feet from Gilman's, and I just hit a wall."

The boy and the guide disappeared, and Livingstone and I resumed climbing. Slowly, slowly. I still had no headache or nausea. I began to believe I could make it to the rim—it was just a matter of time. But Gilman's seemed to be drifting away. About 7:30, I asked Livingstone how much longer we had to go, thinking he'd say 20 minutes. "I think two hours," he said, and I felt crushed.

Back to matching breaths to steps, back to praying. *"Dear God, let me not quit from lack of will. . . ."* By now, I was mostly shuffling, resting nearly as long between steps as the steps took. About 200 feet below Gilman's Point, I hit my own wall. Maybe I wouldn't make it, after all; it really was too hard; I was running out of stamina.

Then I saw the last of the faster climbers starting down, and they made an irresistible picture. I grabbed my camera, shot a few frames and felt energized. Being distracted helped. I started climbing again.

That left only Livingstone and me heading upward. Everyone else—perhaps half a dozen of the sixteen who had started out—was on the trail back down to Kibo Hut or already past it, hustling toward Horombo, nearly nine miles beyond. For a little while, I realized, the two of us would be the only people in Africa with the whole continent at our feet.

Then the gravel gave way to a jumble of golden boulders, the only dangerous stretch of the climb, and then we were there.

There. The rim. The top.

I scrambled over the last boulders and onto the narrow crater edge and caught my first glimpse of the perpetual ice inside the lip of the crater: the real snows of Kilimanjaro.

I felt radiant. Now it all seemed worthwhile, all. "Happy?" Livingstone asked, hugging me. "Oh, yes!" I said, and then, of course, burst into tears.

"Since I was seven years old!" I sobbed to the mountain. "Since I was seven years old!"

Off to the right, the glaciers lay in terraces, tier on tier of white snow and blue ice stretched out in the crystal sunlight. Below, the caldera of the volcano dropped away like a deep, lopsided bowl, dry and Tibet-brown, with a puddle of ice in the bottom.

At my toes, the wreckage of a wooden sign proclaimed "Gilman's Point." There was a small, flattish space around it, littered with plastic bottles, candy wrappers and other bits of climber trash.

Garbage on the roof of Africa. Wherever it is, I thought, people always manage to mess it up. But sometimes nature takes advantage: A big black bird with a white splash on his nape was also here, picking through the mess for a meal.

Livingstone and I took pictures—pictures of the glaciers, pictures of each other, pictures of the rocks, pictures of each other sitting on the rocks. Then we shared a communion of water and Rice Krispie bars.

I had one bar left over, so I tossed it to the big black bird, which was instantly mobbed by five other big black birds, all shrieking and scrabbling for the treat, until the whole feathered knot of them tumbled off the crater rim and into the air.

"Crow," Livingston observed. How fitting, I thought. Maybe I could write a famous short story too. Call it "The Crows of Kilimanjaro." I found that hysterically funny.

But the mountain wasn't over. "Where is Uhuru?" I asked, finally able to think about going on. Livingstone pointed across the crater, and I squinted at the other side of the rim. The highest point in Africa didn't look all that high. In fact, it looked lower than where we were.

I gazed at Uhuru and was surprised to feel no emotion— no challenge from it, no yearning toward it. My lustful American voice was silent. I had no doubt that I could walk over there—no doubt at all. I felt great, energized even. But all my macho reasons for going there had vanished.

As I looked at that brown ridge, I understood, as clearly as if I'd read it in a letter from God, that Uhuru was not where I was supposed to go that day. I already stood where I needed to be. There was nothing more to prove. And no point in proving it.

I looked at Uhuru, and I let it go. That was something I'd never done before: get close to a major goal and deliberately stop short. It felt strange, almost perverse. But freeing. This is what our culture doesn't encourage: simply saying "enough."

I turned around and faced east again and felt the African sun blast through the thin air onto my skin and smiled. I had climbed my mountain. And the mountain had shown me a truth I hadn't learned on flat land:

Sometimes standing on the highest point isn't the point at all.

The Night Before New Year's Eve

1986

———

THIS IS THE MOST ROMANTIC CITY in Europe, maybe in all the world—a place rich in art and flowers, intimate cafes and quiet parks, love stories and famous lovers. Think Heloise and Abelard, Napoleon and Josephine, la Dame aux Camelias; there have been countless others.

My own Parisian love affair isn't with someone in the city, though—it's with the city itself. I like it best in winter, "when it drizzles," as the old song says. It doesn't matter if the weather's bad—Paris is its own climate.

Once, my husband and I spent the week after Christmas there, and I remember the city as if it were a secret: Paris seemed empty. It wasn't, of course, but the winter was so bitter that the French complain about it still, and that is what kept them indoors and tourists away.

In front of the bars and bistros, a few forlorn tables huddled tenantless on the sidewalk, and that made the interiors seem more crowded, brighter and smokier than they are in summer. We ducked into cafes more often too, to warm our hands and bellies with big cups of *chocolat chaud* and tiny ones of *café express*.

The Eiffel Tower, that ultimate Christmas tree, wore spangles for the holidays, with scallops of lights on its flanks and the season's dual greetings spelled out in capitals: JOYEUX NOEL. BONNE ANNEE.

Restaurants from the grandest down to the holes in the wall had posted hand-made signs announcing Reveillon—the traditional New Year's Eve repast for which chefs all over France pull out the stops. We had reservations at the Tour D'Argent, a respected institution on the Left Bank, where Reveillon demanded tuxedos and evening gowns.

That night was romantic, as we'd expected, but the night before New Year's Eve was more so, in a humbler way. We had spent the late afternoon exploring Montmartre, one of the "villages" of Paris—neighborhoods so self-contained that they are towns within town.

In warmer weather, this one crawls with international tourists, and I'd always avoided it then. But Montmartre on December 30 was stripped of tourists, as bare as its trees were bare of leaves. A few artists and pseudo-artists were still shivering beside their canvases in the Place du Tertre (shades of Utrillo! echoes of Lautrec!), but there were few browsers.

As dusk deepened, the little square and the deliberately quaint cafes around it looked more and more genuine, less and less touristy. We softened toward them and finally succumbed to Le Consulat, a restaurant usually jammed with foreigners because it "looks so French."

We had no expectations about the food, and, true, the duck with orange sauce was overcooked, and the *pommes frites* weren't up to Paris par. But the atmosphere more than compensated. There was even the proverbial guy at the piano, singing

Edith Piaf ballads with a cigarette dangling from his lips and occasionally adding a few ballads of his own.

The tables lining the walls were packed, but with Frenchmen, not tourists, and everybody in the place seemed to know each other. Soon we did too.

A heavy-set, gloomy-looking man at the next table suddenly leaned over, wine bottle in hand, grinned at us and asked jovially if we'd like some. Sure, we said, amazed at this sudden rip in the interpersonal curtain.

He said his name was Marco, and he was there with his son. "Here, meet my son! These people are Americans! Hey, Gerard"—he called across the room to the piano player—"come over when you get a break!"

We spent the rest of the evening pouring wine back and forth and chatting about "la Butte," as Montmartre people call their hilltop. Gerard, the piano player, composed a poem for me and scrawled it on the paper tablecloth. (I have it still, framed on a wall at home.)

Next to the poem, Marco drew a cartoon map of Paris, explaining that that's how Montmartre residents view the surrounding city—with their neighborhood dominating everything else. "Are those trees?" I asked, pointing to some pine-like squiggles he'd drawn in the Bois de Boulogne. "No," he laughed, "prostitutes!" (The map's on my wall too, and it still makes me smile.)

We closed the place down that night, enjoying to the end a conviviality I hadn't experienced before in Paris. We even exchanged phone numbers and added those common, hopeless tourist invitations. "If you're ever in the States . . ." we said. "I'll call you," Marco promised.

But such commitments are difficult to keep. The wine wears

off, the good mood with it, and the travelers leave and the locals forget and their paths don't cross again. We knew that, but this time it made us sad; we regretted, all the way back to the hotel, that it was over.

Two days later, at a decent hour on the afternoon of New Year's Day, the telephone rang. "This is Marco!" a familiar voice bellowed. He hadn't forgotten, any more than we had. "I promised I'd call you! Bonne Année!" It was indeed a happy new year—he had made it so.

Along the Great River

2001

———

I GREW UP within walking distance of the Mississippi, and it spoiled me. It made me prefer rivers to lakes. Lakes stay put, after all. Lakes look inward. But rivers move. They are permanently impermanent—always there, always leaving.

When you grow up beside a river, you grow up knowing you can leave, too, even if you choose to stay. The way out flows right past your doorstep.

The river that has always flowed past mine is supposed to be civilized now. But down on its banks, from Minnesota to the Gulf of Mexico, the Mississippi is still wild—a green, damp place, smelling of mud and fish, where turtles doze on stranded logs, where blue herons and white egrets wade in shadow, and leaves scatter sunlight over murky water.

Down there, the river still has its own climate, sings its own songs, goes its own way. Always has. Always will.

For a brief time, as I drove the Great River Road from Minneapolis to the end of the pavement in Louisiana, I got to go along.

I bypassed the big cities. I wanted river towns and river

hamlets, river lore and river rats. All those, the Mississippi gave me—with a few life lessons along the way.

You can't, pretty obviously, drive both sides at once. So I kept criss-crossing it, trying to stay as close to the water as I could, taking lonely gravel roads through steamy bottomlands and often getting lost.

This gave me the strange illusion that I was actually driving in a straight line—while the great Mississippi itself kept switching from side to side, like an enormous snake flip-flopping its blue coils over my head.

Another truth: No matter how you try, you cannot see everything along its banks. No one can. The Mississippi is so long, so varied, so rich in history and towns and characters, that you could drive it from source to mouth a hundred times, a thousand times, and each time it would still be fresh and new.

That makes the river *personal*, a matter not of geography but of coincidence. My Mississippi is a scrapook of private serendipities that couldn't happen to someone else, or even to me if I set out to do the trip again.

The best memory—and the most important lesson—came early, in the middle of the Mississippi bridge at Lansing, Iowa, on the night of the full moon in July.

It was the exact moment when day and night are so close you can touch them both. The bridge ran right between them. I started up the short, steep ramp, and the view was instantly so lovely that I slowed to a dazzled crawl.

Upstream, the sky still glowed, and the last of the sunset was painting the water a deep orange and gentle blue. The colors flowed like the river itself, into sloughs and among islands, making them stand out like black lace against twilit silk.

Downstream, the full moon was blessing the river with wide white light, so the surface looked like shifting mercury, flickering from silver to pewter to silver again, brighter and darker, as the current subtly moved the water.

There is no place to pull over on the Lansing bridge. No walkway to perch on. No realistic way to park somewhere and run back with a camera. And no point: The light was changing too fast.

"Sometimes you take pictures with your eyes," a wise woman once told me. This was one of those times. I drove on, photoless, marveling.

You do not need to travel the world for the sublime. It may be waiting for you in your own back yard.